THE WAR JOURNAL (1999-2010)
Volume I

THE WAR JOURNAL
(1999-2010)
Volume I

**The Visions, Dreams And Prophecies
From Almighty God
Concerning
War IN America**

Paula Matthews

S̸L
Spirit & Life
Publications

The War Journal (1999-2010) Volume I
© 2010 Paula Matthews

The Narrative And Edited Version Of
The War Journal (1999-2002)
© 2002 Paula Matthews

Published by
Spirit & Life Publications
Los Angeles

Unless otherwise noted, Scripture quotations are from
The Holy Bible: Authorized King James Version, © 2003 Thomas Nelson, Inc.

Printed In The United States
ISBN 978-0-9851172-0-7

'IN THE NAME OF GOD, AMEN
We whose names are underwritten, the loyal subjects of our Dread
Sovereign Lord King James, by the Grace of God of Great Britain,
France, and Ireland, King Defender of the Faith, etc.
Having Undertaken,
For the Glory of God
And
Advancement of the Christian Faith
And
Honor of our King and Country,
A Voyage to Plant the First Colony in the Northern Parts of Virginia,
Do by These Presents Solemnly and Mutually
In the Presence of God and One of Another,
Covenant and Combine ourselves together
into a Civil Body Politic . . . '

Translated Excerpt of the Mayflower Compact of 1620
The First Recorded Governing Document of America—Source:
www.mayflowerhistory.com/PrimarySources/MayflowerCompact.php

'God Shall Judge The Righteous And The Wicked:

For There Is A Time There

For Every Purpose And For Every Work.'

Ecclesiastes 3:17 KJV

EXHORTATION FOR PRESIDENT TRUMP

Mr. President, it is with great honor that I address you as the forty-fifth President of the United States. The message of this book was originally prepared for President George W. Bush. It was presented to President Obama and now to you.

This book is a prophetic documentation about things that are coming upon our nation and the nations of the world in the last days before Jesus returns.

Concerning your presidency, Sir, God gave a powerful prophetic word. On the night of the 2016 Presidential Elections, I received a vision of the Lord placing a crown upon your head. It was then that I knew that God had chosen you for such a time as this.

After the election, the Lord explained why He had chosen you to lead these United States. He said that you, Sir, were ***the only candidate that would fight for the nation*** against our enemies; that you would ***"stand for righteousness."*** The Lord also said that for both you and Vice President Pence, these were more than political positions, ***"this is ministry,"*** unto God.

Thank you, Sir, for your desire and dedication to both our nation and our God. I therefore exhort you to be steadfast to hear from our Lord concerning all matters. Be determined to obey what you hear. Then stand immoveable in what have heard and done in obedience to our God.

Finally, I do not know you, nor has the Lord revealed anything about you other than what I have shared, but I believe the word of God that says that *"The king's heart is in the hand of the Lord, as the rivers of water, he turneth it whithersoever he will* (Proverbs 21:1).*"* I will continue to pray for you and Mr. Pence, knowing that God's will, is being done in your terms of office.

A MESSAGE FOR PRESIDENT OBAMA

Mr. President, I am honored to address you as presiding Commander and Chief of the United States Armed Forces. This book was originally dedicated to President Bush, and slated to go to press in July 2007, but a series of tragic events delayed the process, and subsequently we have a new administration in the White House, but still an urgent message of national concern to be addressed.

I begin by congratulating you Sir, for your efforts at restoring faith in the American Dream. Your presidency is also a fulfillment of prophecy about God bringing someone out of obscurity to be our next president. In 2008 I stepped into the voting booth and asked God to lead me to His choice. Your name immediately arose off the ballot page and The Spirit of the Lord said, ***"This is the one. My Hand is on him."***

I thank God because your presidency is also a sign for those of us who have been preparing for a change in America. The Lord promised that He was changing both religious and political leadership in America. The old guard was about power and greed at the expense of others. God promised to place in power those who had a heart of compassion to aid those who are suffering; and place in leadership, those who would use their wealth and resources to help their brothers fulfill their dreams. We need that in America now more than ever. Some would say that this is the American Dream, but God would say, that this is the core message of the Gospel of His Kingdom.

I pray that you continue to let God lead you, as you lead His people. May God's blessings continue to flow from Heaven upon you and the first family, and from that abundance may it flow upon our nation, and from that abundance may it flow out to the nations of the world.

DEDICATION

To President George W. Bush, Former Commander and Chief of the United States Armed Forces;

It is in obedience to the Lord Jesus Christ that I have written this journal. The Lord specifically commanded me to prepare it for you, Mr. President.

I thank God for you and pray for you often. Never in the history of this country or of the world has there been such importance placed upon human integrity as in this time of turmoil. May I remind you of something you know very well? God is still on the throne and in control of the events that will come upon each of our lives in this nation. We are indeed in the end-times involving wars and rumors of war that Jesus mentioned in the Bible: a time when nations will rise against nations and kingdoms against kingdoms.[1]

Things in this world according to the Bible will worsen until Jesus returns for His church. Our only hope as a people and a nation is Jesus, the Light of the world. Indeed the world will become increasingly dark. Isaiah says that *gross darkness* will be upon the people, but the *glorious light* of God will be upon His people.[2] Understand that God is our only hope. This battle we fight with terrorism is spiritual. It's a battle of Good versus Evil, and we will prevail as one victorious nation under the rule and authority of Almighty God.

Destruction is coming, but the Lord says that a house built upon the rock will not be destroyed. America was once built upon the Rock (Jesus Christ) and Biblical values. But, as a nation we have slowly chipped away at the solid rock of our foundation that our fore fathers established. They had a strong belief in God and built this nation upon the motto: 'In God We Trust.'[3] This was not a blind trust, but a trust built upon the moral law that lined the very fabric of their lives. They developed similar principles in our government and constitution. They found certain 'truths to be self evident.'[4] These very truths came from the Holy Bible. We have seen the erosion of moral values in our country and a strong desire on the part of our leaders not to retain the knowledge of God, in order to appear politically non-offensive.

One only has to tour our capitol buildings, memorials and courtrooms to observe our historical reverence for the Holy Scriptures. These words of God's Truth are engraved everywhere. There was even a time that American newspaper publications printed a daily Bible verse as part of the front-page headline. Yet, in our day and time, there has been a relentless outcry against the public display of anything godly. The huddled masses have enjoyed the benefits of our liberty in America, but we as beneficiaries, are offended by the God from whom this liberty flows.

Christianity is not a doctrine easily embraced by the masses. It prescribes a narrow path to God.[*] Jesus is called the 'Rock of Offense.'[α] He offends those who want to exalt themselves above the knowledge of God. Jesus said He did not come to bring peace, but a sword.[β] America was never supposed to bend its knee to those who are offended by the God of our strength. We were called to defend the liberty on which we were founded: a liberty that comes from our faith in God our Creator. Our faith is offensive to those who care not to be reminded that there is a God. Men who reject God do so because they secretly desire evil rather than good, and want their deeds to remain hidden. The acknowledgment of a Holy God in the presence of an immoral people is condemning, yet the Hand of God has never been far from us.

There is much evidence of God's Hand upon our nation beckoning us to return to Him. When I began to write this dedication, the Lord immediately began speaking specifically about two works from American history, the *Pledge of Allegiance*[χ], and the *Battle Hymn of the Republic*.[δ] He told me that His hand was strong upon the individuals who wrote them. I was led to do some research to learn more. These works represented our nation's solidarity in its covenant of peace made with God. Both were written to unify our country around God and the faith of our founding fathers.

THE PLEDGE OF ALLEGIANCE

I pledge allegiance, to the flag of the United States of America, and to the Republic for which it stands; One nation under God, indivisible, with liberty and justice for all.

****

After doing research, I found some interesting facts about the *Pledge of Allegiance*. First of all, the author, Francis Bellamy was a Baptist Preacher.[*] He wrote the Pledge in an effort to bring unity back to the United States after the Civil War. He got the idea from the 'Oath of Allegiance'[α] required of Southern rebels in order to regain citizenship and political rights in the United States. It was the heinous aftermath of the Civil War that inspired the writing of the *Pledge of Allegiance*. Bellamy's desire was to bring the nation back to the unity that the founding fathers had once established. The words 'One Nation Under God'[β] were added after another devastating war; World War II. This change in the Pledge was granted in 1954 after the Knights of Columbus started a campaign to remind Americans that during this crisis, our country needed to be both spiritually and physically strong.

Shortly after America was attacked on September 11, 2001, we sent combat troops to Afghanistan to pursue Al- Qaeda and Osama Bin Laden. Later, we went after Saddam Hussein in Iraq. Our military actions in the Middle East have stirred up the most dangerous enemies our nation has ever encountered. Muslims around the world have proclaimed jihad against America; calling for a showdown between their god and our God, meanwhile we have positioned our nation for defeat by wanting no visible connection to the God of our fathers. We have ignorantly disarmed ourselves in the face of a determined enemy, in what will prove to be the bloodiest battle on U.S. soil since the Civil War. And yet, as our history shows, there is still hope.

During the Civil War, Americans in the South twisted the Bible to support their stand on slavery. The North strongly supported the declaration that all men were created equal; a right they knew came from the Creator God. It was only through those who knew God and what this nation stood for, that the war was won. The Lord had mighty warriors that prayed and led this nation back to God. One such person was Julia Ward Howe. I was deeply moved when the Lord first began revealing how His Hand was upon Julia Ward Howe, when she wrote the *Battle Hymn of the Republic*. Like Bellamy, her inspiration was the Civil War. In 1861, Mrs. Howe visited some troops near the nation's capitol. In her own words, she saw the 'grim Demon of War face-to-face.'[*] To keep themselves stirred on, the soldiers sang war songs. Their favorite was about John Brown.[α]

What motivated the soldiers was the martyrdom of a man who understood what God intended for our country. Mrs. Howe said that the tune of *'John Brown's Body'* remained in her head while she slept. The words to the *Battle Hymn of Republic* came to her upon waking. Mrs. Howe was a strong Christian woman who allowed the Lord to move through her to inspire hope in the midst of great tragedy. Her song became the symbol of strength for the union army and an enduring anthem for our nation.

THE BATTLE HYMN OF THE REPUBLIC*

Mine eyes have seen the glory of the coming of the Lord: He is trampling out the vintage where the grapes of wrath are stored; He has loosed the fateful lightning of his terrible swift sword.
His truth is marching on.

I have seen Him in the watch fires of a hundred circling camps; They have builded Him an altar in the evening dews and damps; I can read His righteous sentence by the dim and flaring lamps.
His day is marching on.

I have read the fiery gospel, writ in burnished rows of steel; As ye deal with my contempters so with you my grace shall deal; Let the Hero, born of woman, crush the serpent with his heel.
Since God is marching on.

He has sounded forth the trumpet that shall never call retreat; He is sifting out the hearts of men before His judgment seat; Oh! Be swift, my soul, to answer Him! Be jubilant, my feet!
Our God is marching on.

In the beauty of the lilies Christ was born across the sea;
With a glory in his bosom that transfigures you and me;
As He died to make men holy, let us die to make men free,
While God is marching on.

The Battle Hymn of the Republic says that God's truth is marching on. May I remind you Mr. President, that Jesus is the Truth.[*] He is marching on to victory in America. We will see His Glory and His Wrath. Why now? God says its time. We will see the wrath of God fall upon our nation and upon the nations of the world. He will judge us all; shaking every person and every nation. What we will experience will not be the performance of evil men, but acts of a just God who will execute justice upon all people; both the good and the evil.

How America measures up to God's justice is up to us. Unfortunately, we have forgotten the impact we have made on the nations of the world. Immigrants have flocked to us for political and religious asylum, viewing the American way of life as a virtual Promised Land of freedom and prosperity. Yet, Americans have taken our prosperity and freedoms for granted, forgetting that we are not prosperous or free because of who we are, or what we have done by our own power. We live free because the Spirit of the Lord was with the founders of this nation, and where the Spirit of the Lord is, there is liberty—freedom to live the abundant life God desired for all men on the earth.[α] The Spirit <u>has</u> to be Lord, and He will be Lord again in America, even during times of war.

Once again we will see the Hand of God upon our nation as men like John Brown, give their lives to uphold our freedoms. We will see many like Julia Ward Howe and Francis Bellamy who will document their witness of the battles and give glory and honor to the Sovereign God whose grace remains upon our nation.

God loves America. Our founding fathers created our nation to be free to serve Him without fear of government retaliation. Imagine how it grieves the Spirit of God when American court decisions favor those who persecute people holding firm to this foundational belief. Yet, while some have tried to sever our relationship with God, He will honor the prayers of the covenanted few on the behalf of an entire nation which in times past believed in God's purpose and plan for our lives.

The wave of persecution of Christians living in America has been astounding. Some Christian based community organizations have been under attack for their firm commitment to the very values on which they were founded. Others who preach the Gospel of Jesus Christ are being attacked, ostracized and treated like extremists. Standing up for godly values is no longer acceptable in America. This is an outrage in the eyes of God and He will execute a severe penalty against America for her actions against Him.

I am reminded of the Children of Israel before they entered into the Promised Land. God told them that He alone gave them power to get wealth. Like America, God prospered them with vast economic wealth and superior military strength against their enemies. This is God's covenant with His people. They were also given a warning, and that warning applies to America today. God said that in the day that they choose to forget Him and His Commandments, He would turn them over to their enemies to destroy them in the land which He gave them.[β] I declare to America that we are in that day; the day of vengeance of our God; because we want no part of Him.

Americans will learn that we have wealth and protection because our fathers had a promise from God; not mere words of men among men, but God spoke from heaven and our fathers agreed to promises that were sealed with the precious Blood of Jesus. Many men, women and children have also shed their blood in war, race riots, lynching and murders to uphold America's godly values. Their blood is crying out to God to avenge their lives. The Blood of Jesus is also moving to avenge all those who have died to uphold God's promise in the earth. America has forgotten God, therefore we will be attacked in the land that God gave us, and many will perish. For those of us who honor the promise and obey our God, we will do great exploits and give Him the honor due His Name.

Mr. President, there will be war in America, says the Lord. God will prove that He is indeed not only <u>The Supreme Power</u>; but, He will prove that He is the <u>Only Power</u> that will rule the nations. God will bring America and all the nations of the world to their knees. His Hand will move forcefully around the world, showing mercy only to those who abide in His Will and to those who call upon His Name with a pure heart.

As the Bible says, the Lord is with us while we are with Him. If we seek Him, He will be found of us, but if we forsake Him, He will forsake us.[*] America has forsaken God, but not all. We will win this spiritual battle but not with human physical strength alone. We will wage a mighty battle with fervent prayer and earnest obedience to Almighty God, who has already given us the victory.

Mister President, Sir, you know the voice of God and can hear from Him. I pray that you have the strength to obey Him as He directs your path. God has now appointed Donald J. Trump, Commander and Chief to lead America into the next phase of this spiritual battle. God's Hand is on President Trump, a fellow believer in Jesus Christ, who is determined to correct the injustices in our country and restore the America for the sake of all people. I pray that he continues to let the Spirit of the Lord guide him so that all Americans may have a quiet and peaceable life in godliness and honesty according to 1Timothy 2:1-3.

We will continue to pray for peace, but please understand that Jesus Christ is the **PRINCE OF PEACE**[*], not peace as the world knows it, but the peace that only God can provide; complete and total reconciliation with a Holy God; for without Him we will have no peace.

May God bless and keep you, and uphold you with the Mighty Power of His Right Hand, Jesus Christ, Our Lord and Savior. I leave you with the powerful words of the last stanza of Francis Scott Key's *Star Spangled Banner*[α]

> *O thus be it ever when free man shall stand*
> *Between their loved homes and the war's desolation.*
> *Blest with vict'ry and peace, may the heav'n rescued land.*
> *Praise the Power that hath made and preserved us a nation!*
> *Then conquer we must when our cause it is just.*
> *And this be our motto, "In God is our Trust!"*
> *And the star spangled banner in triumph shall wave.*
> *O'er the land of the free and the home of the brave.*

TO THE BRAVE MEN AND WOMEN OF THE UNITED STATES MILITARY AND IT'S ALLIED TROOPS IN THE WAR AGAINST TERRORISM

We thank you and honor you. We are grateful for your demonstrated courage and dedication to fight for the world's freedom from terrorism. You are heroes to all of us who cannot serve in this battle. Our prayers are with each of you and your loved ones night and day. May God keep you under the wings of His protection as you uphold peace, justice and godliness for all mankind. May He soon bring you home, safe and victorious.

TO THE AFGHAN AND IRAQI PEOPLE, OUR ARAB AND MUSLIM BROTHERS AND SISTERS, AND OTHER VICTIMS OF THE CROSSFIRES OF THE WAR ON TERRORISM

This war is not against Arab people. It is not even a war waged by Christians against Muslims. It is strictly a war against the tyrannical reign of terror over the nations of the world. War is always costly in human lives; however, terrorism must be stopped. There can be no negotiation with terrorists.

We apologize for any and all prejudice, hate or revenge directed at you just because you are of Arab descent or Muslim religion. There are many Americans who are against this war. They understand that the real enemy is terrorism and the fear it creates. Fear deposits evil into the hearts of men causing them to turn against friends, neighbors, and even their own brothers.

We pray that the Living God reveal the truth of His love to Arab and Muslim people around the world, especially those who are determined to wage jihad against Americans. May you be among the nations who will walk in God's light, bringing glory and honor before Him, and freely partaking of the tree of life in the midst of the Paradise of God; whose leaves are for the healing of the nations.*

SPECIAL ACKNOWLEDGMENTS
To the members of the Body of our Lord Jesus Christ;

I admonish you to seek God with your whole heart. Strive to obey Him at heights never before attempted by mortal men. God is calling you to display HIS POWER and HIS WILL in the 'greater works.' We are being called to perform at the top of our game. Not in the human sense of performance, but in the godly sense of denying ourselves and demonstrating HIS LOVE and COMPASSION for the lost. No longer can HIS Church choose to be isolated from darkness. But we are being called to dominate the darkness of this world by letting our lights burn brighter and longer than ever before.

To the leaders who are stepping up to take their rightful place IN HIM. Be strong and courageous IN HIM. The Lord has equipped you with an anointing exclusively for this season of darkness. It is more powerful than human comprehension. Meditate on what He has told you and strive for that promise. Do not compare yourself with those who have preceded you. You do not look like, talk like, nor behave like leaders of the traditional church. God is calling His True Sons out of Egypt. You have been trained specifically to survive the extremely dark and evil situations that the traditional church has long feared.

You have been called for such a time as this, therefore stand firm when men arise to persecute and reject you. Like Saul, they will see the Davidic anointing on your life and desire it for themselves. Know that God has indeed anointed you to lead His people. Do not fear men or their attempts on your life. Do not repay evil for evil as they do. Persecution is your cross to bear. Pray for your enemies because the wrath of God is against them. Obey God, praise Him often and He will remove the evil ones from your path.

Some of you were almost destroyed by discontent, not understanding that your pain and difficulties were because of the call on your life and not because of what you did. I exhort you to deny yourself the comfort of complaining, seeking revenge or murmuring against the church. Offense will steal the promise of God from you and give Satan victory in his plot against your life and ministry. I urge you to fight the good fight of faith and obey God. He chose you according to His Will and His Purpose, not yours. Look to Jesus as your example. He left His throne in heaven, and took on the likeness of man. Jesus humbly served man although He was God. He was persecuted and spat upon, yet Jesus was obedient to God all the way to the cross. A true disciple will be as his master, and follow His example.

Abide in Him and let His word abide in you. Hold on to the words that He spoke to you. The Lord gave you visions and dreams that seemed impossible for you to achieve. I exhort each of you to pull out those dreams, holdfast to the promises and watch them manifest in your lives. Let the Glory of God shine upon all you do. You saw things in a way similar to Ezekiel, where the Lord would take you by the spirit and tell you what was to come. Then you arose to the occasion and spoke boldly like Elijah. What you heard and saw came directly from the throne of God, but when you spoke and it fell on deaf ears. You spoke a truth before its season to those who did not have an ear to hear the truth.

Remember how Joseph shared what God showed him and it nearly cost him his life. The Bible said that his brothers hated Joseph because their father favored him.* They hated him even more because of his dreams and words Joseph received from the Lord. Your confidants, pastors and leaders called your visions demonic and made you an outcast. This was not because they thought you could not see or hear with spiritual accuracy. They did it out of jealousy. They saw the anointing (favor) on your life and coveted the dreams and visions God gave you. They had no desire to support you. They persecuted you in an attempt to destroy your dreams from God.

To appease your leaders, some of you have agreed to call your visions demonic. I caution you not to blaspheme the Holy Ghost by claiming that your prophetic Word was from Satan when you know it was from God. This is very dangerous. You will be held accountable for the Word you have been given. Don't let your mouth cause your flesh to sin. Don't say before God that you spoke in error by His Spirit. To do so will cause God to be angry at your words and cause Him to destroy the work of your hands.[α] Keep yourself from speaking such evil words. Fear God, because by your own words you will either be justified or condemned. God will judge you.

God wants you to know that the reason your trusted leaders could not see, is because they are not anointed nor called to see. Their spiritual blindness is ordained of God. Because their hearts cause them to constantly rebel, God is taking them out of power and raising up a Davidic order of leaders who will accomplish all of God's Will in the earth.

The current leaders are blinded by their own ambition and will attempt do to you what Saul tried to do to David. They will plot to kill you and take the anointing for themselves. Do not fear those who can kill the body. Fear God who can destroy both your body and soul in Hell. The Lord says that in your obedience, He will destroy the enemy before your eyes. Like Saul, these leaders will die in their sin if they do not repent.

I have been commanded to declare before all heaven and earth that you are the chosen and faithful for this final hour. Blessed are your eyes for they see what you see and blessed are your ears to hear what you hear. Indeed there are kings and princes and mighty leaders who desire to see and hear these great things, and won't. My sisters and brothers arise and take your rightful place. The nations of this world cannot survive without your gift, and, the church cannot move into the greater works without you. Arise and go forth, in the Name of Jesus!

To the sisters of Good Shepherd;
Sister Julia Mary the visionary who exudes the presence and compassion of Jesus Christ. Sister Patricia, you demonstrated so much love and fed me much wisdom. Special blessings to The Sisters of the Lovers of the Resurrected Cross, who left their homeland of Vietnam to serve Jesus in the United States; Sisters Virginia, Jennifer, Francesca, Cecilia, and Bernadette, especially to Sister Marian, evangelist and teacher, who often spoke of the love and cleansing power of Jesus Christ. To each of you, Margarita and staff, I send much love. I pray that the Lord sends an abundance of blessings your way, because, when I was yet a stranger, you took me in, fed and clothed me and nursed my wounds. May the Peace of God rule and reign in your midst, now and forever.

Special Acknowledgments

To the Hernandez-Reyes Clan;
Tony, Mercedes, Claudia, GiGi, Ignacio, Shellie, Christina, Vanessa, Tony Jr., Jorge (Baby Boy) and Lucy (LoLo), Christian, Walter and of course Letisha and Christopher. I love you all. I am forever grateful that God brought us together. Thank you for making me a part of your family. Mercedes, tu es mi hermana, ahora y siempre. Te amo.

To the HBH Crew;
Pam Norton, Mercedes, Monica, Angelo, Danny, Mayra, Marta, Brenda, Joanna, Elizabeth and the gang. Thanks for all your support in completing this project. I could not have finished it without your help.

To the Staff at Kawada Hotel:
Thanks to John Marco, Saori, Paula, Mary, Mike, Stephen, Derek, Rudy, Luis, Mario, Kevin, Patricia, Victor, Havalino, and the entire staff for providing me a home away from home. It was the perfect place to write this book. Thanks for wonderful service and friendship.

To the Staff of PLB Management;
For those of you that wondered what I was so intently writing at my desk, and for those who asked, 'Paula, when can I read your book?' here is the finished product. May it enlighten you as to how I could patiently perform a job in the midst of periodic craziness and turmoil. It was God's plan and purpose for my life. It was a labor of love for Him that I worked with each of you, prayed for you, and shared the love. I will never forget our time together. It was a blessing.

To my family, the Scotts and Randles;
You've always known that I was a little different than most people and was led by a voice that many did not hear. I pray that you now understand that God was always in control of every trauma and tragedy I experienced. It was never about me, but about what He was calling me to do. I love you all and pray that each and every one of you also endures to see the Glory of God manifested through these fragile lives.

To my spiritual parents, Apostle Fred and Dr. Betty Price;
It was a difficulty and a shock when the Lord dropped me at your doorstep with such a controversial project. Even though I looked and sounded like a stepchild, God's plan was to reunite me with the family at Crenshaw Christian Center, to do a mighty work for His Glory. I honor, respect and love you both so much. May the perfect will of God manifest in all that you are and all that you do.

To Pastor Argie Taylor;
The spiritual midwife that helped me birth this new phase in my call to ministry. Thank you for your example of obedience, compassion and love for God's people. Thank you for allowing the Spirit to be Lord in your life and ministry. You are a rare and precious gem in the Kingdom of God. May God continue to demonstrate His miracle working power through you in ways far beyond anything you could ask or think.

Special Acknowledgments

To Pastor Gary Greenwald;
Thank you for confirming God's enormous end-time plan for my life. The Lord declared that I would successfully complete this call before He returned. You also echoed the same words that shook me the first time God spoke to me; words about forcibly removing anyone or anything that got in the way of my finishing this work. After you spoke those words, you and I both knew that it was of utmost importance that I obeyed God. Thank you for speaking the truth as you saw it, both the good and the bad. May God bless you immensely for delivering His prophetic word with keen spiritual integrity and discernment.

To Pastor Gary Gregor;
Thank you for obeying God and sending me back east to complete this project. It was a pleasure being with you, Vivian and the family. Our time together was brief, yet profound. May God continue to bless you, the family and the powerful prophetic ministry He has entrusted to you.

To My Los Angeles Ministry Support Team;
These are the people of God who were assigned to give me spiritual support and guidance.

Pastor Garry Ziegler, and Pastor James Price;
Thank you for the many prayers, answered phone calls and emails while I was in Ohio. Your support was essential during this time of preparation for this project. May the seeds of time, prayers and good tidings be multiplied back to you, your families and ministries, one hundred-fold. You are the best!!

Special Acknowledgments

Mindy Reid, in honor of your husband, Pastor Mike Reid;
When I returned to Los Angeles, the Lord told me that Mike would watch my back. He called him *'an obedient soldier.'* The Lord said that Mike would pray and do whatever he was told in order to assist me. With Mike watching my back, I felt at ease while traveling in some of the most wretched places of darkness. In honor of Mike, may God bless you Mindy, with your heart's desire in life and ministry.

Pastors Alice Gier and Mark McVay;
May God bless both of you for your prayers and support. You lovingly confirmed the heart of God during my transition and new assignment in Los Angeles. Thank you.

Drs. IV and Bridgett Hilliard;
One October morning in 2003, I awoke to powerful praying on my behalf. The Lord showed the two of you alongside Dr. Fred and Dr. Betty, praying over my assignment. After the praying ceased, a heavy mantle felt upon my shoulders. I praise God for you all for helping equip me for the work the Lord destined for my completion.

Bishop Clarence McClendon;
In 1998 the Lord gave me a command concerning you. He said, *'this is your brother, watch his back'*. I had never heard of you, yet the Lord had me praying for you. One day I was talking to the Lord about my assignment, and your spirit joined in the conversation. I admired how you could not only see in the spirit, but you enquired of the Lord about what you saw. This proved helpful when the Lord had you praying for me. Although the hoards of hell were sent against me and you were at times repulsed by what you saw, you remained on point and prayed me to safety. I will always be grateful for your faithfulness to God and the task He assigned to you on this project.

Special Acknowledgments

<u>To the Ohio Project Team</u>: Pastors Bill Davis, RA Vernon, Ozzie Arroyo, Lyle and Ernest, Reggie and Regina, Dorothy Carmack, Dove, Daniel James, Darrell and Edwina Carew, and Sister Obie and our Nigerian family at Mountain of Fire Ministries of Ohio;
The Lord said that my assignment in Ohio was complete and victory was won. As co-laborers together, we share in that victory. May the heavens remain open, pouring out immense blessings on all that you do. Rest in the victory of a job well done.

<u>The Ohio Scott Klan</u>: Pastors Darrell and Belinda Scott; Darrell and Lynne Scott; and Gwen Scott;
I was born into the Scott family on earth but born again into the heavenly family of God. What we share is greater than any name or blood of mere men on earth. May you all continue to do good works and glorify the name of our Lord Jesus Christ, to the glory of God our heavenly Father.

To Gwen McCurry and family;
It was a blessing working with you all. Gwen, thank you for your faithfulness, both to the Word and to loving God's people. God has knit us together in heart and ministry. I cherish and love you dearly.

To Rod Parsley;
When the Lord sent me to your church, my first assignment was to pray for you. As I prayed, the Lord revealed something about you I had not expected. He showed me your heart. I saw a pure heart that loved God and desired to obey Him. God loves you and showed great things being birthed for you from His Spirit. I am confident that He that began a great work in you will be faithful to complete it until the day of Jesus Christ.

xxxiii

Special Acknowledgments

To Pastors David Scott, Kelvin Scott, Dennis and Denise Givens;
Who could have even imagined that the Lord would take us from
Pilgrim Baptist Church in South Bend, Indiana; fill us with His Spirit,
equip us for ministry and have us boldly doing what we are doing
today. Give God the glory for what He has, is and will be doing in our
lives and in the lives of others who are eager to do His Will under this
apostolic anointing.

To Jacob's Daughters: Marian, Carlotta, Diana, Helen, Mary,
Dorothy, and Marcella;
The mighty women of God sent to Los Angeles to work on this project
and take off in claiming their kingdom inheritance. Let nothing short
of God's plan and purpose be manifested richly in each of your lives.
May the blessings of Abraham be your reward for answering the call
to get out of your country, from your family, and from your father's
house, to a land that the Lord would later show you. May you birth
nations of obedient, loving and prosperous followers, the savor of
whose fruit will impact the world for our Lord Jesus Christ.

To Marcella Marks;
A faithful soldier and valiant warrior of the kingdom. Thank you for
all the loyalty and un-compromised service you have bestowed upon
me. May the blessings of God continue to rest upon your life because
of your diligence and steadfastness in the faith of our Lord Jesus
Christ.

Special Acknowledgments

To My Son Jeffrey;
I painfully, yet obediently gave you to the Lord the same way God gave His only begotten son Jesus. Thank you for the love and prayers over the years while we were separated. The Lord said that He was raising you to become His prophet and deliverer of many souls. I am forever grateful that the same grace and peace of God that rests on my life has kept you all these years. You are indeed a precious gift from God, a powerful arrow flung from the bow of the Almighty Himself.

Special Acknowledgments

To All Those I Don't Know by Name:
Everyone that God anointed to pray and support this project. Please know that your labor of love was not in vain. May God abundantly multiply fruit to your account. May He make all grace abound toward you, that you may always have all sufficiency in all things for every good work, now and forever.

And to My Lord Jesus Christ;
There are no words that could ever describe the depth of my love for you. I will, however, give my life in obedience to you as a declaration of that love. Regardless of pain, suffering and persecution, I will live and die so that others might experience that same love. I will forever worship You, whom God has highly exalted and given the name which is above every name, that at the name of Jesus, every knee should bow, of those in heaven, and of those on earth, and of those under the earth, and that every tongue should confess that Jesus Christ is Lord, to the glory of God the Father. For Yours is the kingdom and the power and the glory forever. Amen.

Table of Contents

EXHORTATION FOR PRESIDENT TRUMP

DEDICATION   xiii

SPECIAL ACKNOWLEDGMENTS   xxv

FROM THE AUTHOR
My Commission From God 1
Labor Of Love 5
Counting The Cost 9
My Heart's Desire 19

ABOUT THE JOURNAL
The Purpose For This Journal 27
The Way I Receive Information 29
Notes About The Journal 31
Warning To The Skeptic 33
Warning To Those Eager 43

INTRODUCTION
The Real Matrix 57

THE DARKNESS AND THE GLORY
PART I: The Judgment Of God Revealed 71
PART II: The Love Of God Manifested 81

THE WAR JOURNAL ENTRIES
YEAR 1999: *Exit From Los Angeles* 99
YEAR 2000: *Move To Ohio* 109
YEAR 2001: *Preparation For War* 139
YEAR 2002: *The Enemy Exposed* 171
YEAR 2003: *The Storm Is Coming!* 199
YEAR 2004: *The Year Of Completion* 217
YEAR 2005: *The Glory Is Here!* 249
YEAR 2006: *Possessing The Land* 267
YEAR 2007: *A Day Of Rest* 311
YEAR 2008: *The European Connection Defined* 333
YEAR 2009: *A Better Understanding* 341

THE CONCLUSION OF THE WHOLE MATTER
    Final Exhortation 365
    Conclusion 383

APPENDIX
    BIBLIOGRAPHY .... cdxxxvii
    RECOMMENDED BOOKS .... cdxxxix
    OTHER RESOURCES .... cdxli
    TOPICAL INDEX .... cdxliii
    ENDNOTES .... cdxlv

FROM THE AUTHOR

'And He Put Forth The Form Of An Hand . . . And

Brought Me In The Visions Of God . . . '

Ezekiel 8:3 KJV

My Commission From God

In 1998, the Lord took me by the spirit and showed me a small powerful congregation of no more than 200-300 men and women, all of whom had worldwide ministries. The Lord declared this to be <u>His Church</u> that He was raising up in our midst. When I saw these leaders, I was awestruck. They were mighty men and women of valor. Not only did they possess tremendous financial wealth, but superior spiritual strength. <u>All</u> of the ministry gifts and <u>all</u> of the gifts of the Spirit operated through <u>each</u> individual as the Lord willed. They did not seem to be human. They were so much like supernatural beings, that I asked the Lord if they were angels. He told me these were the believers who lived only by His Word and obeyed His Spirit. The Lord said that they would do whatever He asked them to do, without considering themselves or their situations. They were pure and yielded vessels. Each of them performed the greater works Jesus spoke about in John 14:12. They also walked in an unusual power of God that surpassed the works of Moses, Elijah, Elisha, Jesus, and all the Apostles combined.

Immediately following this vision, the Lord commissioned me to '***teach***' His Church. I asked the Lord what it was that I could teach such a powerful group of believers. He said that there were many things about the spirit realm He taught me over the years that they would need to know in order to carry out their assignments. Then the Lord gave me yet another vision and explained that this was to be my assignment until Jesus returned. He showed me standing before His Church at three distinct times of my life. I could only estimate my age based on how I looked in the vision.

The vision began with me in the pulpit teaching. I looked just like I do today except I was pregnant at that time and my husband was standing behind the pulpit listening and doing church business. The Lord then zeroed in on my eyes while I was in the pulpit. Then He pulls away from those same eyes and the vision shows Paula with silver hair. I assumed that my age was somewhere between 60-70 years old based on how my parents turned completely silver at the same age. I was preparing to teach and someone was helping gather my things to walk out before the congregation. A woman, whose face I did not recognize was fixing my stray hairs and tugging at my dress. Then the Lord zeroed in on my eyes again and this time when He pulled away from my eyes I saw a very old and thin woman standing behind the pulpit. By this time in the vision, I am somewhat overwhelmed by seeing the aging process of Paula. If the Lord had not shown my eyes in each of the different ages, I would have easily denied the identity of this old woman. Although it was eerie, I knew it was Paula. I looked to be about 90 –100 years old; thin and frail, but moving with little need for assistance.

A few months following these visions, the Lord said that He was sending me out like He did the first Apostles to find the ones He is calling to His Church. He called me to first *__heal and deliver__* them, then teach them what He needed them to know to carry out His Will. My first mission was to several pastors throughout Southern California. Since that time, the Lord has continuously sent me out according to this commission. The Word about war is only one of many given to me to speak during this season. In God's perspective, the war in America will be one platform from which His Church will demonstrate His Awesome Power.

The Word about war does mention specific geographic locations that the enemy will target. These locations include, but are not limited to, the northern half of Ohio, Southern and Northern California, and Las Vegas. The Lord also gave me specific instruction for His people. He said prepare them for war, and prepare them for persecution similar to that in nations hostile to Christianity. The Lord said that the church as it exists today is not capable of withstanding the darkness destined for our world. But, His Church, like a powerful army, will arise and boldly occupy, until Jesus returns. It will seize the enemy and produce kingdom results regardless of what evils befall the nations of the world.

Labor Of Love

This book is just a portion of my personal prayer journal that contains, among other things, messages from Almighty God concerning war in America. Like any type of journal, this is a diary of events and thoughts. The only difference is that this journal focuses on my prayer time with the Lord. Some of the events are future events, and many of the thoughts were from God, as spoken by His Holy Spirit. The Lord told me years ago that the Bible contains promises that are possible for any believer, but what He speaks to me by His Spirit are promises that are specifically for my life. He said that these specific promises are sure to come to pass if I obey His instructions. A prayer journal is the perfect way to keep track of those spoken promises. It is also an effective way of measuring the outcome of prayers and events that the Lord said would occur.

Included in this journal is an account my carrying out God's commission to find His leaders. This commission was significant to the preparation for war. God's leaders must be freed from entanglements, in position and ready to carry out their specific assignments. Some refused to be free while others subordinated their duties. Those prepared to obey are in position and awaiting God's final command.

Also, in this journal are events surrounding the development, presentation and subsequent publishing of this journal. There are details of my struggle to write and publish this book in the midst of extreme jealousy, envy and overall threats to stop this message from going forth. Both the commission to find leaders and the commission to prepare this journal for the president were met with much opposition although the final outcome was successful for both assignments.

My personal account of prophetic events as revealed by God in visions, dreams and prophecies, and other supernatural occurrences, came about through Spirit led public and private prayer, fasting and praise sessions that occurred from 1999-2010. Spirit led means that at no time did the author or those involve conjure up these spiritual occurrences through our own desire or motivation. The Lord spoke and moved us for His purposes, later He revealed events to us. Explanations given for events came directly from the Holy Spirit. Where there are no explanations, none were given by the Lord. Unless urged by His Spirit, I rarely asked for explanations. My job was to carry out His orders.

Please note that events throughout this journal may be referred to as either *spiritual, natural* or *prophetic*. Spiritual events are those seen or experienced in the realm of God's spirit by way of prayer or some other spiritual experience. These are events that cannot be seen with the human eye. Natural events are those that humans can experience with their natural senses. Prophetic events are things that have not yet occurred, but are predicted to occur at some future point in time. Prophetic events can be either spiritual, or natural, or both.

Finally, in this journal are notes of the author's instruction from the Lord detailing specific preparation for war. Mentioned are vulnerabilities in America where the enemy could possibly attack. The Lord stated which events could not be prevented by His supernatural intervention; one such event was the war and the events that would ignite the war in our nation. In these cases the Lord gave instruction on how to counterattack the enemy's plans.

It is my desire that the reader walk away from this journal understanding that war begins in the human heart. The Bible says that out of the good treasure of a good man's heart, he brings forth good things and out of the evil treasure of an evil man's heart, he brings forth evil things.* Every human on the face of the earth knows what it is to battle with the evil within us. When we know what is right to do, but fail to do it, our conscious is disturbed. A battle ensues within our minds and hearts. Americans also know the battle with the circumstances of everyday life. It may sometimes feel like a losing battle when you can't make ends meet and have a family depending upon you. Whether it is a battle with violent crime ridden neighborhoods, or drug infested schools, Americans understand what it means to be at war. Then there are countries that hate our nation because God has blessed us with so much. They have become our enemies because they meditate on war and hatred in their hearts. They want to come to America and put fear in our hearts and minds. But, this is a battle that the Lord will not permit without His Hand protecting America.

When Jesus walked the earth two thousand years ago, He spoke of God's Kingdom existing within the hearts of men.$^{\alpha}$ It was, and still is, a revolutionary idea that nations can be ruled from the inside out. When God's love rules the hearts of men, then external circumstances will change. This is the message that is demonstrated on the pages of this journal. God wants to demonstrate His Kingdom in America, and with the diligence of a few faithful believers, He will show His mighty power to our nation and to the world.

Counting The Cost
Forsaking All For God's Kingdom Sake

The Lord commanded a group of prophets and intercessors to watch over our cities and the nation in 2001. Our unique gathering in Ohio knew only that the call was to usher in the next move of God in the United States. A few months later, we were told to prepare for war.[*] The Lord told me specifically that He was sending me an army that could call bombs out of the sky[α], but none of us could have imagined the events that followed. We were commanded to stay on the walls of the city and pray without ceasing. Once we accepted the call, we were no longer in control. The unction of the Holy Spirit remained on us continually for many months throughout early 2002. Whether we slept or wake, our spirits were constantly praying in concert with the Holy Spirit.

Members of our prayer group could be called the Lord's reconnaissance team. While the US was hunting for Osama Bin Laden, the Holy Spirit talked only about Saddam Hussein and nuclear war.[β] A few days after the September 11th attacks, the Lord showed American cities occupied by organized Arab military soldiers with tanks, and missiles.[χ] Other team members had visions of enemy hideouts, weapons warehouses and nuclear warheads.

God revealed to us very specific <u>war</u> activity that was being planned against the United States and its allies. Not only did we see them, but also the Lord taught us through many visions how we as Spirit-filled believers could overcome the evil weapons of the enemy. The visions and dreams emphasized numerous demonstrations of God's power to overcome armed men, bombs and flying bullets. Our prayer team saw themselves performing specific rescue missions in their own neighborhoods. It was as though we were all rehearsing for the extraordinary events to come. No matter what we saw, each of us knew that our job was to pray for God's Will to prevail in this conflict. The Lord repeatedly told us not to fear; that He would be a very present help in our time of need. Darkness was indeed coming, but He assured us that prayer would overcome the grotesque evil.

From the outside it would seem that we were blessed to have seen and heard from God at this level, however, the more grotesque the scenes appeared, the more painful hearing from God became. Many members of our prayer team were not able to handle the graphic and violent spiritual images. We all saw hundreds of military planes in formation bombing American cities.* The Lord showed dozens of nations uniting to war against the United States. We saw the Russia, North Korea and China militarily supporting the war against America.$^{\alpha}$ Such knowledge weighted heavily on the hearts and minds of the prayer team.

The Lord had me privately discuss with each member what God showed him or her. These sessions were designed to compare what was heard with what the Bible said, teaching them how to discern God's voice and act appropriately to His message. One of the biggest challenges as prayer leader was reassuring the team that they did not have abnormal gifts. The Lord was calling each of us into military service for our country. The gifts of the Spirit are to be used as a demonstration that Jesus is alive and the Kingdom of God is operating in our midst. The church is accustomed to using the gifts to entertain congregations on Sunday mornings. But, from the beginning of the church, the gifts were used to draw non-believers into the kingdom. And, so it will be during this coming war. The Lord will use His people to guide our country and military to victory, and prove once and for all that Jesus is alive and reigning in America.

Our team experienced what God desires for all His sons on this earth. Unfortunately most Christians experience a small taste of the spiritual gifts and they get into pride, or operate in their human understanding and move further away from God. But, those who go after God with a pure and honest heart desiring His Will can experience the extremes of supernatural abundant life on earth. This abundance is not just physical, but it is also spiritual. It is the same oneness with God that Adam had in Eden and Jesus demonstrated on earth during His ministry. This is the greatest part of our inheritance in God: the ability to see, hear and respond to life's challenges on earth like our Father operates in Heaven. The fullness of God resides in every believer. We will see the manifestation of that fullness only if we abide in Him.

Even with one-on-one sessions and Biblical support for what we heard, there were still major challenges for the team. Team members began to share their visions and dreams with leaders whom they respected. The results were disastrous. Some were left devastated and humiliated by the same leaders they trusted. Others could not reconcile the fact that their bishops, pastors or church leaders did not acknowledge the team member's gifts or calling. Nor did their leaders discern the signs of the times. A tremendous event was being exposed in the spirit realm, yet the spiritual leaders of the churches were unaware of it. Strong religious backgrounds prohibited others from acting on God's prophetic Word unless a man of God from a 'mega' ministry confirmed that prophetic Word. Some members also had many conflicts between what they were being taught in church and what they were hearing from God, and chose to ignore what they received from God in order to please their leaders.

What was amazing is that none of the trusted leaders had any knowledge of spiritual things at this level, yet none offered to pray and seek God's guidance in these matters. Men of God spoke from their human understanding to explain away the visions and dreams that were sent to prepare God's people for devastation to come. Some of the team members were told that to even speak about such evil things evokes fear and not faith. Still, others were pressured by leadership to put away all spiritual gifts for fear that further revelation that would confuse the church. But, these messages were not initially given to the church. They were given to intercessors for prayer and intervention.

Others were told that God speaks only to encourage and exhort His people and any message about death and war were labeled as evil and not from God. They failed to see that God was showing how human obedience allows the Spirit of God to triumph over evil, death and war. Through the Spirit, God was exhorting us to obey the Word and walk by faith, even in war.

There are very few people who are chosen to spiritually see and hear at this level and during this hour. God is urgently calling the chosen and faithful few into their positions before war begins. At least two team members, after being ostracized began to renounce all gifts of the Spirit. A visiting pastor gave a strong Word of correction from the Lord; accusing these members of blaspheming the Holy Spirit. They not only saw visions of war and devastation, but also were given instructions on how to prepare for war. Others were told to remain hidden in Christ through obedience. This would allow one to go on stealth missions to disarm the enemy or rescue others without being seen.

Assuredly, the care and safety of others was placed in the team member's hands, yet some contemplated suicide in order to get out of their assignments. They began to question their sanity while experiencing what God showed them, and desired to kill themselves rather than to stand and fight for the kingdom and our nation. They could not handle the responsibility needed in order to perform mighty exploits in the earth, bringing glory to God's Name. To know God's Will in this hour and do nothing, will cause God's wrath to be against the chosen ones. It is my prayer that this book resurrects the seed of greatness that the Lord sowed in their hearts for this hour.

As a prayer leader with vast experience in supernatural manifestations of the Spirit, I could sympathize with those suffering team members. But, if one hopes to increase in the spiritual things of God, he or she should never lean on his or her own understanding to explain a supernatural phenomenon. Nor should one should share with another what they have seen in the spirit unless the Lord instructs them to do so. If the message is meant only for prayer, it could confuse the hearts and minds of those not called to hear the message. It also invites undiscerning people to interpret the message in error. Only the Spirit of the Lord can accurately interpret things of the spirit. But, once one is sure God has spoken then one must only follow His instructions concerning the Word that was received. To do otherwise could result in major consequences that could impede the spiritual progress that God is initiating. This usually means that people will began praying against you, your gifts and the assignment God gave you. Out of their ignorance they will begin to pray against the Will of God to their own hurt.

I also cautioned team members to never use the Bible to quench the Spirit of God. Satan knows the Bible. He even battled Jesus with God's written word.[*] Jesus won the battle because He was led by the Spirit of God as to which specific scriptures to use against Satan. A specific word or scripture provided by the Spirit of God at a specific time for a specific reason, is call a *Rhema*[α] word. Jesus had a *Rhema* word from God that defeated Satan.

Unless someone has *Rhema* from God concerning an experience, the Bible alone may not be sufficient enough interpretation. The Bible is vital to knowing God's general will. But, without a personal relationship that comes from fasting, prayer, and meditation on the scriptures, or without the leading of the Spirit of God, one will never know God's specific will (*Rhema*) in a specific situation.

When Jesus prepared the disciples for persecution after His death, He told them to expect a *Rhema* word from God. Jesus told them not to think of what to say, but that He would give them a mouth and wisdom that all the adversaries would not be able to resist.[*] If Jesus was gone from the earth, how could He give them wisdom to speak specific things? The Spirit of God within them would do the speaking for them.[α] Jesus told them that although He would be gone, they would not be left comfortless.[β] He was sending another comforter who was called the Spirit of Truth, who would dwell with us and be in us forever. Jesus said that the Holy Spirit would guide us into all truth and would speak what Jesus said.[χ] Likewise, God wants to speak through us and guide us today, especially in times or war or tragedy.

When I first began this assignment the Lord told me that He was '*infinite.*' That is more than the human mind can comprehend. I trust what the Lord tells me more than I trust my own thoughts. He told me not to put Him in a box. This is a command that I cannot violate no matter what.

In this particular assignment, I was often overwhelmed by what the Lord was saying. I prayed for His guidance to put things into perspective. Later, I was commanded to write down what I saw and heard. Until this project, I was not consistent at keeping a prayer journal. My time with the Lord is very private and personal to me. When He leads me into prayer for the nations or for leaders, or for the church, I keep His confidences. I never speak what He tells me unless He says so. In the past I never recorded much of what God said because I knew that the Holy Spirit would bring to my mind whatever I needed to remember.

Writing a journal and then making it available for others to read was like bearing my soul to the world. It was painful. The persecution and severe criticism were more than I care to recall. And, when I thought the journal for President Bush was done, the Lord then commanded me to write a book for publication.* He made it very clear that if I did not speak His Word of warning to the rebellious, their blood would be on my hands. It is because of this godly fear that my journal was recorded and this book was written and made available for distribution.

I fully understood that my assignment was not a glamorous one, yet it was essential that I obeyed at all costs. The Lord sent me out like He did the first apostles. I would deliver the Word He instructed and then move on to the next city. The purpose of my assignment was to prepare leaders for the next move of God's Spirit upon the nations. It has only been during the past nine years that the Lord instructed me to deliver the message concerning preparation for war in America.

My plan was always to keep as low of profile as possible. Any unnecessary attention could cause jealousy and retaliation from the enemy. My acceptance in most churches was overwhelmingly positive until I delivered the Word. The Lord said He was sending me to the most rebellious of His people, so not to be shocked by the rejection. According to the Lord, those who reject the Word He gives me to speak will perish in the destruction that is coming on the earth. God wants His people to obey. If they refuse to obey, they alone are responsible for the consequences they face. I am determined that their blood not be on my hands.

Since taking on this project, the persecution has been unbelievable. Public ridicule was bad enough, and then there were death threats too numerous to count. The Lord has had me deliver the word and flee before the death threats could be executed. I have been thrown out of churches and asked to leave many. I have been called demonic, a witch and a liar. I was physically accosted and locked in a room while visiting one church. One pastor's wife wanted to run over me with her car. Another pastor's wife called herself the devil and threatened to throw me down a flight of stairs. Someone else tried to force my car off a cliff on a back road.

Then there was the pastor who threw a punch at me while my head was turned. I turned around by the Spirit and blocked the punch. Several pastors and prophets have tried to steal my journal. One actually broke into my hotel room and stole my computer disks. She said the Lord told her to do it. The devil retaliated because of my assignment, but out of all these things the Lord has brought me unharmed.

These responses are typical of what I have experienced in the church. God's people spend more time slandering their brothers and sisters, lying, gossiping, cheating and seeking positions, than perfecting the things of God and displaying love for one another. The best reception I have had with the Word has been with those outside of the church. Wherever the Lord sent me, I carried His Word. It may not have been about war, but it is always about the kingdom. I have delivered the Word to business leaders, office workers, and to the man on the street. These people are hungry for the Word. I have had gang bangers and street hoods ask me about God and how His Spirit speaks. There are many people that know God and have experienced His Spirit, but they will not step foot into a church. They want to see the real Jesus. They know that Jesus and His power are real. They just don't want to be part of a hypocritical church.

The war in America will cause the true worshippers to step forward and demonstrate His love and mercy to the hurting masses. The true church of Jesus Christ will appear in our midst, and it won't be church as usual. In fact, being part of the true church will put us in direct opposition to the religious establishment of our time. If you want to be part of <u>this</u> church, it will cost you everything. Jesus said that if you don't forsake all for the kingdom, you could not be His disciple.* Forsaking all is the least we can do for our Savior who gave all He had, even His very life that we might be all we can be in Him. If we sacrifice our desires in this world for His sake, He will give us His desires that will satisfy our souls for an eternity.$^\alpha$

My Heart's Desire

The writing of this book has been quite an adventure on many levels. Most authors get an idea and spend days, perhaps years developing that idea and translating it on to paper. As a prophetic writer led by the Spirit of God, this was also a time of translating God's Words on to paper, but the power of the words I wrote began transforming everything in and around me.

When God speaks, people and things hearing His words are forced to change from their initial position, to end up at God's desired position. The force of truth as spoken by God propels things into another mode of operation. Truly, my mind has been renewed throughout the writing of this book. Sometimes the transformation has been very painful. There are many who heard what I heard and were in agreement with me on this project. Very few of those people remained with me until the completion. The most painful was the man of God whose help I needed to write this book. Because the book required a leap of faith far beyond his religious understanding, he abandoned this project and me, but not before conspiring with others to pray against me to stop this book from going forth. A battle ensued and I was attacked with deliberate hostile, yet *friendly fire*. The Lord let me know that this man left me to die on the battlefield with a few other faithful laborers. We are still alive today because of obedience to the word of God that we heard.

Then there were the ones who were sent to help me, but somewhere along the process became jealous and wanted to sabotage this project; believing they could do things their way because they are called of God. This is not how Jesus lived. He did only as He was told, but they believed that God somehow made an exception in their case.

Along with these were the detractors who had nonsense prayer requests or teaching requests, but had no desire to hear from God. Their only desire was to take my focus away from what God was calling me to do. There were those in my inner circle who ridiculed me and my dreams from God because of my background. The plan was to discourage me enough so that I would abandon this project. I even had threats that if I ever became famous, they would make millions off my name by making up lies and selling them to the press.

Then there was the ex-husband who declared himself to be the only god that I would ever serve. When I continued to pursue God, this man kidnapped my son. When that did not stop me, he hired perverted men to follow me with cameras hoping to find me doing something. When they found nothing, they decided to humiliate me by showing up on my job with pictures taken while I was showering; using emotional blackmail to hurt me knowing that exposing those pictures to the public would hinder this project. And then, there was the witchcraft, Voodoo and numerous death threats on our lives. The Lord said that it was Satan's plan to murder us before the book was released. But, in all these things we have been more than conquerors.

This book was successfully completed because the Word of God had within itself, the power to transform and protect the messengers. This is the victory that overcomes the world and its evil; our faith. My focus was always on delivering this message, no matter the consequence. I saw this word supernaturally moving through our lives and I knew it would do the same for others. Throughout the pain and suffering, I remained on task. God was faithful to change our circumstances as we obeyed His word with a pure heart.

This word catapulted me beyond my fears of retaliation and humiliation. It even pushed me beyond my fears of discovering the darkness that still remained within my soul. God called His Word a *__mine sweeper.__* It has the ability to go within the depths of our beings detonating and defusing things that would have destroyed us from the inside out. I therefore present this book not just as a writer, but also as a transformed product of this word. There were many days that I started to write, yet spent hours on my face in travail before God. There were other days when I wrestled with the word because it greatly challenged what I wanted for my life. In the end, the word conquered my will and changed my desires.

I have learned many great lessons while writing this book. The more that God reveals to me in vision and dreams, the more I realize that while I understand much about Him, I truly have just scratched the surface of His understanding. I am humbled more and more each time He speaks.

I am convinced that I will never understand the entire purpose of anything He commands me to do, until I see Him face-to-face. Yet, I am also convinced that God's thrill is when we as His children pursue Him in order to search His infinite wisdom. This I believe is the joy of His heart. He desires that we pursue Him, and when we do, He pours out revelations from heaven too great to utter.

My heart's desire is that readers of this book would pursue God's dream for their lives. Pursue Him with all the passion of your being. Then, hold onto whatever He tells you. This is a precious gem from heaven given to you to glorify God in this earth.

God's thoughts and ways are far beyond our thoughts and our ways. In the human mind, it is impossible, but God has placed within you all the faith to make it possible, otherwise, He would not have given it to you. Hold on to the word in spite of criticism, disappointment and hardship. The dream will come to pass if you don't give up. Rely on God's faithfulness to His word. Do not rely on your abilities to bring the dream forth. Let God do it. It is His dream and His plan for your life. Who best would know how to bring it to pass?

Beloved, pursue God and His ways of doing things, and you will never see the world the same way again. You will see as God sees. You will understand as God understands. You will be immensely blessed and supernaturally transformed for an eternity!

ABOUT THE JOURNAL

'Write The Vision, And Make It Plain ...

For The Vision Is Yet For An Appointed Time

... At The End It Shall Speak, And Not Lie ... '

Habakkuk 2:2-3 KJV

The Purpose For This Journal

It is in obedience to God that I have written a narrative version of my prayer journal. The Lord labeled it my *"War Journal."* It is a chronological record of many of the visions, dreams, prophecies and other spiritual encounters I received directly from the Almighty God concerning war in America.

The purpose of this journal is to provide evidence that God is tracking the plans of the enemy in war; both in our personal difficulties and those of America. Despite the apparent horror of what appears in this journal, there are several repetitive truths demonstrated throughout:

1) God's people are protected
2) God's people will prosper
3) The miraculous power of God will be evident
4) The judgment of God will be executed with boldness against His enemies.

The Lord has something to prove to the church and to the world. America wants God to bless her, but she continues to rebel against the knowledge of His existence until a tragedy occurs. The Lord faults the church for the condition of America. God's people are very rebellious. They too, want God to bless them, but they won't obey His Word. They don't love Him and won't love their neighbors. The church refuses to live the gospel that they preach. If they had been standing boldly for what's right in God's eyes and had been praying without ceasing for our nation's leaders, we could have prevented much of what is to come.

I have had many sleepless and sorrowful nights over what the Lord has shown me in the spirit. The various visions of planes and bombings in the sky were repeated not only every day, but sometimes throughout the day for weeks at a time. Some things were so graphic in nature that I did not want to remember them, let alone put them on paper. It was with the help of the Holy Spirit that I have completed this project. What He has shown me is evidence that these attacks on America have been planned over a period of years. It is not humanly possible to undo the enemy's laborious plans.

Likewise, the Lord shows in my personal life that attacks had been planned over a period of years before I knew what I was called to do. There are graphic details about the war tactics launched against me and my husband while trying to produce a book and setting up not for profit organizations to help the suffering. Whether it's a personal situation or problems of our nation, prayer for supernatural intervention is our only hope for resolution.

The Lord wants to prove that neither judicial, political nor will military authority be able to save America from the death and devastation that is coming. Only God can save America!! He is calling His Kingdom army to boldly arise. They are coming armed with faith-powered words and taking dominion. America will be saved and the great commission to seek and save the lost will continue, because Jesus will rule and reign in America!!

The Way I Receive Information
From The Holy Spirit

Most of what is recorded in this journal occurred during my personal prayer time or during prayer with other intercessors, unless otherwise noted. The methods and timing used by God to speak to me were unpredictable. God does what He chooses to do because it's His Spirit and His Word.

I've had flashes of information in **visions** along with a spoken Word of God. Other times it's an open vision (**translation**) where I am taken by the spirit to a location and shown detail. Friends and family have witnessed some of the unusual spiritual occurrences. They saw me blank out while in conversation with them, and I came back speaking as though I was a million miles away in another conversation. Oftentimes I could not tell exactly where the Lord took me, but I could recall what happened.

I have had detailed night visions (**dreams**) during a deep sleep where I can feel, touch and smell all that is around me, while asleep. During prayer, I often go into trances by the Spirit of the Lord, where I speak (**prophesy**) and do things by His Spirit. I also have recorded several **angelic visitations**. In any case, whether a vision, prophecy or visitation, there are over one hundred such occurrences recorded in this journal.

It is my sincere belief that the following visions and dreams and other spiritual events were given solely for the purpose of interceding in prayer for our nation.   The only exceptions are when the Lord specifically stated that an event would happen and prayer could not be made to intercede.

I also believe that the visions and dreams portrayed are the worst possible scenarios that the enemy could plan. I know that the effectual fervent prayers of the righteous will always change situations in the earth to reflect the Will of Almighty God. Our country's success in intercession is the sole reason the war will not manifest to a greater degree.

Notes About The Journal

In May 2002 the Spirit of the Lord told me to *__prepare a war journal for the president.__*[*] It was then that I immediately asked the Holy Spirit to bring to my remembrance all that the Lord told me by His Spirit since 1999. One obvious difficulty in preparing this journal was matching the exact dates for all the entries. With the help of prayer groups and others who were witnesses to what the Lord was saying through me at the time, most of the entries could be approximated to at least the exact month of occurrence.

In retrospect, it is apparent that God was indeed in control. I was led by the Spirit of the Lord to begin prayer groups in March 2001,[α] but did not get the direct word on war[β] until July of that same year. Even the weekend before September 11th, we were just told to pray for the nation[χ] as we had done months before. There were no specific dreams or visions given concerning war details until after September 11th attack. Once the attack occurred, the visions and dreams bombarded our spirits daily for months. Some of my prayer group members have also seen similar visions and dreams. Only the ones I received directly are included in this journal. The majority of journal entries during the October 2001 through July 2002 periods contained details about specific war activities that would occur in the future. Many of these were rescue missions and revelations of the enemy's planned attacks on our nation. What is recorded is not conclusive.

Numerous new visions have been recorded since preparing this document; some vary slightly from the previous ones. The most outstanding of these unrecorded visions included those showing bombs being placed under the structures of bridges and in various buildings throughout the US. There were also visions concerning the wealth transfer. The Holy Spirit did not bring this back to my memory until the final writing of this journal. The absence of these occurrences in no way changes the message the Lord wants to convey concerning the upcoming war.

In addition this journal chronicles the personal warfare of the writer. The names of people and places in these particular instances have been changed to protect their privacy.

Finally, I apologize for the fragmented journal entry style. In the handwritten journal, the fragmented sentences were used only to capture the general thought of the vision or dream that the Holy Spirit emphasized. Further detail and explanation is included in this edited version where necessary. Endnotes are symbolically annotated and listed in the Appendix and categorized by chapter.

Warning To The Skeptic

To those in the church who do not believe that God speaks to men today, I congratulate you for opening this book. You are at least curious about what has been written. There is much scripture quoted and documented in this book. I encourage you to get your Bible and read the scriptures that support what is recorded in this journal. If you still are not satisfied with what you've read, then commit it to God in prayer and let Him reveal it to you. That is, if there is a breath of hope within you for God to answer prayers and reveal Himself to you.

If you are reading just to poke fun at something you don't understand, I pray that the Spirit of God overtakes you with such a significant hunger and thirst for Him that it spills over on everyone in your path. May He open the eyes of your understanding to see Him as He wishes to be known by you; not as you think He is, but as He truly desires to be known.

The Lord desires to fellowship with man. The Lord walked with Adam and Eve in the Garden of Eden.*When Adam sinned, that fellowship was broken. When Jesus came to reconcile us back to God, fellowship was part of the deal. After all, the veil of the temple, which separated mere men from the holiness of God, was torn so that we could have direct access to God.[α] The Apostle John had fellowship with God. He exhorted the church to walk in the light as God is in the Light, and have fellowship with God.[β]

The word fellowship, used in these passages, is translated from the Greek language as *koinonia*,[*] which means a direct communication, or social interaction. Jesus said that if we obey Him, He and the Father would abide with us and would manifest Himself to us.[α] If Jesus is in your house (or in your heart), and He is not speaking, something is wrong. You would never invite someone into your home without expect to hold a conversation with them. So, why would invite Jesus into your heart and not expect Him to answer? Something is terribly wrong. Either Jesus lied in the scriptures, or you are walking in darkness. You may not be committing obvious sins, like fornication or murder, but unbelief is indeed a sin. Unbelief is common among Christians, but the Bible calls this it as "an evil heart of unbelief".[β]

Now, there are some who believe that God only speaks by bearing witness with your spirit the Truths of the Bible. These people don't believe in the gifts of the Spirit that Apostle Paul discussed.[χ] These people do not accept the idea that God would move upon men supernaturally by His Spirit. Then there are those who believe that all they need to know about God is written in the Bible. They don't believe any prophecy other than those contained in the Bible. Anything beyond what is written they consider not of God.

Let me remind you what John said about Jesus' ministry on earth. He said that Jesus did many more signs than those recorded in the book of John. This was only a sampling of Jesus' work on earth. They were written so that men would believe Jesus was the Son of God so that they might have eternal life.[*] But, if you truly love God with all your heart, wouldn't you desire to know Him even more?

John ended his book by saying there were many other things that Jesus did, if they all would have been written, the world could not contain the books that would be written.[α] John purposely mentions the vastness of Jesus' work on earth. John in his three-year walk with Jesus could not record all that He did in the earth. And, if John said that to do so would be impossible, why would anyone who claims to know God think all they need to know about Him exists only on the pages of the Bible? Are not God's thoughts and ways are above ours?[β] For mere men to think they know God based solely on what they have read is preposterous. God's ways are infinite.[χ]

Listen, if you do not believe God speaks to men today then God won't speak to you; faith comes by hearing of the Word.[δ] It's very simple. How many times did Jesus say, 'he that hath ears to hear let him hear?'[ε] If you don't believe, you won't receive! But, for those who want to receive, let's move on to how Jesus dealt with the skeptics of his day.

Look at Jesus' life. It was His custom to go into the synagogue and read the scriptures.* The written word was of such value to Jesus that when He was tempted of Satan in the wilderness, He overcame temptation by saying 'it is written.'[α] God definitely speaks through the Bible, but He also speaks by His Spirit directly to men. Jesus said that His sheep recognize and understand His voice.[β] The Bible reveals God's mind and character, but you can memorize the entire Bible and still never know God or hear His voice. How sad! Reading and studying about God is not the same as knowing Him. Jesus said that eternal life means having intimate knowledge of the true God and of Jesus whom God sent.[χ]

Recall a discourse Jesus had with the Pharisees. They sought to kill Jesus because He said that He was the Son of God. Jesus told them to search the scriptures all they wanted, but the scriptures spoke of Him and they refused to believe Him.[δ] They knew what was written, but when God was speaking directly to them, they could not hear. Jesus said this was because they read and studied the word, but the word was not abiding in them. God forbid that those elected to Know God during our day and time would not recognize Him, nor hear His voice when He comes the second time.

The religious skeptic would say, that Jesus learned all He knew from studying the scriptures, but Jesus did and said what He saw the Father do.* If Jesus was on earth, and the Father was in heaven, how did He see what the Father did? When Jesus went into the wilderness to be tempted by Satan[α] did He read on page 352 of His Holy Scriptures; *thou shalt go into the wilderness and be tempted*? NO! The Bible said that the Holy Spirit led Jesus into the wilderness. And, when He needed go to Samaria[β] did Jesus read that in the scriptures or did the Spirit of the Lord speak to Him? When Jesus raised Lazarus from the dead, how did He know that it was going to be done for the glory of God?[χ] None of these actions of Jesus were written in an instruction book. God sent the Holy Spirit to lead Jesus on earth. The Lord gives His Spirit to lead men on earth. He did it for His Son Jesus, why not also for us who are predestinated to be conformed to the image of Jesus?[δ]

God, the Father explained to me that it is impossible for earthly men to accomplish His plan without the Holy Spirit. God said that just as Jesus needed the Holy Spirit to live on earth. Godly men cannot live successfully in this life without Him. God said that He is Spirit. Jesus is His Body. The Holy Spirit is His Mind. Neither the Father, nor the Son, or nor the Holy Spirit operate apart from the other. They are one.

To perfectly carry out the will of God on earth we must also be one with God the Father, God the Son, and God the Holy Spirit. This is only possible when we give our body and mind to God and allow the Holy Spirit (the Mind of God) leads us. The Lord said that the Bible is the Christian's operating manual just like the driver's handbook is to those who drive an automobile. He said that you don't learn to drive by memorizing the handbook. It merely sets forth basic rules by which you can legally operate on the road. In the same way, He said that the Bible sets the basic rules by which Christians should legally operate in life.

We learn to drive by getting into the car and gaining experience in handling the road based on various circumstances involving other drivers on the road. Likewise, a Christian learns how to operate by gaining life experiences handling others we encounter on a daily basis. And guess what? Not everything is in the Book!

For example, what do you do when the green light tells you to go, but a peace officer standing in the middle of the intersection commands you to stop? Which do you obey? The handbook says that the green light in your direction means go. But there was no mention of what happens when a peace officer is in the middle of the road. So, how do you decide what to do? It is in the experience of being on the road that you learn the application of the rules which are written in the book.

A handbook gives us basic rules, but we adapt what we have read to what we see and experience in each situation. And so it is with the Christian life. When we meditate on the word and attempt to do it, the Holy Spirit helps us adapt what we've read to each situation. His voice should be given highest priority when we are driving on the highway of life. He is the heavenly peace officer sent to warn us of danger ahead. He guides us to a better way of doing things in this earth. He is our comforter and helper. The world cannot receive him because they don't see Him or know Him.* But, if a Christian cannot receive him either, it's because they don't believe.

Nowhere in the Bible does it say that God no longer speaks to men, yet this is a belief held by men who have used I Corinthians 13:8-11 to justify the belief that God no longer speaks to men. They argue that this chapter is proof that prophecies, the gift of tongues, and the gift of knowledge cease to exist today. Why? Because they say that humans today have outgrown the gifts of God. Now that we are mature we should put away childish things. They actually think that God speaking through men is childish. These people stop reading that passage too soon. There's more explanation in the next Chapter. I Corinthians chapter 14 continues the discussion of spiritual gifts. The very first verse of this chapter says to pursue love and spiritual gifts. In particular, Paul stresses the need to prophesy. An honest student of the Bible would question why Paul would spend so much time discussing the importance of spiritual gifts if he felt they were childish and vanishing away. Does Paul contradiction himself? No!

Those who use these verses to oppose spiritual gifts are not spirit-filled Christians being led and guided by the Holy Spirit. Otherwise, they would understand how love is necessary in order for the gifts of the Spirit to operate in the earth. The Holy Spirit is the earnest[*] promise and a sign of what is to come when all things are perfected in Jesus. We can only know in part until we are reunited with the Lord in heaven. When we see Jesus, we will be like Him.[α] There will be no need for the Holy Spirit to show us of the Lord because we will be with Him. There will be no need for the gifts or tongues because we will speak to Him face to face.[β]

Not only will there be no tongues or prophecy in heaven. Hey, there will be no churches or denominations either. Imagine, no more arguments about which day is the Sabbath because there will be no sun or moon because there will be no night to distinguish the days in heaven. So, how will you know which day is the Sabbath? The Bible says that the Father and Son are the temple and the illumination of everything in heaven.[*] Therefore everyday in the presence of the Father will be a Sabbath in heaven. We will worship and praise him without ceasing for an eternity. Hallelujah!

Finally, there are those that have been so embarrassed by charismatic drama that they want no part of the Holy Ghost or the spiritual gifts. Please understand that to do so is doing a disservice to a Holy God who desires to show His Glory in the earth. It is the plan of Satan to keep the church powerless. Without spiritual gifts, the church has no power. The Apostle Paul tells us to avoid those appearing godly yet they deny the power of God from operating.[α] In this time of war, America needs the full power of God to be in operation if our country is to survive. The Lord is calling His sons out of Egypt to lead the battle. They will take dominion for the kingdom because their hearts are honest and pure before God. Their only desire is to see God move upon the face of the earth in order to transform the lives of men.

Those who received Jesus, have been given the power to become sons of God,[β] but not everyone will walk in that power. Many are hindered by their minds and their lusts, yet God has reserved for Himself a remnant of sons, birthed by His Spirit. They will glorify Him mightily in the earth during the season of darkness.

These are the men and women who understand the power of stepping out of a boat in the midst of a turbulent storm. It takes little faith to believe in what Jesus did, but it takes even greater faith to walk on water as the Lord commands us to "Come". God in this hour is calling His sons to step out of the boat and keep their minds fixed on His power and not on the storm around us. This will be a true test of our faith.

If you desire to intimately know God as Father and want to operate on earth as His son, seek His Face. Seek to know more about the workings of the Holy Ghost. Earnestly seek the Lord and ask Him to reveal His truth. He rewards those that diligently seek Him.[*] But you must believe that God is what the Word says He is, not what you think He is, nor what you have been told. Seek Him with your whole heart and you will find Him. Seek only the Truth and the Lord will reveal Himself.

When Daniel sought the mercies of God concerning the secret of Nebuchadnezzar's dream, he did so that he and his friends would not perish. How much more should we seek God today concerning the secrets of what is to come so that our nation will not perish. When God revealed the secret to Daniel (Daniel 2:19-22) he blessed God and said,[α]

'Blessed be the name of God forever and ever: for wisdom and might are his: and he changeth the times and the seasons: he removeth kings and setteth up kings: he giveth wisdom to the wise and knowledge to them that know understanding: he revealeth deep and secret things: he knoweth what is in the darkness, and light dwelleth with him.'

Seek God with your whole heart. Take the limits off of the infinite God and let Him show His face. Blessed are the pure in heart,[β] for they shall see God move miraculously on earth, and they will appear victorious before Him in heaven.

Warning To Those Eager
To Explore The Spirit Realm

There will be some of you that will read this book and be anxious to seek visions and dreams and plunge into the intrigue of the spirit realm. **STOP and CONSIDER!!!** What are your motivations for seeking visions and dreams or any supernatural experience?

Are you seeking a thrill? Do you seek notoriety? Do you seek power and personal gain? **BEWARE!!!** Do you have legal permission to enter the spirit realm? If not. **BEWARE!!!** Under whose authority and by what means are you entering in? Is it by God or by Satan? Are you using godly prayer, witchcraft (ungodly prayers) or tarot cards? **BEWARE!!!** If you enter into the spirit realm with wrong motives, without legal access, or by ungodly authority and means, there will be demonic spirits eager to oblige you and satisfy your desire for visions, dreams and prophetic utterances.

In this section, we will explore the correct manner in which to seek spiritual revelation from God. We will also give Biblical and real life examples of what happens when human beings enter into the spirit realm illegally.

Many in the church have backed away from spiritual things because of what a few cracked pots did in the past. But it was the Potter's original plan to place within us the fullness of His Spirit, a glory that would be revealed from vessels who obey His Will.

The Apostle Paul said that within the believer is the hidden wisdom[*] of God that cannot be seen, heard or perceived by the human senses. The Holy Spirit reveals this wisdom to those who love God. Jesus said that if we love Him, we will keep His commandments, and He would ask the Father to send the Holy Spirit to dwell in us and be with us forever.[α]

He also said that if we love and obey Him, He would reveal Himself to us.[*] Therefore, obedience to God's Word results in divine revelation as given by the Holy Spirit. The Holy Spirit is God's proof that we are His for an eternity. So, if we come to God in obedience, we can expect the Holy Spirit to reveal spiritual truths to us anyway God chooses, whether through a dream, vision, or prophetic utterances.

Since access into the spirit realm is part of the inheritance of the believer, it is important for us to discuss the correct way to enter into this heavenly realm. There are spirit filled believers who actually think they can go in and out of the spirit realm and only find God. Wrong! How you enter into the spirit realm will determine who or what you tap into. You must understand that the supernatural realm is not only where God and His angels operate. Satan and His angels are there too. Jesus said that He is the door by which you should enter in. Anyone who enters in the spirit realm any other way is a thief and robber who comes only to steal, kill and to destroy.[α] Jesus is the only way to God <u>and</u> the things of the spirit that provide abundant life. Any other entrance into the heavenlies is illegal according to the Bible and will result in destruction.

Now that we have established that Jesus is the only Door for entering into the spirit realm, let's see who is qualified to enter through that Door. Jesus said that only sheep could enter through the door.[β] But who are the sheep? Jesus described the sheep as those who hear and obey his voice. So, in order to legally enter the spirit realm one has to become a sheep (follower) of Jesus Christ.

A sheep is one who is led and guided by a shepherd. Without the shepherd, the sheep would be aimlessly scattered, and slaughtered by wolves. A sheep is totally dependent upon the shepherd for daily provision, protection and guidance. The Psalmist David knew first hand that if the Lord was his shepherd, everything he wanted would be provided for by God.[α] The Lord also gave David much spiritual revelation. David wrote that the man who fears (obeys) God would receive secrets from the Lord.[β] Jesus is telling us today to follow Him and do what He tells us and God would provide everything we need, whether it is answers to spiritual secrets or other provision in this world.

So this is what we know from the Bible. To legally enter the spirit realm and to receive the spiritual knowledge of God, one must come through Jesus by becoming a follower of Jesus and by obeying His commandments.

God is very clear that He does not want us following any other voice but His. In our day of information overload, there are voices speaking quite persuasively everywhere you turn. Many have chosen to listen to the voices that make human sense. You may have heeded some the voices of talk show hosts, celebrities, witches, psychics, horoscopes, séances and other mediums. Mediums and the media are just that; an avenue for transferring information from a source to a recipient for a specific purpose.

If the voice you heed is not God's, it is either a voice speaking the words of man (his world and culture), or the words of demons. Their purpose is to entertain you, amuse you, take your money, and ultimately your life. Some of these voices may even seem to help humanity and the culture of their day. But if these voices do not point you to God, their ultimate purpose is to get you to follow them and exalt their thrones above the throne of God. They want to be god in your life.

If you choose not to follow the voice of God, whose voice are you following? God asked Adam the same thing after they ate from the tree of the knowledge of good and evil. The most devastating sin they committed against God was trying to get knowledge from a source other than God. Imagine this. God, the Creator gave them all the wealth, dominion, and knowledge they would have ever needed to flourish in the earth. And yet, when Adam and Eve wanted to know more about creation, they talked to a serpent. They chose the serpent as their source rather than the Creator who knows all things. Think it not strange, because the same thing happens in our day.

When Adam and Eve sinned against God, a sacred trust had been violated and the communications line between God and man was severed. It is important for God to be in relationship with man. This is what God designed from the beginning of creation. It is also important for human beings to understand that if they are not obeying the voice God, it is because they obeying another voice. To heed another voice will separate man from God now <u>and</u> for an eternity.

Let's briefly go back and see why man's source of information is important to God. When Adam and Eve got their information from the serpent, they ceased to be followers of God and became followers of the serpent who represented Satan in the earth.

The Bible says that whomever we submit our bodies to obey, become our master, and we are enslaved to that thing.[α] So while they were created to serve God as children and receive all the knowledge and goodness God had, when they submitted to serpent they became enslaved to sin and evil.

What is sad about Adam and Eve is that they had access to all the knowledge of God from the very beginning. They spoke with God daily in the garden. Anything they wanted to know God would have told them. God had the knowledge and understanding of all that He created in the heavens and earth. Satan had limited knowledge of things he did not create. Yet, Satan (who was using the Serpent) was clever enough to seduce Adam and Eve into believing he knew more than God.

Today, people still listen to and obey a snake. They listen to false prophets, psychics, witches and those who consult familiar spirits. The demonic spirit associated with such practices is called the spirit of divination.[*] The Greek word for divination is python (a snake).

In the Bible, when God's people went to possess the Promised Land, the Lord told them not to consult witches, diviners, charmers, wizards, or anyone who consults the stars or familiar spirits. To do so was an abomination to God. He said that He would raise up a prophet among the people who would speak the words of God and anyone who did not obey that prophet would die.[α] Jesus is that prophet whom God raised in the earth. We are called to obey Him or die. God made it clear that hearing and obeying any words other than His Words would be a cause for death. These are strong words, but understand that God is not killing people. It's the python that is feeding people words that lead to death. It was Jesus who came to earth saying that His words were spirit and life. And His were living bread sent from heaven to feed humans with the abundant life of God.[ε]

Let me pause for a moment. Now, if any of you have a background in practicing or consulting witchcraft or divination, you have been partaking evil venom from a python and it will kill you. But it's not too late to turn around and starting partaking from the Bread of Life.

48

I might add that the python is very active in churches around the world. It can be seen in people who use the Bible to control and manipulate people to follow after them instead of God. Many have used the Bible as a weapon to intentionally place bondages on others. This too is witchcraft, and the churches that practice such are called cults.

Now, for anyone who has been heeding voices other than God and you want to turn around, the steps to change are very simple. First of all, you must renounce all forms of witchcraft and the occult from your past. If you have family or friends that still practice, separate yourself and find a local church with some strong Christian prayer warriors to keep you in a supportive family environment while you transition from death to life. Then, you must ask Jesus to be your Lord; the source of all you do and need to know.

Here is a simple prayer to pray out loud and from your heart.

Dear God, I'm sorry that I looked to others as my source of information and not to you, the Creator of the Universe, and All Knowing God. Today, I make up my mind to change from hearing words of death to hearing and obeying your words of life. So, I ask that Jesus be Lord over my life. I want Him to be my source and shepherd in this life. Fill me with your Spirit and I ask that the Holy Spirit operate thru me. Thank you for hearing and answering my prayer. I ask these things in the Name of Jesus, your son, my Lord and Savior. AMEN.

Now that you have acknowledged Jesus as Lord, turn everything, every thought and every habit over to Him. You life is no longer your own. Your mind and body is no longer your own. You now belong to God, body and spirit. Your purpose now is to glorify God in your body.

In God's family, you now are freely given legal access[*] to our Father and all He has. Since God is our Father, you get what you need by asking Him. Don't try to get things in your own strength. If you don't know what to ask for or how to ask, ask the Holy Spirit to guide you to the will of God for your life. The Bible says if we lack wisdom in God's Will to ask in faith and God will reveal it to us.[α] We do this by praying to God and expecting to receive an answer in whatever form God desires. In plain talk, prayer is just our way of talking to God. It does not have to be with fancy words, but it does have to be from a sincere heart with truth from God's Word. God will answer what is in your heart. Just share your heart with Him and watch Him work in your life.

You must understand that Almighty God is the Creator of the heavens and the earth.[β] As Creator, He has set forth rules on how to operate in the heavens and the earth. The Bible is our earthly guide to living according to God's rules on earth. So, get a Bible and began reading about God's promises to His people. If you don't have one and can't afford to buy one, check our Appendix for Bible resources.

I encourage you to learn of God and let Him lead you through the spirit realm. God Himself will provide the narration as the Bible scripture are being played out before you. There is nothing more reassuring to your faith then seeing the Word of God manifested before your very eyes. God is Real!!! The Bible is Real!!!

Some people want information. But I want the Truth and Wisdom of God. I want to understand the secret things of God. This is the greatest treasure we can ever obtain from God. Daniel knew that God was the revealer of secrets. He was one of the Hebrew boys held in Babylonian captivity. God gave these boys knowledge and skill in all learning and wisdom. Daniel was given understanding in all visions and dreams. The king found these boys ten times wiser than all the Babylonian magicians and astrologers in matters of wisdom and understanding.[*]

Let the Creator of the universe guide you through the heavenlies and reveal His secrets. Seek His wisdom and understanding. God's wisdom makes human wisdom foolishness, and nullifies the understanding of those exalted in the earth.[α] The wisdom of God created the heavens and earth, and all things visible and invisible. God's wisdom is infinite. His Words and ways are higher than any human can understand.[β] In the upcoming season of war, God will demonstrate that even the wisest voices in the earth will not be able to advise nor comfort America. Only those who know God and heed His voice will have the wisdom to triumph in these last days. Man will no longer be glorified. God alone will be glorified in America!

INTRODUCTION

'I invite you to take a step into the <u>Real</u> Matrix; a place where

Anything is possible and anyone who dares to trust God can be a

Supernatural hero!'

Paula Matthews, Expert Author, Ezinearticles.com
From her article entitled, "The Real Matrix: Your Path to a
Supernatural Lifestyle."

The Real Matrix
A Modern Analogy Of Life In Christ

One of my teachers began discussing a prophetic dream she had about God's end time army: a powerful group of believers possessing supernatural abilities. She was particularly impressed with one dream where these believers were flying from one place to another just like Philip was caught up in the Spirit and taken from one city to another.[*] She saw God's people moving by the Spirit and saving the lost by any means heaven felt necessary. They were defying every law of nature and fulfilling the will of God. It was an amazing time of sharing because several of us had had similar dreams. I had even been caught up several times and sent to remote places in China, Africa and India. It was a blast!

Shortly after these teaching began, Warner Brothers studios released a film entitled *The Matrix.*[1] My teacher told me that her grandchildren had taken her to see the movie. She did not understand a thing that was going on. In fact, the violence and supernatural feats made it hard for her to sit through the movie. I thought it odd that after receiving dreams by the Holy Spirit of coming violence and supernatural feats, she would be shocked by seeing something similar in a Hollywood film. It wasn't until I arrived in Cleveland in September of 1999, that I finally saw *The Matrix* on video. My curiosity was aroused as I watched. What I saw and heard thoroughly captivated me.

This was a pivotal time for me because everything the Lord previously said about His end-time church was making more sense; how they would do whatever God wanted regardless of the circumstance. These humans would operate in the earth with the power of heaven backing their every move. The Holy Spirit would teach them what they need to know to get the job done.

It was at this time that the Lord told me to write a new book. He would later have me to write the prayer journal beginning with the series of events that occurred in 1999. The Lord also said that I would someday teach what He called **"The _Real_ Matrix."** This chapter contains an abbreviated version of what the Lord gave me. We will discuss several key points of *The Matrix* movie, making parallels to the gospel of Jesus Christ.

Let me preface this teaching by saying that in no way do I condone the violence, foul language nor graphic images contained in the movie. The movie is Rated R[2], and does not contain the brief sexual scenes that appear in *The Matrix: Reloaded*[3] or in *The Matrix: Revolutions.*[4] The *Matrix* was originally written as a Japanese science fiction animation. Hollywood took this idea and made it into a futuristic Kung Phu thriller. There are dramatically choreographed fight scenes, big guns, exploding building and crash scenes. You will also recognize similar scenes in this journal. The difference is that what appears on the movie screen is from a Hollywood script. What appears in this journal was written from heaven of future violence that is coming upon the earth. The violence that is coming is real, but it comes with a Kingdom message of love, redemption and restoration. It is the story of a God who will do mighty exploits on the behalf of His faithful followers.

I understand that some people may be offended by any comparison being made between a secular Hollywood film and the gospel of Jesus Christ, but the Lord will use any available medium to reach the lost.[*] Most people don't choose God's way, because they don't know God's way. Instead, people heed the world for answers that only God can give them.

Jesus had a similar challenge in His day. The religious leaders thought they understood the ways of God, but in actuality they practiced traditions and ignored God's Word.[α] On the other hand, the common people were willing to hear God's Word because Jesus taught in terms they understood. Jesus taught by parables.[β] A parable is a hyperbole or metaphor; an analogy or simple story used to explain a more complex concept. Jesus used things that were familiar to men of His day to explain truths of the Kingdom of God. In reading through this chapter, take note of this modern day parable designed to help you see, hear, and perceive the ways of God.

We begin the teaching by introducing the premise of the movie *The Matrix*. There was war between man and the artificial intelligence he created. The machines destroyed the earth and its inhabitants.[5] The only surviving human city is located near the earth's core. This city is called Zion. The action centers on the crew aboard the ship Nebuchadnezzar. Their leader is Morpheus. Their mission is to protect Zion, and find "The One",[6] the man prophesied to come back from the dead to Zion and save them from destruction and end the war.

The matrix is described as a computer-generated program.[7] designed by the machines to deceive the surviving humans into believing that the earth still exists. The cities look and feel real, but in actuality are only electrical impulses sent to the brain to simulate reality. Humans learning the truth about the matrix are sought and destroyed by program agents and sentinels (gatekeepers).[8] The agent's job is to find the traitors and dispatch sentinels to destroy them before others are made aware of the truth.

A computer hacker named Neo hacked into a program and heard of life forms outside of the matrix. Neo's curiosity led him to find the answer to one question[9]: What is the matrix? In his quest, Neo meets Morpheus, who is convinced that Neo is "the one" whom the Oracle[10] prophesied would return and save them. The movie continues with Neo joining Morpheus and his crew, while the agents and sentinels follow after to destroy them.

We begin our analogy by exploring Neo's question: <u>What is the matrix?</u> The Bible defines a matrix as a womb.[*] It is a loving place where life is conceived, protected and nurtured before being expelled into this world. Every human on earth came through the matrix of a human mother. In the film, the matrix is a place where humans are conceived, nurtured and generated by machines. Did you know that the very first matrix was the womb of God? It was not a physical womb, but it was a spiritual one. God is love[α] and from His bowels of love, the Lord desired, conceived, and birthed man all by Himself. He created man for a heavenly purpose.[β]

God desired a family on earth; created in His image and likeness, having dominion on the earth and experiencing all the blessings of heaven.[*]

God, who is a spirit,[α] created man from the dust of the ground, but only after He breathed His breath into man's nostrils, did he become a living, speaking spirit[β] just like his father, God the Creator. The first Son of God was named Adam.[χ]

God's Matrix was a place of love, blessing and provision. He created a garden on earth to replicate an everlasting Matrix, a place where man would never die, but he would be in God's presence forever. God called His earthly Matrix, Eden. God put man in Eden and gave him commandments to obey. God expected man to birth children of His Spirit, and bless them until the entire earth was filled. This was God's plan for all humans, but something went wrong. Adam wanted out of God's Matrix and wanted to do his own thing. He rebelled against God's command thereby committing sin within the Matrix. God threw Adam and Eve out of Eden because their sin could have perverted the ways of men on earth for an eternity. No longer were they living by God's Spirit and being blessed. Now, they were cast into the evil *world* matrix and subjected to physical death and the curse.[δ] Adam and Eve were fruitful and multiplied; however, they spawned humans not born of God's Spirit, but of sin in the world. This *world* matrix looks similar to the one in the movie because looks and feels real, but is a place of human bondage that ultimately results in death.

In the movie, there was hope in the midst of the evil in the matrix. Morpheus said that there was a man[11] born in the matrix that had the power to change it as he saw fit. He said that the man freed them and taught them the truth. The man died, but it was prophesied that he would return and end the war against mankind. Similarly, Jesus was born in the *world* matrix with the power to change it as God the Father saw fit. Jesus came to destroy the works of the devil,[*] and to restore all that Adam lost.[α] While on earth, Jesus freed men from bondage to sin, demons, sickness, and disease. Jesus not only came to be a witness of the truth, but He also declared Himself to be the Truth.[β] Jesus died on the cross and arose from the grave possessing all power of heaven and of earth.[χ] He then gave earthly dominion and power back to men on earth. Jesus prophesied that He would return to earth with the power and glory of His Father[δ] and His Kingdom would reign upon the earth.

Jesus changed the *world* matrix, so that men on earth no longer had to live the curse and die in sin, separated from God for an eternity. He was our example. Jesus was the firstborn of God's Spirit on earth, and firstborn from the dead,[ε] thereby taking dominion over sin and death in order to reestablish the full authority of God's Matrix on the earth.

Now, no matter how men are born into the earth, they can be born again of God and live-forever in God's Kingdom. God loved us so much, that He sent Jesus into the world so that whoever believes (obeys) in Him, shall not die, but have eternal life.[*] This is the <u>Real</u> Matrix. Jesus is the Door, or the portal to the <u>Real</u> Matrix. He is the Way, the Truth and The Life; no man can come to God, except through Him.[α]

Once a person hears and believes the truth about the <u>Real</u> Matrix, and makes a choice to follow Jesus, a conversion process occurs. The light of the gospel[β] is placed in the heart of a new believer, creating a desire for more of God. A similar process occurred in the *Matrix*. When Neo believed, what he heard, he made the choice to step out of the matrix and step into the real world.[12] Neo goes through a conversion process where he is literally born again as a different species.[13] In his new body, Neo had to retrain his mind to adjust to his new life. His training consisted of computer programs being downloaded to his brain. He also learned that in his new body, he was no longer confined by mind, space or circumstance.[14] Neo's greatest challenge was letting go of the knowledge of the previous life in the matrix. Likewise, everyone who is born into Christ is a new creation[χ] capable of receiving from God. The Spirit of God teaches them what they need to know, through prayer and the reading of the Bible. They are commanded to no longer live like the world, but to renew the mind[δ] with God's knowledge so that His will may be done in their lives.

All who come into the <u>Real</u> Matrix are delivered out of the power of darkness and translated into the Kingdom of God.* In that kingdom abides a new creation birthed by the Spirit of God. A man or woman in the <u>Real</u> Matrix is conformed into the image and likeness of Jesus Christ. Their blessed new life in Christ Jesus makes them free from the curse of sin and death.$^\alpha$ They have the ability through the Holy Spirit to operate like sons of God in the earth.$^\beta$ Wicked men will imitate their father the devil, but sons of God will be imitators of their Father like dear children;$^\chi$ walking in love, taking dominion upon the earth and being fruitful in every good work.

The sons of God are those who are led by the Spirit of God; just like Abraham was led to leave his home and journey to an unknown land; just like Moses was led to leave Pharaoh's palace and journey into the wilderness with the Children of Israel; and just like Jesus left the comforts of heaven to save men on earth.$^\delta$ The Children of the <u>Real</u> Matrix will do whatever is necessary to obtain the promises of God. They will deny themselves, take up their cross and follow the Lord.$^\varepsilon$ They will keep His commandment of love and abided In Him, just like Jesus kept His Father's commandment and abode in His Father's love. Then Jesus and the Father will love them, reveal things to them, and make their abode with them.$^\phi$ They will live bountifully upon the earth and be at peace with God for all eternity.

This is life in the Real Matrix, God's plan and purpose for man on earth. It began with Adam and extends to everyone who will come to Jesus and give his or her life to Him. If you are not living in God's Matrix upon the earth, you can make the decision to be born again right now. Maybe you have accepted Jesus as savior, but are not living in the blessings of God's Matrix; you can also make the decision to make things right with God now.

Just stop what you doing right now, and ask the Lord to forgive you for doing your own thing. Ask Jesus to come into your heart and restore all that Adam lost in the garden. Ask Him to fill you with the Holy Spirit and ask the Holy Spirit to lead you into God's perfect plan for your life. Now, everyday talk to God in prayer and read your Bible. If you don't have one, there are resources listed in the Appendix of this book.

Ask the Holy Spirit to teach you God's ways. He will also help you to remember whatever you read in the Bible. And most of all do whatever the Bible and the Spirit of God tells you to do. Obedience to God is the key to the blessings of God. If you happen to make a mistake, repent. God you're sorry. And, don't intentionally sin again. God will forgive anyone whose heart is sincere.

Remember, God loves you and wants the best for you, but you have to do it His way and not yours. Surrender your will and ambitions to Him, and He will give you more than you could have ever dreamed of obtaining on your own. That is how much God loves each and every one of us.

THE DARKNESS AND THE GLORY

' . . . Darkness Shall Cover The Earth, And

Gross Darkness The People: But The Lord Shall Arise Upon Thee,

And His Glory Shall Be Seen Upon Thee.'

Isaiah 60:2 KJV

PART I: The Judgment Of God Revealed

Dramatically portrayed throughout this journal is a theme of extreme darkness and magnificent glory. The darkness can be described as the blatant demonstration of evil in the lives of human beings. The glory is the overwhelming manifested goodness and mercy of God on behalf of those oppressed by darkness. The Lord has declared this coming season as His time of Justice in the earth: a time in which God will reward both the good and evil according to the persistence of their hearts.[*] This is neither the end of the world nor the final judgment that is mentioned in the Bible.[α] This is merely a season of God's glory coming into the earth to prepare a way for Jesus' return. The world, as we know it, will end. King Jesus is returning soon to the earth to rule with justice and judgment.[β] The Glory is a precursor or sign of God's kingdom rule that is coming to overtake the earth.

God has purposed to set up His Kingdom on the earth and destroy all ungodly kingdoms that are in existence.[χ] The Lord said that violence is occurring in the heavens to fulfill this end. This same violence must come to the earth before Jesus returns. According to the Bible, ungodly men will grow worse and will continue to violently resist Jesus.[δ] Because of this persistence of evil and violence, God's Kingdom will respond with even more violence throughout the earth. God's Kingdom is coming to overthrow all forces that oppose God's Law.

71

The closer we are to Jesus' return, the more violence we will see in the earth as we transition from the rule of darkness to the rule of the Kingdom of God. It is not God's desire that anyone be destroyed, so He is warning us to change our hearts now and turn from sin in order to be saved from the approaching violence that is coming upon the earth.

Jesus is coming to restore God's Kingdom upon the earth. But, before He can return, a path of righteousness (godliness) must be prepared or else the entire earth will be destroyed. God's glory is coming go prepare the way of the Lord. This coming season of glory will teach men to fear God and return their hearts to Him, lest Jesus return and curse the entire earth. This curse will destroy all evil men in God's wrath.[*] This curse of destruction will not only affect those who don't know God, but it will also affect the hypocrites and all those who profess the name of Jesus falsely.[α] The Lord is calling upon all men to repent if they want to be protected from the wrath to come.

In this journal you will see the glory displayed as God's Justice. God will execute His Justice by exposing evil, destroying the effects of darkness, punishing the guilty parties, and rewarding those who seek refuge in God's Kingdom and His Righteousness. What the reader will witness on the following pages is a foretelling of phenomenal spiritual violence. As great as it appears, what you will read pales in comparison to the ultimate battle between good (God) and evil (Satan) that is coming to the earth when Jesus returns.[β]

Many instances of death and destruction don the pages of this journal. Yet, great manifestations of God's Glory abound in every instance. Be cautioned not to focus on the evil events that are recorded. Just know that our country has a brutal enemy that has no regard for human life. God will allow this enemy to attack us on our own soil. They will compass about us and siege our cities with a passion for blood. This will be God's judgment against our nation. Neither the military nor our leaders will be able to help us in this time of danger. Our only hope of survival will be in the hands of a merciful God.

Judgment must be executed against the people of America because we have arrogantly made ourselves mighty by exploiting and oppressing the weak. We have spoiled many nations therefore we will be spoiled in our land.* We built this nation on the blood of Native Americans, African and Asian slaves, indentured servants and others. We are an adulterous and hypocritical nation that professes God in times of trouble and yet historically we have destroyed our neighbors in order to gain political advantage and profit. Exploiting the weak for a profit is evident throughout our entire economy. God will not allow America to continue to operate in this manner without severe repercussions.

God will punish us because it is our penalty for violating His Law, but once our nation cries out to God and repents, He will remember His Covenant with our forefathers and rescue America. He will not let our enemies completely destroy us.

The prayers of a faithful remnant of believers in America will move the hand of God in our favor. He will show His mighty power against our enemies and the world will rejoice. The God of the Bible, the God that many have heard and read about, will show up and do justice against our enemies. He will do what seems impossible, for those who trust Him. The message of this journal is therefore designed to be one of great hope, faith and triumph in the midst of much tragedy, pain and devastation. What the enemy meant for our destruction, God will turn into our victory. It will make us a stronger nation. It will make us a God fearing nation, and God alone will get the glory.

Jesus said that wars and other tragedies would continue until the end of the world.* Wars and conflicts have been an inevitable part of human history. Since the time that Cain slew his brother Abel,ᵅ men have fought against one another: brother against brother, and nation against nation. But, any time there is war or any tragedy, people inquire of God. "Does God really exist?" "If God does exist, why did He allow this to happen?" "If there is a God, how could He stand by and do nothing?" Some conclude that either God does not care, or God is powerless to stop evil men on earth. One thing is for sure; during tragedy man's first instinct is to turn to God: whether for His help, or to point the finger of blame at Him. To further explain why tragic events occur, we must take a closer look at how the judgment of God comes upon men.

The occurrence of evil is never the fault of God. The Bible says that the ways of the Lord are perfect (true and just).[*] So, if God's actions do not cause tragedy, then man's actions must be at fault. From Genesis to Revelation, the Bible reveals that men who do not obey God always cause darkness and evil to prevail. There are numerous accounts of wars and calamities in the Bible that came about as a result of sin: humans rebelling against God and His will on earth. Man's sin will cut him off from God's protection and make him prey of his enemies. The Lord told Cain that if he obeyed His Word, then God would be pleased with him. But if Cain did not obey, then sin would be allowed to overtake him. He disobeyed God; sin overtook him causing him to murder his brother Abel. As a result of his sin Cain was cursed from the face of the earth.[α]

The Bible urges us to live peaceable with all men knowing that vengeance belongs to God, and He will repay.[β] Yet, war and murder is man's choice method for settling disputes. But, wars don't start with nations, they start in the hearts of individual men who choose to hate rather than love. It was jealously and hatred that led Cain to disobey God and kill his brother. Hatred filled Cain's heart and he chose to murder. But, the Bible said that Abel pleased God,[χ] so why would God allow him to be killed? What did Abel do to deserve death? Abel was not killed because of anything he did. He was killed because of his family curse.

When Adam and Eve sinned, God told them that they would surely die.[*] Adam sinned and his son was the first to die as a result of that sin. How many people appear to be innocently killed in wars and tragedies today? Yet, the Bible says that if they or their parents worship anything other than the true and living God; a curse of death would be upon the family up to four generations.[α] When Adam and Eve sinned in the garden, rebellion dominated their household resulting in one son murdering the other.

Did you know that according to God's Law the only weapon you need in order to commit murder is a mouth that speaks hatred against another?[β] The Bible also tells us to submit to the governing authority and whoever resists that authority resists God and shall receive judgment.[χ] How many have spoken evil of the president and other leaders? Americans call it freedom of speech, but God's Law calls it murder. God wants us to pray for those in authority so that we may have a quiet and peaceable life in all godliness and honesty.[δ] Let God take vengeance on the leader, but keep your hands clean of murder. Speaking against our leaders makes you an enemy of God to be judged. In America, we have laws that can be overturned by a court judgment. In God's court of law, His Word Stands. God, Himself cannot violate a law that He has placed in the earth. If God cannot violate His own laws, why does man think he can violate God's Laws and not reap the consequences?

We mentioned that tragedies are often evil consequences of a violation of God's Law. The Bible mentions two tragedies that occurred during Jesus' day. He discussed them with His followers. One tragedy was the murder of Jews whose blood was mixed with the animal sacrifices.* Jesus asked His followers if they thought that these Jews were sinners more than others. He said, no, but if they (His followers) did not repent, they would likewise perish.

Then there was mentioned of the eighteen (18) people upon whom the tower of Siloam fell and killed. Jesus asked His followers if they thought these eighteen (18) were more sinful than all that lived in Jerusalem. He again said no, but if they (His followers) did not repent, they all would perish in the same manner.

Likewise, should we think that those that tragically died on September 11th, or in Hurricane Katrina were more sinful than all those that lived in the United States? Jesus would say, no, but unless we all repent, we are all subject to perish like they did.

As it was in the days of Noah, and in the days of Lot, so it is in our day. People are still eating, drinking, marrying and doing business as usual.[α] Americans carry out their daily activities as if everything is right with God. There is no fear of God, and no motivation to repent for sin, and yet we have been warned that the wages of sin is death; and payday is soon coming.

There is even an expectation among believers that they will be removed before the wrath of God comes. No one knows when the final tribulation will occur, or when Jesus will return. But we do know that we are expected to endure hardship in this earth. This is consistent with other tragedies recorded in the Bible.

Noah's family was not taken from the earth, yet they were shielded from the storm within the ark.[*] When Moses delivered the Children of Israel from Egypt, God did not take the people out right away. Instead, He performed great signs and wonders to make a distinction between His people and the people of Egypt.[α] He kept His people in the midst of great danger in order to show His Hand to the world; that the world might desire Him as its God. He did it with Daniel in the lion's den, and with the three Hebrew boys in the fiery furnace.[β] God receives great glory when He does the impossible for His people, in the midst of the trouble. The faith of His people is strengthened and the heathen sees the glory and desires to know Him as God. The Lord indeed has established the coming season for His glory. But, how long we are expected to endure such hardships, God the Father only knows.

Knowing the times and season of war in America is just part of a more crucial message to the world; the Gospel of God's Kingdom and His final judgment of men on earth. This message was given first to God's people, the Jews, when John the Baptist came preaching, '*Repent for the kingdom of heaven is at hand.*'[∂]

John urged the people to repent in order to prepare themselves for the coming of the Lord. John further warned that the King (Jesus) was coming and would baptize them in the Holy Ghost and with fire. Those who repent He would gather to Himself, but those who don't repent the Lord would burn with unquenchable fire.[x] The times have changed, but the gospel message is the same. God has appointed Jesus as Judge and Savior of all mankind on earth. Those who believe and obey Him will be saved from the wrath that is coming to earth. Those who don't will be destroyed and spend an eternity in hell. People everywhere are being exhorted to repent (change their evil hearts and ways), and obey God for the Kingdom of God is at hand.

The Lord is merciful and longsuffering. It is not His desire that anyone be lost, but He cannot go against His Word. If He said it, it will come to pass, maybe not today or tomorrow, but it will come to pass. Jesus told the churches in Revelation Chapters 2-3 to repent of their sin or suffer the consequences. He is saying the same to us today. If the church is barely saved, what hope is there for the rest of the world?[*] Paul told believers to hold fast to their faith. He says do not refuse Him who speaks. If they were destroyed who refused to obey God when He spoke from the fiery mountain in the day of Moses. How can we escape the wrath of Him who speaks from heaven saying, *'Yet once more I shake not only the earth, but also heaven?'* Paul concludes that we have received a kingdom that cannot be shaken. Our refuge is within that kingdom. Therefore let us have grace and serve God with reverence and godly fear, *'For our God is a consuming fire.'*[α]

PART II: The Love Of God Manifested

Every earthly kingdom has its pomp and circumstance, a majestic entourage of splendor, and showcase of military strength that precedes the entrance of its monarchy. All of this grandeur serves as an announcement of the eminent arrival of the King or Queen. There may appear trumpeters, musical fanfares and processions of kingdom military guards and processions of distinguished dignitaries. Regardless of what precedes the monarchy, it is required that certain protocol be followed by all subjects of the kingdom. This protocol is simply the etiquette or code of behavior expected by all who are in the presence the King and his royal entourage. The entire kingdom is expected to humbly prepare and follow protocol in honor of the approaching monarch. Those who refuse to follow protocol, dishonor the King, which results in shame and punishment upon themselves and their families.

The Kingdom of God is a spiritual kingdom that exists in the hearts of men on earth. The ruling monarch of this spiritual kingdom is Jesus, the Son of God. Like other kingdoms, there is also a majestic entourage of splendor and a showcase of military strength that precedes the appearance of King Jesus. This pomp and splendor that precedes Jesus, is called the Glory of God. The Glory of God as seen on earth is merely a reflection of God's kingdom that exists in heaven, just like Jesus is the reflection on earth of the glory of His Father, which is in heaven.

God appointed Jesus as King,[*] but the kingdom is under the ruler ship or domain of God. Therefore, the glory that precedes Jesus' coming, is not His, but that of God the Father. Jesus said that when He comes to earth again, He is coming in the glory of His Father. What is the glory of God and what does it look like? The glory of God could be described as the reflection of His nature, word or character in the earth. The glory is evidence of God's presence on earth. Since God is a Spirit,[β] His presence cannot be seen with human eyes. But, the evidence of God's presence is obvious. The Bible says that God created the heavens and the earth.[χ] The Spirit of God hovered over the face of the waters of the earth in anticipation of bringing into existence whatever God spoke. So, when God said, *'let there be light'*, it was the Holy Spirit moving upon the earth and the waters that brought light to the earth.

God spoke into existence everything that we see in the heavens and earth today. All of God's creation reflects His glory because they are the manifestation of His word in the earth. Humans may have never seen God, but we do have evidence that He was here from the very beginning. The Holy Spirit also moved upon a young virgin named Mary, and Jesus, the Son of God was born. Jesus was the glory of God and the only begotten of the Father.[δ] Today, the Holy Spirit moves upon the hearts of obedient men in order to produce whatever God speaks to their hearts. God speaks, but it is the Spirit of God that brings about the glory.

Jesus said that if we love Him, we would obey Him. Then He would love us and manifest Himself to us and He and God would abide with us.[*] In this chapter we will see how the glory of God is the manifested love of God, sent as a response to our obedience to His Word.

Kingdom protocol requires strict obedience to God's Word. This makes a way for the Spirit of God to send the glory as a sign that the Kingdom of God is in the earth. We saw this throughout Jesus' ministry. Jesus was full of the Holy Spirit. It was the Holy Spirit who led Jesus to obey His Father when He walked on the earth.[α] Jesus said that He did always what pleased His Father, because the Father was with Him.[β] With the help of the Holy Spirit Jesus spoke what God told Him to speak.[χ] Jesus said that it was the Father that dwelled within Him that did the miraculous works on earth.

When Jesus came to earth speaking the Words of God and acting like God, miracles happened. The blind began to see. The lame could walk, and the dead came back to life. This was evidence that the kingdom of God in all its glory, had come to earth. After His resurrection, Jesus said that these same signs would follow those who believed.[δ] The disciples went forth and obeyed Jesus' command to preach the gospel and when they did, the Lord worked with them by showing these signs, just as He said He would.

Jesus desires that all believers follow His example. He said that men should keep His commandments and abide in His love, just like He kept His Father's commandment and abode in His love.* When we speak and act like Jesus, the glory of God will be seen upon our lives, as it was upon His life. The glory manifested in us will be greater[α] than that which Jesus had when He walked the earth because of the Holy Spirit working through many more sons of God in the earth.

In this journal, there are many examples of how the glory of God will be evidenced by His goodness and protection during war. Men and women will hear and obey the voice of God, causing miraculous healings, deliverances and provision to be manifested. The Holy Spirit will quicken the hearts men to defy nature and circumstances. They will do greater works because the Father and the Son will be giving orders from heaven, and the Holy Spirit will make it happen on the earth!

The light of God's glory will spring forth from His obedient sons, in the midst of the prevailing darkness of terror, death and destruction. The glory is coming to confirm the truth of God's Word. When men hear the gospel and see miraculous signs as proof that the gospel is true, many will repent and turn their hearts back to God.

As the Lord directed me to write this chapter on His glory, He took me back to the creation and compared it with the message of the gospel. The kingdom that Jesus taught about is a replica of God's glory as it appeared in the Garden of Eden. Both Eden and the kingdom reflect God's immeasurable goodness designed to benefit men on the earth. The Lord took me to the Garden of Eden and spoke about His original plan for men on earth.

The Lord explained that the glory at creation appeared upon the face of the earth exactly as it appeared in heaven. Adam was one with God and His love. From that oneness, abundance and power was available for man to have days of heaven on earth. God's will was done in earth just like it was in heaven. Eden was more than a beautiful abundant garden, it was the place on the earth where God walked and communed with man, one on one. There was no distance between God and man. God gave everything He was and everything He had to man. Eden was the place where the heavens were continuously open and pouring God's glory (love and voluminous provision) upon man and upon the entire earth. God predestined man to be one with Him in a loving family relationship for all eternity. This concept of eternal life flowing from of heaven's abundance has always been God's desire for men on earth.

Eden was a place where there was no sin, and there was no death. There was only goodness and abundant life flowing from the bowels of God, the Father unto His children in the Garden of Eden. When Adam sinned in the garden, the heavens were shut off from earth. The glory (presence) of God left. Man was cut off from God's Eternal life and was then destined to die.

The Lord was very frank with me concerning the Gospel of the Kingdom. God loves us. We are commanded to love God with all that is within us. The proof of our love for God is our continual obedience to His Word.* To disobey God's Word is sin. And when we say we believe and do not walk in the Word, but continue to sin after having knowledge of the truth, then the blood of Jesus is mocked and judgment is certain.$^{\alpha}$ The Bible also says that when we sin, we need to repent.

Repent means not only being sorry for what we have done, but it means having a changed heart and behavior. If we confess our sins, then God will be faithful to forgive us and cleanse us.$^\beta$

Imagine inviting someone into your house to be part of your family. Now imagine that same person, whom you love, moving in and immediately disobeying your rules and upsetting your home. You would tell that person that as long as they were under your roof they had to follow your rules. If they continued to upset your household, you would throw them out. The same is true in the kingdom of God. If you want to do your own thing, you will not be allowed to remain in the kingdom. Paul often used the analogy of running a race to describe the Christian journey in this life. He said that we are in Christ to run the race and receive the prize. So, Paul said we are to master our walk with Jesus on order to obtain the crown. This requires that we subject our personal desires to the Word or else we become kingdom castaways like Adam.$^\chi$ Paul uses the example of the Children of Israel who died in the wilderness because they were disobedient murmurers and complainers.

The Christian life can be compared to an athletic race that requires faith and endurance. Everyone entering the race must know the rules and follow them faithfully in order to successfully complete the race. Why be disqualified from such an important race when the rulebook is available, and the author of the rulebook is waiting for you to ask Him for specifics concerning your race. Jesus is King and we must know Him and His rules pertaining to entering and remaining in the kingdom.

God loves us and wants to manifest Himself through everyone who comes to Him. Before Jesus went to the cross, He announced that the time had come that He should be glorified. Then Jesus said to God, *'Father, glorify thy name.'* A voice answered from heaven saying, *'I have both glorified it and will glorify it again.'** When Jesus obeyed His Father all the way to death on the cross, He glorified (honored) God. Because Jesus obeyed, God knew that many sons would come to know Him and also glorify God again in the earth.

The Lord gave me a two-part vision that demonstrates why believers need to glorify (honor and obey) God in the earth. In the first part of the vision, the Lord showed how the glory appeared in the earth during the time of Adam before the fall. There were open heavens and all creation was in one accord with the Spirit of God. There appeared to be a vast light coming directly out of heaven and covering the entire earth. It looked like a powerful force field that began in heaven and ended on earth. Everywhere on earth the glory was full because darkness had been subdued at creation.

When Adam sinned, the glory left the earth and darkness reigned until Jesus came to earth. Jesus took dominion over the darkness of this world. Jesus now reigns in heaven, but He gave the dominion over darkness back to believers on earth. We are called to reign on Jesus' behalf until He returns to the earth. He told His Father, *'I do not pray that You should take them out of the world, but that You should keep them from the evil one.'* Jesus gave us the glory that He had in the earth,* so that we could be the light in the midst of darkness.

After Adam sinned, darkness also reigned in the hearts of men. The Lord explained that the only way His glory could return to earth was that it had to be replaced inside the hearts of men just like it was placed inside of Adam at creation. Once men accept Jesus Christ as Lord and Savior, the glory of God is manifested as a light in the midst of darkness. That light is placed within the hearts of men on earth. This was demonstrated in the second part of the vision from God concerning the glory.

The Lord showed circular beams of light coming from heaven to the earth. These beams of light were the glory of individual believers sparsely located all around the world. New beams appeared in seemingly random order all over the earth. Then some of the beams began to enlarge in diameter to the point that they appeared to connect to other beams. The Lord said that the beams increased in size according to the obedience of the believer. The more obedient the believer, the larger the glory beam appeared from heaven.

As one obedient believer connected with another obedient believer, the glory of those believers seemed to be woven together into an even larger beam of light. This weaving of beams multiplied in the earth blocking out all signs of darkness in their midst. This began happening all over the earth. The final result was the appearance of one solid beam of light coming from heaven and covering the entire earth, just as it was in the beginning when God created Adam. The glory in the earth appeared as the fullness of God flowing directly from heaven, destroying the darkness and unhindered by the sin of man.

Today, our assignment is to eradicate the darkness. The light in each of us will manifest in the earth when we are obedient to God. As we practice obedience and develop the likeness of Christ, the brighter our light becomes, and the more darkness we subdue. When our light connects with another's, we collectively subdue even more darkness. The Lord called this the unity of the faith. The result will be an earth where the glory of God looks like it did before Adam fell. The Lord said that the gospel has to be preached in every nation, it's the only way the light from heaven will replicate what was on earth in Adam's day. It's about all of us working as one Body, in one accord with His Spirit until the glory once again covers the whole earth.

We are valuable to God, but He wants us to understand that obeying Him should be of utmost importance to us. In order for God to fulfill His plans in the earth, He needs us to manifest His love through obedience to His word. God loves us and is not willing that anyone perishes, but He will not tolerate the rebellion and stubbornness of man for long.*

Jesus told His disciples to find a donkey and a colt on which He would display His glory.* He chose the most stubborn animal known to man. He commanded that it be loosed and let go. Why? Jesus had need of it. He does not loose us from the darkness without a reason. He loosens us so that His glory can be seen on us. If He can loosen a donkey and use it, how much more would He desire to loosen a man made in the image and likeness of God the Father, and use him to do mighty exploits in the earth?

Remember when Lazarus became ill, Jesus said that the sickness was not unto death, but it was for the glory of God, that the Son might be glorified. Even at the darkest hour for Mary and Martha when their brother Lazarus died, Jesus told the disciples that Lazarus was sleeping and He had to go wake him.[α] Jesus had also told them earlier that the sickness was not unto death, yet Lazarus died. So it should have been obvious that something miraculous was about to happen, but neither the disciples, nor Mary nor Martha understood. If we are In Christ, the things that afflict us in this world are not unto death. Even if they kill the body, in Christ we will be resurrected in the last day. And, to be absent from this body is to be present with the Lord.[β] In Christ, we win no matter what happens on earth; so don't be moved by afflictions. Our job is to overcome the evils of the world by faith so that our Father will be glorified. Jesus gave words of encouragement to the disciples. He said that in this world we would have tribulation, but to be of good cheer because he had overcome the world.[χ]

The apostle Paul was terribly afflicted and persecuted throughout His ministry but he never complained. Paul always encouraged others by saying that the Lord delivered him out of all that he endured. He explained that all who live godly in Christ Jesus would be persecuted.[*] Jesus said blessed are those who are persecuted for righteousness sake because their reward is the kingdom of heaven. He said to rejoice and be exceedingly glad for great is your reward in heaven. You are also told to leap for joy when you are persecuted.[α]

Let's go back to the story of Lazarus and the death that glorified God. In the midst of faithless 'believers,' Jesus declared that they would see the glory of God.[β] When Jesus cried 'Lazarus come forth, Lazarus walked out of the tomb bound with grave clothes. The Lord commanded the people to 'loose him and let him go.'

Today, God's people answer the call to come forth when they get saved, but they are still wearing grave clothes and stink. Where is their faith? They hear the word, yet they remain faithless. They see the provision and miracles of God that have been done for them, and still they are in unbelief. They study and pray but can't overcome sin. These are the defeated saints who claim victory in Jesus with their mouths, but their lives have little or no proof.

I had a vision years ago about God's people. They were sitting in prison cells waiting to be freed, yet the cell doors were wide open. There were no prison guards and nothing preventing them from exiting the cells. They just sat in the cell waiting for God to do something miraculous to let them out. In the spirit I began to shout, 'OBEY GOD' repeatedly. Finally, each one walked out of the cells praising God and ready to obey His purpose in the earth.

Now is the time for all of God's people to arise and demonstrate the Word of God in their lives. Let God's glory be seen so all men will marvel! The Lord is commanding you to be loosed and let go so His glory can be seen on you. You may be out of the tomb, but if you are walking in darkness, you are still bound in grave clothes with a napkin covering your face. You act like you're alive, but you're look like, dress like and smell like a dead person. You have not put on righteousness yet you still profess belief in Jesus. Where is your faith?

You may call Him savior, and maybe He is, but He is definitely not your Lord. You refuse to let God heal and deliver you from fear, not realizing that healing and deliverance brings glory to His name.

And, why are you waiting for God to miraculously transform you? The Bible says that you are transformed by the renewing of your mind.* Get in the Bible and see what God has to say about your situation. Put that Word in your mouth and speak the faith of God into your situation. Faith comes by hearing the word,$^\alpha$ so keep speaking, hearing and meditating on what you have read until the Holy Spirit energizes your heart with faith. During your meditation be open to God speaking His desires to your heart. Then obey whatever you have heard. This is how faith works!

Everyone who is born of God overcomes the problems of the world by faith in God's Word.* Know beyond a shadow of a doubt that God's Word will come to pass no matter what! For with God nothing shall be impossible!$^\alpha$ Understand that when we give our lives to the Lord this is just the first step in manifesting God's will. He desires that all men be saved and come to the knowledge of the truth.$^\beta$ You are saved but you must come to know the truth. Jesus said if you abide in His Word, then you will be His disciple, and you will know the truth, and the truth will make you free. God's Word is the Truth.$^\chi$ It washes$^\delta$ the darkness from our minds and hearts and sets us free from spiritual bondage.

When you began to obey the Word, you will live free. Free from the world. Free from the darkness of your past. Free from any thought or idea that is not consistent with God's plan for your life. Each of us must make the decision to put on the new man[ε] and be transformed in order for God's glory and purpose to be revealed in their lives. This transformation often comes with much travail, pain and sorrow, just as Jesus sorrowed on the cross and died. But! In His suffering, Jesus pierced the darkness of this world with the light of God's glory. How? When Jesus arose from the dead He had been transformed into a glorified body. In this new body, Jesus had flesh and bone, and could eat and drink like any human, but supernaturally this body could walk thru closed doors, appear and vanish out of human sight, and was carried up to heaven in plain sight.[5] Jesus' glorified body was evidence that another power was unleashed in the earth, so that whatever became sick or died due to Satan's power could now be brought back to life thru Jesus Christ and the power of His resurrection! The kingdom of darkness no longer reigned on the earth.

That same resurrection power is now available to all who obey God! But! Each of us has to enter into God's Kingdom by accepting Jesus Christ as Lord of our lives. When each of us decides to obey God and accept the pain and suffering necessary to show forth God's glory, that same resurrection power will work thru our human bodies. And here is the good news!! We don't have to die to go to heaven in order to show forth this power. We just have to believe and obey God. With human strength there are numerous impossibilities, but with God's power, there are no impossibilities. And, as children of God, we are called to walk in the realm where all things are possible.

Jesus said that the Kingdom of God is like a man who found a treasure hid in a field. He valued it so much that he sold all that he had to buy that field.[*] My brothers and sisters, Jesus found the treasure in us and paid all He had, even His life, to purchase us. Then the treasure of the Holy Spirit was placed within us to help us show forth the Father's glory on earth. We are valuable to Him.

In the eyes of our Father, which is in heaven, we are more valuable than silver, gold and diamonds. Even the diamond, which is considered rare and beautiful, is hidden in the earth inside a dirty piece of coal. The coal has to undergo intense heat to bring forth the brilliance of the diamond. If a piece of coal can be transformed into a beautiful diamond, how much more can we, who have the indwelling of the Spirit of the Living God leading us through the fire, be transformed into the image of His Son? Are you willing to sell out to God?

Are you willing to sell all that you hold precious in this world to obtain the Kingdom of God that resides within you? Are you willing to hold on to the prophecies concerning your purpose in Christ, and fight the good fight of faith to obtain it, no matter the cost? Then arise, take up your cross and follow Jesus' example![µ]

These last days will truly be the glory days; the days to be excited about the kingdom message, for the Lord will hasten to perform His Word for all those who believe. We will run to the battle with spiritual weapons in hand, our spiritual armor secured, subduing the darkness while taking back territory and rescuing the lost. Our battle cry will be heard around the world and God alone will get all the glory!!

THE WAR JOURNAL ENTRIES

'... When He, The Spirit Of Truth Is Come,

He Will Guide You Into All Truth ...

And He Will Shew You Things To Come.'

John 16:13 KJV

THE WAR JOURNAL

YEAR 1999: *Exit From Los Angeles*

THE WAR JOURNAL
YEAR 1999: *Exit From Los Angeles*

8/1/99 It was time for the next assignment. I had been told by the Lord to pack and prepare to leave LA, but I was not sure where I was going, or for what length of time. I assumed that it was for short period due to the fact that He also told me to apply for school in the fall.

8/8/99 At Sunday service, Dr. Gary Gregor, of Living Faith Fellowship, under the direction of the Holy Spirit, sent me out on assignment and prophesied: 'God is sending you back east . . . healing and teaching to multitudes. . . '

8/10/99 I began final preparation for entering school. It was the Lord that told me that I had to receive something from Dr. Price in order to fulfill my assignment. He led me to apply for training at MTI. He told me to complete the application and submit it for the fall session.

8/15/99 I received a call from my sister to come to Indy for her wedding in September. I told her I had to pray about what to do.

8/15/99 That evening I received another call, this time from Cleveland. My brother's wife was pregnant. They wanted me to stay with them until the baby was born in October. I also told them I needed to pray about coming. I began praying immediately after these two phone calls. I needed clarification from the Lord on what to do. He was calling me to go east, yet He also told me to plan on entering MTI training in 2 weeks with Dr. Price.

8/16/99 *(A Change of Plans)*
The Lord urged me to call MTI about my application. I called and was told that all new classes were cancelled for the fall. I did not understand why the Lord had me apply for school if they were planning to cancel all new classes. At the Lord's urging, I called my family and agreed to go back east.

8/16/99 *(Preparing to Leave: Reflecting on the Past)*
I will never forget the strange events that occurred before I came to LA. The Lord told me to **_"GO"_** and I had purchased a plane ticket to LA, and was waiting for money to come through. My mother battled viciously with me about leaving. She threatened to stop me from going to LA. Then a friend invited me over for dinner in an effort to beg me not to go, when in the middle of her plea, the Spirit of the Lord came upon her and she said, 'you have to go. If you don't leave, I am afraid of what will happen to you.'

Then the next day I got a call from a business associate who lived in Kansas City saying that she had a word from the Lord for me and was told to deliver it in person. She flew into town and we met for lunch the following day. This woman said, 'you are in real danger. If you don't leave soon, you will be dead. You have until Tuesday to leave town.' Before the night ended, I received a disturbing call saying that my cousin was struck with a heart attack and a stroke and it was uncertain whether she would survive.

8/16/99 *(Continued)*

My mother told me point blank, that if I left to LA that meant that I did not love my family or care about my cousin. I was asked one simple question, 'will we see you later?' I answered, 'yes', but I could not tell them how much later, nor I could not tell them that it would not be in Minneapolis. I felt pressed on every side. I needed the Lord's help. If my family did not see me in Minnesota the next day, all hell would break loose. I spent the night at my sister-in-law's house seeking peace and directions from the Lord. All night long there was an evil presence hovering over me. it disturbed the entire house. The Lord identified my ex-husband lurking outside of my sister-in-law's home. The evil was so intense that she got up and said, 'you have to leave town right away.' I told her that I had no more money to travel and my car needed to be checked out to see if it will take the cross-country trip but I did promise to leave in the morning.

That next morning I still had no peace. On one hand, I had my orders from God. On the other hand, the words of friends, family pressures, the sudden illness of my cousin, and the evil appearance my ex-husband came against me with astounding intensity. When I asked the Lord what to do, He asked just one question that put things into perspective, *'__Are you going to believe them or obey Me?__'* This one question rang loudly in my spirit. I obeyed immediately. With my car packed, $50 cash and an emergency credit card in my pocket, I headed for Los Angeles.

8/16/99 *(Continued)*
When I arrived in LA, the Lord told me to separate myself from my family and have no direct contact with them for a while. That was two years ago. And now, it was time to see them again face-to-face. I began to understand that this next assignment would be another test of my ability to stand in obedience to God in the midst of unbelieving family members who habitually try to control and manipulate my life whenever the Lord wants to take control. But this I know, if God is calling me to go, then I am more than able, by His Spirit, to fulfill the call. He said that I would see the positive results of my prayers for them.

9/4/99 *(Praying for a Clear Path)*
I spent Labor Day in prayer at a local hotel, and then went to Prayer Mountain. I prayed and fasted for safe passage out of LA. There was a powerful spiritual barrier that was attempting to abort my assignment and prevent my travel back east. After several hours of intense prayer and travail, the barrier lifted. There was much peace all about me, but I still did not get the green light from the Lord to leave LA just yet. My only option was to wait and listen for the Spirit of the Lord to give further instruction. That night the power of God fell upon me like a heavy weight. Then the Lord let me know that it was time to leave LA and head east.

9/9/99 I left LA on an ATA Flight and arrived in Indy for my sister's wedding. I remained there until she and her husband returned from their honeymoon. It was an enjoyable time reuniting with family and friends. I especially enjoyed seeing what the Lord had done in breaking demonic strongholds off my family.

9/22/99 I took a bus to Cleveland and arrived that evening. The spiritual atmosphere was so evil that I could barely stand up on my feet. There was oppression everywhere. The people on the street looked like the walking dead.

9/99 *(Word of the Lord Concerning New Book)*
During the first days in Ohio, The Lord said, 'Write a new book'. He gave me a title and gave a detailed outline of what to write.

My only activities for six months in Cleveland:
• Babysitting---some evenings.
• Prayer 8 a.m. – 3 p.m. (with personal Bible study).
• Church service on Sundays and Tuesdays.
• Some family dinners and outings.

9/99-12/99 *(Destroying Satan's Strongholds)*
I prayed and travailed intensely for Cleveland, trying to penetrate the mean evil heavens. There were times when all I could do was travail in the spirit continuously for days at a time. There were two major demons that fought with me constantly. One was clearly defined as the spirit of witchcraft. In fact, the Lord showed me that by coming to Cleveland I had entered into heavy satanic territory. He identified three leaders of a satanic order that I had first encountered in Illinois. This particular group was in the habit of performing human sacrifices. They were also active in California in sacrificing children.

9/9-12/99 *(Continued)*

While in Cleveland, the Lord had me pray to interrupt the satanic ritual sacrifice of a young woman. I don't know what happened to that woman, but the satanic leaders became angry and began to direct their witchcraft at me in grand fashion. The Holy Spirit helped me land a powerful blow in prayer. Much to my surprise, when I stopped praying, others began praying a follow up blow in the spirit. This devil of witchcraft was dealt two devastating blows, one in Cleveland and one from California. The satanic leaders, although stunned, did not give up easily. They came after me again. I threw a powerful blow followed by another's blow. This continued for about an hour or two before the battle ceased.

After the battle with the Satanist, there still remained much institutional witchcraft activity throughout the city. It demonstrated itself in the church community by strong religious leaders (Jezebel spirit) who were attempting to destroy the leaders that were being led by the Spirit of the Lord. The Lord had me pray to destroy this hold on the church. The battle had a strange but definite pattern. When my prayer subdued the power of Jezebel, another unidentified yet stronger spirit would appear. It never came against me. It just showed up and pressed upon my head and left. I could tell by the spirit that this was a rather large and powerful demon, but he refused to come against me with any force. I had a strong sense that he feared if he identified himself by striking first, I would destroy him. This spirit chose instead to play a game of cat and mouse with me. In my spirit, there was something very familiar about this demon. I knew that we had fought before. I just did not know who he was.

9/9-12/99 *(Continued)*

When Jezebel recuperated from the blows I dealt, the battle would begin once more. This battle with Jezebel went on for weeks, and each time I subdued her, the unknown spirit would return and press upon my head with a little more force. Then one day I totally defeated Jezebel. She never came back at me. By now, the unknown demon had my full attention. I had to know who he was. I waited patiently for his typical reaction, but there was none. I began calling him out and taking jabs at him in the spirit just to get a reaction. It was my goal to anger this spirit to the point that he would identify himself and I would destroy him. Still there was no response from this spirit. The battle apparently was over.

I let out travail in the spirit and pierced an unhindered path in the spirit that created open heavens over Cleveland. The only thing that was flowing was the power of the Living God. I was in the process of praising and celebrating the victory when the Lord gently hushed me up. A few moments of silence had passed when a powerful reaction came out of nowhere. It came like powerful angry fist; he hit me hard and retreated. I got the full blow from this demon and I knew by the way he hit me that it was no fist; it was a swat from a large and heavy tail. It was the python; spirit of divination and witchcraft that rules many major cities. This demon hates the Spirit of God. Python will literally squeeze the life out of a leader and suffocate him to death. He wants to kill every dream or Word from God before it can come to pass.

12/99 *(Victory over Python)*

By obeying the voice of the Lord, I have learned how to break the power of python off my life and continue to break this demon wherever the Lord leads me. When I bore a gaping hole through the evil heavens over Cleveland, python hit me and ran. He knew he had no power to coil around me or squeeze the life out of me anymore. So, I laughed at him and declared an end to his rule and reign in Cleveland. Python left immediately and the battle was won. The battle was not mine, but the Lord's. I fought in the name of the Lord Jesus Christ; my strength and my shield. In Him, I am more than a conqueror every time!

Now that the battle was won over python, the peace of God was free to rule the city of Cleveland. God's healing power, protection, and provision can freely flow to those in need. The enemy stronghold is destroyed. God's people are free from enemy bondages and can go forth with God's Kingdom Agenda.

THE WAR JOURNAL

YEAR 2000: *Move To Ohio*

THE WAR JOURNAL
YEAR 2000: *Move To Ohio*

1/2000 *(Word about Studying the Gospels)*
The Lord told me to study the gospels but He did not tell me how or for what purpose. A few days passed when I just happened to read[1] where Oral Roberts read the gospels and the book of Acts three times in 30 days. He read on his knees and the Lord taught him much about Jesus. This truly amazed me, but I was not convinced that the Lord would have me do the same. I never did a thing just because another person did it. I only did a thing if the Lord told me to do it.

A few more days went by and I still did not hear from the Lord on how He wanted me to study the gospels. So I told Him that if it was His will that I read the gospels three times in 30 days to give me confirmation. It was not even a week later when I was given a set of Kenneth Copeland tapes on the topic of faith.[2] These tapes must have been at least ten years old. On one of the tapes Kenneth Copeland talks about how his wife Gloria read that Oral Roberts read the gospels and the book of Acts three times in 30 days on his knees. Gloria did the same thing, although I don't know if she read on her knees. The Lord gave her supernatural revelation and she had enough spare time to take care of family, and refinish several pieces of furniture. I received confirmation in my spirit and proceeded to read the gospels and Acts three times in 30 days.

1/00 (*Abundance of Holy Ghost Power*)
The study of the gospels (Matthew, Mark, Luke and John) and the book of Acts was the most fascinating study time I had with the Holy Spirit. I read the gospels and Acts aloud with my audiotapes playing in my ear. The anointing fell heavy during the first reading, and increased right through the third reading. I barely made it through the third reading because while I was reading, revelation knowledge was coming at the speed of Light. I had to stop the tape and stop reading just to hear what the Lord was speaking. In my study I was reading the words and understanding every word I was reading. The Holy Spirit would give me numerous teachings that were off shoots of one verse and take me on an excursion through the entire Bible.

Outside of my study time, another supernatural whirlwind occurred. Prophetic utterances were flowing from my mouth without my being able to predict or control them. I did not get unction to speak. The words bypassed my mind and came directly from my spirit through my mouth so quickly that I had no warning. I would be just as shocked as those hearing me speak at what was coming out of my mouth. I was speaking things I had never heard before. These utterances increased more after reading the third time. My spirit was so full of the Word that it flowed out of my mouth wherever I went.

1/00 (*Vision of the Kingdom of Heaven Suffering Violence*)
I woke one morning to my bed being bounced upon its four posts. I thought it was an earthquake I realized I was in Cleveland and not in LA. I thought to rebuke the devil, and then I discerned that only the Spirit of the Lord was in the room.

When I sat up in shock, the Lord spoke to me saying that '***The Kingdom of Heaven is indeed suffering violence, and that violence will be coming to earth before Jesus returns.***' He said He was coming with a power that would frighten His people. It will be a power never seen before. The Lord told me to know that it would be His power NOT Satan's that would shake the earth. He also said it was time for the 'greater works' to be performed in the earth.

2/00 (*Word about a Television Job*)
The Lord indicated that it was time to leave Cleveland. He wanted me to go to a neighboring city. He told me that a television job was available at a particular ministry in that city. He told me to call the ministry and apply for the job. The Lord also told me that I would have to submit my resume tape. When I called about job openings at the ministry, I was told there were none. The Holy Spirit told me to call again the next day. I obeyed and got the same response from another person in the personnel department of the ministry. The Holy Spirit told me to keep calling. By this time I am sure that I irritated a few people and they directed me to the head of personnel where I still got the same answer.

2/00 *(Continued)*
I called again the next day, but this time I asked for the television department. The television department again told me that there were no jobs available. I asked to speak with the department head. He said there were no positions available. The man paused and said 'well, there is one job coming available, but I don't know what it is.' The man began to explain that the Lord told the pastor to create a new position in the television department. The pastor refused to tell them what the job was. The Lord told this pastor that He was sending someone to fill the position. The person the Lord was sending would know in detail what the position was. This would be a sign to the pastor that the Lord had sent them. Before the man could finish speaking, I responded, 'I know what the position is. That is why I kept calling your people over the past several days.' He gave me the information necessary to submit my resume tape and application letter.

February-March 2000 I prepared my resume tape and letter to send to the ministry. The Holy Spirit told me what to write in my letter. A door opened for me to visit the ministry for several days. I also planned to leave Cleveland and stay with my parents in Michigan until either the job came through or the Lord gave me further instruction.

3/11/00 *(First Visit to Apply for the Job)*
I left Cleveland and stayed with my parents in Michigan. From Michigan, I traveled to visit the ministry in Ohio where I applied for the television job. The Lord told me that the pastor of the church had a key role to play in the coming move of His Spirit. My first assignment upon arrival in the city was to cover the pastor. No one in his church was praying for him. He and his family were totally exposed.

3/11/00 *(Continued)*
My plan was also to attend services at this church, undercover, but that was not to be. Unbeknownst to me, the Lord had put this particular pastor's anointing on me so heavy that many people knew it when I walked into the door. More than one leader prophesied that God had sent me. One visiting pastor called me out and confirmed that Lord put the pastor's spirit on me and brought me to the church to do a work. The anointing was so heavy that every inch of my body was in pain. Even my hair hurt. Then there were leaders close to the pastor who did not like me. They glared at me wherever I went. It was like the more people spoke over me the more the jealously was coming upon some of the leaders.

In another setting, two leaders spoke evil about another leader from the pulpit. They did not mention him by name, but made derogatory comments about one of his books. These ministers also spoke against another Bible school before the congregation. I was puzzled at the open hostility. These people were in Ohio and the other school was in California. I did not understand why there would be territorial issues involving the congregation. I was glad that the leaders did not know that I was connected with these other ministries. If they had known, they would have definitely banned me from their church. There was prophecy and praise from some leaders and hate and jealously from others. Both sides were very intense and closing in on me rapidly. Then there was the hostility toward other ministries. All I wanted was relief from the spiritual pressures that surrounded me. I got only slight relief when I went back to the hotel. Then I could not sleep. The Lord kept speaking to me about what was going on at the church and He kept me in prayer all night long for two nights.

3/00 (*Revealing the Pastor's Heart*)
Sunday morning was the first time that I would see the pastor face to face. I sat in the visitor's section of the church. When the pastor looked at me he gave a long pause. The Lord told me that at that moment he let the pastor know who I was and why I was there. He also let him know that I was the one praying for him and covering his back. After service I was invited to go into a special room to meet the pastor along with other visitors. For some reason, I was lagging behind the crowd because there were so many people. When I found the room and approached to enter, the pastor and his entourage were also coming into the room. The moment I looked into this man's eyes, the Lord showed me his heart. I was shocked at what I saw. On the surface, this pastor seemed harsh and almost rude. In his heart, he was a very gentle and shy man who loved the Lord and had a heart to obey. I knew instantly that his congregation had no idea what was in this man's heart. They have never seen the real man. He was bound by his ministry and the congregation and was not able to obey God to his heart's desire. That evening, the Lord had me pray that this pastor's bondages be broken so he can get into position to obey. His ministry was vital in this next move of the Lord's Spirit on the earth.

3/00 (*The Assignment Revealed*)
On that final night at this ministry, the Lord revealed more of my assignment. The Lord gave me a very disturbing dream. In this dream I came to deliver a message to the pastor. Once the message was delivered, the leaders tried to kill me. As they approached me, the Hand of the Lord pulled me out of harm's way. The pastor's reaction was what got my attention. When he received the message, and rejected it, he turned and let his leaders go after me.

3/00 *(Continued)*

As the Hand of the Lord pulled me out, the pastor saw God and turned around quickly. He panicked and began reaching to pull me out of the Lord's Hand. The pastor wanted me to come back to the ministry. The Lord said *'No.'* The pastor held his head down in remorse. He knew that He had missed God. When the Lord pulled me out, He placed me on the ground behind the pastor. To my surprise, the Lord put me under the protection of another minister. When I woke the next morning, a young prophet I met at the church had a message of confirmation for me. He told me that the Lord had sent me to that church, but to watch my back. He said the leaders were watching me and would hurt me if given the chance. Without sharing what the Lord showed me in the dream, I thanked this man for his concern. I let him know that I would do nothing without consulting the Lord first. My plan was to head back to Michigan with my folks, but the Holy Spirit had another plan. He told me that a friend in Indy was in trouble. When I called there was much confusion going on. I did not ask her much before the Lord said, *'Go.'* I rerouted my ticket and left.

3/00 *(The Attempt to Rescue Mandy)*

I arrived in Indy and met Mandy. Right away I could see that several demons were tormenting her She has a powerful call for the healing ministry. Her church does not teach on spiritual gifts or spiritual warfare but she has been operating by what the Holy Spirit had taught her. The devil would love to keep her bound to crazy men just to abort her call. Mandy had told me at my sister's wedding that she was not seeing anyone. I could tell that not only was she involved, but also this time she was bound by a devil that wanted to take her out.

3/00 *(Continued)*

My visit with Mandy was very brief. The power of God came flowing through me in prophecy and warning almost immediately. Within just a few hours of arriving at Mandy's home, the Lord revealed that she yoked herself to a homosexual man who was practicing bizarre sexual perversion and witchcraft. It was the sexual perversion that had her hooked. She had no sex in her failed marriage because her ex-husband's Christian fanaticism led him to believe that sex was dirty. He and his mother tormented Mandy into believing she was a whore who was going to hell just because she wanted sex with her husband. That word took root in her spirit. Mandy was convinced that God does not want her to be happy because His Word put too many restrictions on her personal freedom. So Mandy purposely chose to rebel against God to satisfy her unfulfilled sexual desires.

There also was the issue of witchcraft. Mandy's sister became a member of WICCA[3]. She and her friends had been pressuring Mandy to leave Jesus and join the 'good witches.' These people were loving and caring to Mandy while the Christians around her were hateful and judgmental. When the Lord moved me to first speak to her, Mandy responded, 'you're different. The words you speak are harsh, but I feel so much love coming from you.' I began to explain that God being the loving Father would correct those He loves. He does not rebuke us to hurt us; it's for our own good. Only He knows what evil is waiting to destroy us. Obeying His corrective measures puts us back into that place of protection and blessing.

3/00 *(Continued)*

Mandy had another plan. Her sister was getting married in a witches' ceremony. They wanted her to be part of the ceremony. Mandy could not say no to her sister. She had more fear of the witches than of God. She feared that they might hurt her. It never occurred to Mandy that the Lord would allow her to be hurt and send her to hell for an eternity.

Before leaving, the Lord had me tell Mandy that He was removing His protection and letting her go. He would return to her only if she returned to Him. Although tormented, she was arrogant enough in her spirit to boldly walk away from all God was offering. She said she had no intention of doing things God's way anymore. I told Mandy that I could have no further contact with her as long as she was in willful rebellion. I loved her, but I had to let her go. Mandy exalted her throne of sexual perversion above God. By doing so she refused the powerful call of God on her life, and forfeited her position for the next move of His Spirit upon the earth. There was no more I could do for her.

3/00 *(Vision about Mom's Tormentor)*

After leaving Mandy, it was my plan to stay in Indy and visit with my nieces and nephew for a while. The Lord showed me in a vision that my mother was grieving the recent death of her brother. He showed me the demon that was tormenting her and commanded me to go home to Michigan. The spiritual battle over my mother was brief yet intense. Like Mandy, my mother was hurting so bad that she told me that she did not want to do things God's way; it was too hard. My mother knew better, but it was her pain that was talking. People have no idea that when we yield to our pain and suffering and don't give it to God, the devil will infiltrate our lives and wreak havoc. Mom's only hope was intercession, and so I continued to do so quietly.

3/00 *(Spring Break with the Kids)*
I stayed with my parents at the lake in Michigan. Most of my time was spent in prayer, writing and relaxation. My nieces and nephews came to the lake during spring break. I had a blast because we talked about Jesus whenever they wanted. These kids will start preaching at you anytime. We had Bible study every morning and discussions about anything they wanted throughout the day. Our subject of the week was the truth about witchcraft.

I helped them search through the Bible for truth. They also wanted to talk about how much they missed my son. They tried to imagine how Jeffrey would look if they saw him that day. His cousins missed him very much and had been praying for his return. They knew for years that the devil tried to take him from us, but could not, so we agreed to celebrate in a big way when he comes home. This was a healing moment for my family because the adults refused to even mention Jeffrey's name. It was too painful for them. Whenever I shared what the Lord told me about his return, they could not hear. But the all the kids knew in their hearts that he would be found and return home.

3/00 Spring was here and so was tax time. I had very little income during the year, except for some employment early in 1999. Since none of my employers sent my W-2 forms, I had to write them. The Holy Spirit also reminded me that I had some unemployment income also that year. So I sent a letter to Employment Development Department (EDD) in California as well.

April-June 2000 (*Assignment Completed*)

I spent time communicating with ministers from the church where I had an application pending. There was a staff member of the church that wanted me to move in with her after I got the job. We spoke by phone often. She said that the Lord told her to confide in me about what was on her heart. For about an hour this woman poured out her heart about her attempts to obey God. Something was very wrong at the ministry and it was affecting her. I told her that I would seek the Lord on her behalf. When I hung up the phone, the Lord told me to sit down and write her a letter. For the next four hours I wrote every word the Lord spoke to my heart. When I was finished, I had typed more than 20 pages in response to this woman's concern. I anointed the letter with oil and prayed for her bondages to be broken. The mail carrier was driving up to the mailbox just as I sealed the envelope. As I reentered the house from the mailbox, the Lord told me that the message I wrote was not for the woman, but for her the pastor. He said that the woman would give it to her pastor and then the leaders would come after me.

3/00 (*Word about Taking Up My Cross*)

The Lord spent the next several days ministering to me about taking up my cross and following Him (Matthew 16:24). He told me that it was part of His plan that I be exposed to danger and organized crime in my personal life. He said that it prepared me to deal with the real criminals: the men and women pretending to be God's leaders. The Lord said they were intentionally killing the people of God for gain. He said that their tactics were similar to those of organized crime. They did not love God or the people of God; instead, their hearts were inclined to extort them.

3/00 *(Continued)*

The Lord said that He was sending me head-to-head with these evil leaders, in order to take them down. They take people's money and lead them away from God. When the people are hurt or dying, these leaders cut them further with religion and eagerly watch them die. When the Lord asked me if I was ready, I told Him to lead me and I would obey His every command. The Lord put a supernatural love in my heart for His people. When I feel the pain God feels for His people it compels me to obey no matter what the cost. A spirit of compassion overwhelms me and I can do nothing, but obey God.

Sometime after the Lord finished ministering to me, I called my brother about a computer question. And I told him that the Lord was sending me to that church in Ohio and I had to obey even if it cost me my life. My brother became relieved to hear my words. He responded, 'so you know that they will try to kill you.' He said that the Lord had told him the same thing earlier that week. He began praying that the Lord not send me in. I asked, 'so what did the Lord tell you?' My brother replied, 'He said this is what you are called to do and I could not interfere.' From that point on I shared with him what the Lord ministered to me about taking up my cross and following Him. When the conversation ended, we both were at peace because we knew the will of the Lord was going forth.

June –July 2000 I enjoyed my final moments by the lake. There were mornings that I would sit for hours in prayer at the end of the pier with the dog, watching the sun come up over the lake. I just loved the peaceful water.

7/4/00 (*Satan's Retaliatory Death Blows*)

My cousins were visiting from Minneapolis. My sister and her husband were due to arrive as well. The family had been visiting every day since the weekend. That morning we got a call saying that our family doctor had died. Later that morning we received another call informing us that a friend of ours had died. He had been ill, but no one expected he would die. Then later that afternoon, I took a phone call from my sister-in-law that one of the nieces was in the hospital in code blue.

She was nineteen years old, just graduated from High School and was expecting a baby in less than a month. By the end of the day, she was gone. The baby would only live for one day. In one day four people I knew had died. And, if it were up to Satan, there would have been yet another death that day.

While I was taking care of the houseguests for my mother, I had a terrible fall in the bathtub. I was sure I had broken something because the pain was excruciating. My niece got me an ice pack, but I could not walk or put pressure on the leg. While sitting down, a very large growth appeared just below my knee. I hit my left shin, but this fist-sized lump suddenly appeared near my knee. I knew in my mind it was a very large blood clot. If this thing traveled I knew it would be fatal. In my heart I was thinking, 'not today devil, no more death.' But before I could open my mouth, the Lord said, *'**Move to Ohio.**'* Obviously He knew I was injured, but my assignment had not changed. At that moment I smiled at the Lord. He knew that all I needed was one word from Him and I could overcome any situation.

7/4/00 *(Continued)*

That night while I slept, the lump in my leg began to move. I began praying in the spirit because it was such a weird sensation in my leg. In less than ten seconds, something traveled from my leg to my brain where it felt like an explosion. There was no pain, but my eyes went blind for a few seconds. The blood clot was gone, but I was still here because the Words the Lord spoke shielded me from the evil that was planned for me that day. Because I chose to obey the word of the Lord, the devil could not kill me. The Word supernaturally protected me.

7/00 *(Supernatural Provision for the Move)*

After my healing experience, I told my parents that the Lord told me to move to Ohio. My mother immediately told me to get a job and begin saving money to move. I explained that the Lord told me to move, not to get a job, save money, and then move. In her mind, you can't move without money and you can't get money without a job. She did not yet understand that God could do the impossible if I just obeyed His voice.

Within a few days, I got a letter from EDD in California stating that I had money that was never claimed. Before I left Los Angeles in 1999, the Lord told me to file for unemployment, but they declined my application. Now they inform me, that yes they did decline my application, but it was a mistake. No one from EDD contacted me and that money had been sitting in my account for almost nine months. Over the next week they held a hearing on my case and determined that I still qualified for every penny of the money.

7/00 *(Continued)*

The caseworker apologized for the confusion, she said, 'it's as if our people were asleep at the wheel and someone else was driving.' I thought to myself that is exactly what happened. God was in control of the entire situation. Over the next two weeks, I sent in all the necessary paper work and received every check that was due me. My mother was appalled. She told me that God would never do a thing like that. She told me to give the money back. There was no way I could explain to her that when I obeyed God, and followed all the rules of EDD, I indeed qualified. My mother refused to hear that God was in control of my life and everything that concerns me. That same week another job became available as well. This one was in Columbus Ohio. Then my sister-in-law in Cleveland called me and offered me a car so that I'd have a way to get to my new job.

7/28/00 *(Satan's Plan Foiled Again)*

My dad and step mom had made arrangements to drive me to Cleveland to pick up the car. We were scheduled to meet at the lake at 4 pm. My mother and step dad decided to run errands earlier that day and I went with them. Around 2 pm my mother began to complain of chest pains and insisted on being taken to the hospital. I called my dad right away and told him what had happened. He was not shocked at what happened, and neither was the rest of the family.

As far back as I could remember, whenever the Lord told me to do something, my mother ended up sick or in the hospital right before I obeyed. The last time she and I battled over her control of my life was when I left Indy for Los Angeles. She threatened to come stop me. I let her talk, but I still obeyed God. My mother was furious. After arriving in Los Angeles, the Lord spoke to me about praying for my mother's deliverance from witchcraft. If she did not get delivered, He was going to have the spirit of death take her.

7/28/00 *(Continued)*

Now, my mother has been in the Baptist church most of her life; to the best of my knowledge she never practiced witchcraft. I asked the Lord to explain what He meant. What He told me frightened me. The Lord said that my mother had a habit of praying against me whenever He told me to do something. He explained that she never prayed His will for my life. My mother prayed <u>her</u> will for my life.

In 1997-8 I obeyed God and prayed for her deliverance, so when my plans to leave for Ohio were delayed, I did not panic. I knew that the power of the devil of control was broken off my mother. When we left the hospital, my mother admitted that nothing was wrong but she just wanted to be sure. For the first time, she apologized for interrupting my plans. I was so proud of her and grateful to God for His faithfulness to get her into line with His plans for her family.

7/29/00 *(Equipping for the Job)*

The next morning I left Michigan and arrived in Cleveland early enough to get the car registered at the DMV. There were many things supposedly wrong with the car. I was told the stereo did not work and the sunroof had not opened in years. Normally, I would not care if the stereo or the sunroof worked, but driving in Los Angeles taught me that drive time was warfare time. While others are spreading their evil music in the atmosphere, I enjoy playing intense gospel R&B or gospel rap on the stereo at full blast. My preference is gospel gangster rap that mentions either the Name or the Blood of Jesus loudly, with much force and repetition. A good car stereo system is necessary for me to do warfare on the road. When I laid hands on this car and anointed it to assist me in my assignment the stereo came on immediately and later the sunroof opened. Praise God, it was time to roll!

8/18/00 *(A New Mantle Falls On Me)*

It took almost three weeks of searching, but I landed a job and found an apartment. I drove back to Cleveland for the rest of my things. The drive wore me out a bit and I sat in a big chair to rest. As soon as I sat down, the power of God fell upon me and restrained me for quite a while. During that time a very heavy spiritual garment fell over my head and landed on my shoulders. I knew from past experience that this meant that a new mantle had fallen upon me. I had obtained a new position in the spirit. The Lord said nothing. The mantle was under another ministry and the anointing was all over it. Several minutes later I was startled out of my spiritual refreshing period when my six year old nephew who had just arrived home from school, enthusiastically jumped into my lap. It was about 3:45 pm. I left Cleveland during rush hour and headed back to Columbus.

8/28/00 *(Word of the Lord Concerning Food Warehouse)*

My second week of job training was held at a local food bank. During a tour of the facility, the Word of the Lord came to me saying, '***My people will need to have food.***' He spoke to me about getting a warehouse facility and distributing food to many cities. The Spirit of the Lord then started speaking to my spirit about running and operating a food distribution center of LARGE PROPORTIONS. The information was coming to me rapidly. It was as though information was being downloaded to my spirit. The Lord explained that there would be a shortage of food; therefore it was necessary that His anointed be over the food just as it was in the story of Joseph in Egypt (Genesis 41:46-57). Nothing was said about how or why a shortage would occur. Over the next several weeks, I met various church leaders. They explained to me that it was prophesied that God was going to start a major move by His Spirit in Ohio that would shake the nation.

9/00 *(Word of the Lord Concerning Money)*
I had an unexpected bill presented to me that had to be paid immediately. The money was nowhere to be found in my bank account, so I asked the Lord where I could find the money. I only needed $50 so I figured it was a simple request. The answer I got from the Lord floored me. The Spirit of the Lord told me to *'make a ledger for $18 million dollars.'* He told me to *'distribute $18 million dollars 'FIRST.'* I knew in my spirit that my measly $50 was insignificant compared to $18 million. But I also knew that the Lord was telling me that the $18 million would be the first of many millions that I was to distribute. Before the night was over, my brother called and asked if I made the ledger for the money. He told me that I was about to get a whole lot of money and the Lord did not want me to be overwhelmed by the dollar amount. He was giving me instruction now so I would know what to do with the money when it came. So, I began making out a ledger and the $50 bill was paid. I also investigated United Way system of assessing needs and distributing funds. They did not distribute to churches, but to independent programs that supported an assessed community need.

9/00 *(Searching for a Church)*
A man on my job said he was Lutheran, but knew of a good church near where he lived. Because he said he was Lutheran, I kindly thanked him and made no further inquiries about the church he was recommending. Several weeks went by and the Lutheran man mentioned the church to me again. He said that he thought that I would like it. By now I was going to another church, but the Lord prompted me to ask more questions. The Lutheran man said that the church he knew was not Lutheran at all. He also said that he did not go there, but some people he knew went and liked it. When I asked why he recommended it, he said that church would come to his mind every time we spoke.

9/00 *(Searching for a Church, Cont.)*
The man said that it was a church that believed in healing like I did and the pastor was a very good teacher of the Bible. The healing church had bought the church building that once belonged to the Lutheran man's congregation. The Lutheran church moved to a new building right next door. I asked the man if he believed it was a good church why didn't he attend himself. He said he was not ready to go that far with God yet. The man suffered a stroke that left him partially crippled in his leg. He was still holding things against God for allowing him to be stricken.

9/00 *(Hostility Revealed)*
For the next few days, the Lord had me pray for the Lutheran man's heart to be healed from bitterness toward God. I also had an intense interest to know more about this little church somewhere on the outskirts of Columbus. So, on the next available Sunday I went searching for the church. After traveling several miles on the back roads, I saw no church. I was on the right road, but it was desolate on this road. I pulled the car over and asked the Lord, 'if it is Your will that I attend this church, let it jump out at me on this desolate road.' I turned the car around and before I could go a quarter of a mile, I saw a little white church sitting just off the road. I don't know how I could have missed it the first time.

When I entered the church praise and worship had already begun. From the time I stepped into church until the time service had ended, I noticed something very familiar about the church. Not only was the anointing on the church somewhat familiar, the congregation appeared to be fairly young yet the spirit of the church seemed to be at least twenty-five years old.

9/00 *(Hostility Revealed, Cont.)*
After the service ended, I remained seated with my head bowed waiting on instruction from the Lord. I sensed a young man seated in the middle of the pew also with his head down. As soon as I stood up this young man came over and introduced himself. By the time the conversation ended, I understood the other church's hostility. It was explained to me that these people left the other church and started this little church in a neighboring city there in Ohio. There was a feud going on in the city and the Lord had me to intercede that that competitive spirit be broken for the sake of the people in that city.

10/00 I was prompted by the Lord to apply for the Assistant Director Position at the food bank. It was a very intense application process involving personal interviews with each board member.

10/00 *($18 Million Ledger Completed)*
I completed the $18 million dollar ledger after investigating community needs unmet by Ohio agencies. As I wrote the ledger, the Lord also gave me a detailed organizational chart on several corporations He wanted me to start and run. He carefully named each company and gave its purpose. Then He gave the names of the other companies that were subsidiaries of those corporations. He had not given me the complete chart. The Lord let me know that what He gave me was just the beginning of what was to come.

10/00 *(Warning From the Lord about Danger)*
The Lord showed four men hiding in my apartment complex. He said that my ex-husband hired them to follow me. One of the men hid a gun in the back of the waistband of his jeans. The man next door was paid to spy on me by camera. He gave himself away because of his intense sexual perversion. I fell asleep on the couch while reading my Bible, when all of a sudden I heard someone talking to me from the other side of the wall. He said, 'I watch you every night and you are so beautiful in your sleep.' I began to beat the wall with my fist and said, 'shut up you pervert.' Another night I was awaken from a deep sleep because it felt like someone was trying to have sex with me. Then I heard the next-door neighbor scream 'what's wrong with you? Why won't you have sex with me?' Again, I shouted, 'shut up you pervert and go to sleep.'

10/00 *(God's Judgment against Perversion)*
The next morning, the Lord told me that this man spies on woman by camera and uses witchcraft to make them respond sexually during their sleep. The idiot could not understand why it didn't work on me. I clearly understood that God was about to intervene on behalf of those who have been victims of this sexual perversion. When God sends me anywhere and reveals the evil around me, He has a plan to eradicate that evil. It is only a matter of time.

11/00 *(Command to Speak to the Camera)*

The pervert is out of control. The Lord told me that when I come home from work, he thinks that I am coming home to him. He actually thinks I am his wife. The man is a lunatic. I had to get police involvement because his conversations through the wall started to become violent. There were nights where he wanted to break down my door. One such night, the Lord told me to speak to the camera. When I did, the man could no longer see me. He began screaming and beating on my walls. I barricaded my door and called the police again.

After the police left, at about 4 a.m. two men came barreling into his apartment. They roughed him up a bit. I heard him say, 'I don't know what happened, the camera just broke. I don't want to do this anymore. Please don't make me do this.' Within moments, the camera was once again working and this man's apartment door slammed shut.

I knew instantly with whom I was dealing. I recognized my ex-husband's mode of operation. Ever since I left him, he has hired people to spy on me. He hates the fact that I work for the Lord. He would do anything to stop me, even kill me; after all he did declare himself to be the only god that I would ever serve. He has to follow me with hired guns and cameras, but the God I serve has only to send His angels and the Holy Spirit. I am not only made aware of danger, but I am also completely protected from every enemy plot. I also remember God's Word to me: about a pool of blood in which this man and his cohorts would be killed.

11/00 *(Miraculous Deliverance for All)*

It was a time of very intense warfare. The Lord told me that since I had a captive audience, let the hired men hear the word day and night. I read aloud. I played tapes on salvation. I played and sang praise music continuously. The Lord even told me to anoint the outside of the building and walk around it several times early one Sunday morning in prayer. A friend picked me up for church. The Lord had her entire family praying for me as well. Later on that evening when I return from a long day of church services, I realized that the demonic and sexual spirits were gone. The spiritual airways were clear. I put on a praise tape and got ready for bed. As I began reading the word and I noticed the most amazing thing. The Spirit of the Lord began flowing throughout every apartment in my building. I could sense the moment people entered into their apartments. There were no demons, only the Spirit of the Lord was flowing.

My heart was overcome with joy. They were still surveilling my apartment, but this time I could feel these people pulling on the anointing and hungering for the Word of God. The more I read aloud, the more they pulled for more Word. I understood at that moment what I Peter 2:2 meant by, 'as newborn babes, desire the pure milk of the word.' These once dangerous criminals were now desperately seeking to hear more of God's word, but unfortunately, this newfound salvation would only last a few days, when all of a sudden, the demons returned more ferocious than before. The Lord told me that my ex-husband and his mob associates were not pleased that the hired guns got Jesus, so they threatened their lives. I thought I was being persecuted because of Jesus, but these men were being threatened with death on the spot if they did not carry out their assignment

11/00 (*United In Prayer*)

Many were praying hard for me in Ohio. At one point, there was such a peace that settled over me that I basked in the presence of God for what seemed to be an eternity. As I lay there, the Lord let me know that my son was praying at the same time. The same peace that was on me was also resting on him. At one point while lay before the Lord, I could sense my son's spirit and my spirit resting in the Lord at the same time. It was as if we were in perfect harmony with God's will and with each other. I had never experienced anything like this before. We were one with God. I could sense our separateness, yet we were one in God. It was a powerful moment. It was just a few years ago that he was kidnapped by his dad. I had no way of seeing my son, and yet God had both me and my son in perfect peace in the midst of this chaos.

11/00 (*Words of a Frustrated Witch*)

I had just finished another successful session in prayer and I don't know all that happened, but the devil was angry. While I sat in the peace of God, a witch appeared in the spirit and commanded me to die. She spoke with the force of intimidation, but it did not move me. I replied, 'I am dead, and it is not I that lives, but Christ in me.' 'You have no power over me. GO!' She left suddenly and I laughed at the devil. For years he tried to scare me into believing he could kill me. The witch tried to command me to die because she knew that they could not kill me. She also knew that her words had no effect on me. Her words were made out of anger and frustration. If I overcame all of Satan's physical acts of violence against me during my marriage to his son, why would I have fear of evil words that have no power, now that I am in perfect obedience to God?

11/00 *(Word about Change of Season)*

My job assignment was ending and my lease would be up soon. I spent time before the Lord to get further instruction about where I was to go next. I got confirmation that day. I heard in the spirit, **'*Paula, are you ready?*'** I scarcely remember what he said. I was distracted by one word he emphasized; something about his needing me to preach. This was new information to me since the Lord had just given me an organizational chart with the corporations He wanted me to start and run. My mind was somewhat overwhelmed. How would I have time to preach and run several major corporations? I conceded by telling the Lord that I would do whatever He wanted me to even if it seems impossible for me at this point in time.

12/00 *(Word of the Lord to Break the Camera Again)*

One evening the pervert neighbor was out of control while I was in prayer. The more I prayed, the crazier he got. The Lord told me to speak to the camera and it broke. This time, the two men came within a minute or two and fixed the camera. It took them longer this time. They left and came back with something and then the camera worked again. Things went back to the way they were and prayer was increased to cover me. I was grateful to have someone covering me because these men were relentless.

The police were also watching my apartment. I was told that there was a ring of men in the area who were spying on their female neighbors by camera and selling the film for Internet viewing. They suspected that these men could have also been involved. It was a high-tech pornography ring. They were very alarmed because these men most often attacked their victims. I was told that women on TV or movies were not good enough for these perverts, but neighbors are familiar and easily accessible. The police had suspected that I was being targeted.

12/00 *(Break the Camera Again, Continued)*

Later in prayer the Lord showed me the women that these men stalked and hurt. They rigged bathrooms and showers with cameras and tortured women's minds and spirits with their perversion. Some of the women could sense someone watching them. I saw one woman in particular who lost her mind trying to figure out what was going on. These men laughed at her and did witchcraft on her mind just to send her over the edge. I have never in my life seen such deliberate and evil hatred of women. I prayed intensely that these women be protected from such violence. And, again, the judgment of God was set against the perpetrators of such evil against women.

12/00 *(Rebellion in the Camp; Covering Broken)*

It was about 2 p.m. and I was working on my computer. The Spirit of the Lord said, *'pray without ceasing.'* A few seconds later, something broke over me in the spirit. The covering broke and the anointing of protection left me. I immediately inquired where the breach was in the covering. The Lord showed a woman in the ministry. I know that she is a woman of God, but when the Lord showed her to me, she was dressed from head to toe like a witch. The Lord said that she did not feel that the pastor could run the ministry and she was attempting to take over. I immediately began praying. The Lord let me know that others involved in this ministry around the world were also in jeopardy. He had me covering them continuously until the Spirit released me at 4 am the following morning. I slept for just a few hours and began praying intensely for the next few days. My prayer was causing the pervert to go even crazier. A co-worker told me how to determine the camera location. I was told to cover the entire wall where I suspected the camera was located, with sheets and if he could no longer see me, I would know that he had a camera secured in the adjoining wall between our apartments.

12/00 *(Covering Broken, Continued)*

I knew that the pervert was out of the apartment because there was no screaming or loud crying going on. I pinned sheets along the entire wall and moldings along the ceiling. When the man got home, he went berserk. He began running back and forth along the wall screaming, 'where are you? I can't see you!' You could hear his footsteps running along the wall back and forth. He started beating on the wall. I called the police again and they were there instantly. When they arrived, the pervert went outside to speak to them. He told them that he did not do anything. The officers came to speak to me. I told them that the man was yelling and banging on the wall. For the next few nights, I slept on the floor in my bathroom because the man kept banging on the walls. The bathroom was on the far side of the apartment. It was also very cold weather and my heater was not working well. The bathroom was quiet, warm and cozy.

12/00 *(The Lord's Undercover Agent)*

One night while sleeping on the bathroom floor, the Holy Spirit told me to go look outside the front window. When I peeked through the blinds carefully, I saw a car parked in the parking lot. It caught my attention because my neighbors usually pull their cars head first in the parking spaces. This particular car was backed into a space and facing my apartment building. I saw the shadow of a man sitting in the driver's seat. When he saw me peering out the window, he turned on his interior light and tipped his finger on the rim of his hat, motioning to me. This man was wearing a big Indiana Jones style hat and a trench coat. He then turned off the light. The Lord said, *'**he is on our side.**'* I closed the blinds, thanking the Lord for confirming that I was safe.

THE WAR JOURNAL

YEAR 2001: *Preparation For War*

THE WAR JOURNAL
YEAR 2001: *Preparation For War*

1/01 *(Twilight Escape from Columbus)*
It was a Friday night and my neighbors were having rowdy parties. The area where I lived was considered a typical middle-to-upper class area, but on a Friday night you would think it was the ghetto. People had money to buy any kind of booze, drug or entertainment for the weekend, but before the weekend would end, someone would be crying, screaming and fighting.

This particular Friday would also be my last night in Columbus. The pervert next door did his usual screaming and beating on the walls. I immediately retreated to my bathroom hideaway to catch a nap before the real fighting began that evening. At about 10 p.m., I was awaken by a camera in my bathroom. It's always easy to know when a pervert is watching you by camera. For the pervert, the minute they see you by camera, they are sexually aroused. I was wrapped in my mother's fur coat, sleeping on top of a pallet on the floor. There was no sexual activity going on, yet in an instant, someone is aroused and masturbating at the sight of me on camera. When I moved the arousal stopped. As soon as I pretended to be sleep, it started up again. I sat up again and it stopped. I lay down again and pretended to sleep and the perverted spirits began to flow. So, I sat up and welcomed my new viewers to Paula's bathroom.

The Lord showed five men watching, including the pervert next door. I announced, 'now that I have your undivided attention, we are going to have a Holy Ghost good time tonight. You boys don't go to church, so since you have tuned in to me, we can have church right here in my bathroom.' I read the Bible until a friend from church came by to assist me. My brother arrived at 1am to take me back to Cleveland.

1/01 *(Satan's Plot of Retaliation)*

On the way to Cleveland I prayed to the Lord for more understanding about the things that occurred with my covering. He explained that there were demons coming from my ex-husband. My ex-husband tried to reclaim me as his wife and took authority. When I asked how that was possible, the Lord mentioned the verse that says that a woman is bound to the law of her husband as long as he is alive (Romans 7:2). The Lord said that is also why He told me that my ex-husband would be killed. It is the only way I can obey God and carry out His call on my life.

The Lord also reminded me that this man does not want me to serve God and will plot another attempt on my life before I do what I am called to do. The Lord said He would strike him down before the murderous thought completes his mind. Then I will be free to serve God. The Lord said that if my ex-husband were alive when I remarried, he would have us both killed. I declare that Satan's plan will <u>never</u> come to pass in our lives or that of our children, or that of our children's children, in Jesus' Name. We are all covered by the Blood of Jesus.

1/2001 *(The Evil Covering Explained)*

I spent the next couple of days in intense prayer before the Lord. My flesh was not pleased to hear what He had to say at this hour. Here I was now again under the evil covering of a man (a professed Satanist and pervert). The Lord said it was because of how He created men and women in the earth.

142

1/2001 *(Evil Covering Explained, Continued)*

Women will always be under some man's spiritual covering whether it is her father, brother or husband. If her covering is not firmly established in the Lord, or if her father, brother or husband is out of order with God, then another man can attempt to take the woman and enslave her spiritually. That was exactly what this man was trying to do to me, but the Lord made it clear that He had another plan. I could not understand how I could work for the Lord and be subjected to an evil covering. The Lord told me to obey His every command and I would see His Hand rip through the enemy's territory. Some would be destroyed and others snatched out of the pit of Hell. The Lord said that what I was doing in the spirit would be bigger than the time He used Moses to take the Children of Israel out of Pharaoh's hands. My spirit rejoiced as the Lord spoke, but my flesh was thinking, 'oh boy here we go again.'

Many years ago the Lord said to me, *'**how can they come out unless I send you in?**'* Now I understand what He meant. In order for Jesus to take the power of death, He had to die and be resurrected. Jesus went through death, conquered it, and came out the victor. In order for Jesus to destroy the works of Satan and Hell, He had to descend into Hell. Jesus saw Satan fall from heaven. No doubt, Satan thought the same had happened to Jesus until the third day when things in Hell were shaken up. Jesus beat Satan on his home turf. Jesus broke through the gates of Hell, taking the keys and some of its captives. Now, here I am on the enemy's turf and he's gloating because he thinks I will be the devil's slave. Not so! God is planning to bust Hell wide open once again and rescue some more captives. If I am to be perfect, I will be as my Master: obedient and victorious in my Heavenly Father's work.

1/01 *(New Assignment Revealed)*

My spiritual senses were operating at an even higher level than before. I was hearing and seeing the demons very clearly. These intense manifestations were everywhere. Many things I could never mention because they are too unbelievable. I was so overwhelmed that I called an apostle friend of mine for covering in prayer. The Lord told me to share a bit with this friend. His wife told me that the devil had taken my mind.

He just prayed and began to prophesy about what the Lord was teaching me. He said by the Spirit, that the Lord had given me, '*a technology anointing. To understand and teach technology in the natural and technology of the spirit.*' This prophecy did not surprise me. Most people don't know that I have had an intense hunger for science and technology since I was a child. I remember being part of some kind of intelligence testing as a small child. I was being tested in math and science at levels well beyond my age. It was the Holy Spirit that taught me. I asked Him the question and discussed the results with Him. The mathematical models lifted off the page while the Lord explained theories and demonstrated motions.

This was just the beginning of my search for God's Word inside of math, physics and computers. As an adult, the Lord has given me inventions. I wrote down what the Lord gave to me. I have no earthly clue how to design anything God showed me, but at the appointed time, He will show me what to do. This prophecy confirmed many things about my life.

1/01 *(The Enemy's Weapon against Me Revealed)*

The next few weeks were tormenting to me because I am used to being able to sense the anointing of God daily. Now, when I pray, the enemy retaliates with evil and vulgar reactions in the spirit. There were demonic jabs to my body every time I prayed or worshipped the Lord. It was the equivalent to living in hell according to the Spirit of the Lord. He explained that Jesus went through the same thing in Hell; surrounded and attacked endlessly by demons.

The Lord showed the weapons the enemy designed to destroy me. The Lord told me that there were evil men following me and watching me by camera. He called them witches. They were doing witchcraft and watching me by camera to see if their spells were working. Several people were praying for me and the Lord showed them the same thing. One of the people watching me was my neighbor downstairs. He was a Jewish man who hated Christians and Blacks. The Lord showed several of us that this man actually broke into my apartment and placed pin-sized cameras throughout so that he could watch me day and night.

The Lord also told me that the enemy was going to convince many men that I was their wife. This was a spirit that, according to God, would only affect fornicators, which would include adulterers, homosexuals, perverts and all twisted sexual practices. Most of the people sent spirits of sexual perversion, rape and murder in an attempt to scare me. I never had fear of them, but feared what God was going to do to them for trying to hurt me.

The Lord also told us that my ex-husband was responsible for the cameras and the perverts. The only thing that surprised us was the type of cameras being used. The Lord showed us what seemed to be heat-sensored equipment that supposedly only the Federal government is allowed to operate. These cameras can detect humans based on body temperature which is actually advantageous for a person given over to sexual perversion. They can watch a person by camera and see where the person's body heat fluctuates. The camera can show them whether their perverted sexual spells are working on their victims. This camera can also pick up limited brain activity, which is why my prayers and praises made the devil mad.

I have never been subjected to such stupidity in my life; grown men stalking women and using witchcraft to torment them. God is watching them as they watch us. He will get revenge on these evil men. This was the law of my evil ex-husband: hatred toward women with perversion, cameras and witchcraft. And, if all else fails, he will murder them. The Lord informed me that since my covering was breached, I was considered a prisoner of war, and must be taught new ways to defend myself in the spirit. Out of the blue, my spirit asked the Lord what seemed to be a strange question. I asked the Lord what it was like being in hell for three days. The Lord responded by saying that I was about to learn what Jesus saw and heard when He descended into hell. I then saw Jesus standing beside me in the spirit and He gave me a very large challis and I eagerly took it and drank it all. Then Jesus handed me an even larger challis. I drank all that was in it as well. When I finished drinking from both cups, the Lord congratulated me and smiled.

1/001 *(Vision of My Cross)*

Shortly after the vision of the challises, I was in prayer and the Lord flashed before me a vision of Him on the cross. Then He flashed what I thought was the same vision, until He flashed it again. Here is what I saw. The first image was of Jesus on the cross. The second image was of Paula on the cross. By drinking from the cups, I was saying, 'not my will Lord, but yours be done.' The cross was the symbol that I had put away every selfish desire to obey God, for a purpose greater than myself.

2/01 *(Vision of the Missile Directed at Me)*

The Lord revealed another enemy plot in a vision. I walked into a house and saw a friend's husband standing near a table in the back of a room. As I walked toward him and smiled, he pulled out a hand held missile and pointed it toward me. I thought he was just showing it to me, until he fired at me. When I moved in one direction, the missile also moved in that direction. I then moved in the other direction and again the missile moved in my direction. Not knowing what else to do, I dove behind a couch, and the missile followed me. As I began to wonder what was going on, the missile hit me. My body exploded in millions of pieces. As it hit me, I rebuked the devil and my body came back together again. The Lord told me to never ask why the enemy is trying to hurt me. He said just know that the weapon is coming and speak the word. I was momentarily distracted by the size and firepower of the weapon. It was the type of missile that could wipe out an entire city block. Why would anyone use that kind of power on me? These questions nearly cost me my life. Whatever the devil planned, it did not prosper, because the Lord was with me.

January-February 2001 *(Another Death Plot Destroyed)*
The Lord revealed a plot by the enemy to kill me. Some strange organism attached itself to my intestine. I watched it happen in the spirit. It took several weeks, but the Lord told me exactly what to do to destroy yet another death plot.

2/01 *(A Chance to See the Devil Face-to-Face)*
It has been a month in Cleveland and the devil has tried every attempted to destroy me. All attempts have failed. After my recovery from the physical attack, I began going on walks in the neighborhood and praying in the spirit. One day, I asked the Lord to let me see the enemy face to face. I saw them by the spirit, but I wanted to get right up in their faces and let them know that Paula was here to stay to complete the assignment. Whenever my ex-husband followed me, someone always lets me know that they work for him. Most think he's a crazy idiot for following around a woman who is not bothering anyone.

After walking two blocks, the Lord said to me, *'**there he is.**'* There was a well-dressed black man walking toward me carrying what seemed to be a portfolio. The closer I came toward him, the more nervous he became. I peered at him although he could not see my eyes under my sunglasses. I could sense that same evil anointing that my ex-husband wears. It is so demonic and unique to him and his cronies. It's a kind of stench that you'll never forget once you get a whiff of it. When the man came near me he nervously said hello. I removed my glasses and looked him dead in the eyes and said, 'May God bless you brother.' That made him so nervous that he walked faster to get away from me. I thanked the Lord for answering my prayer and allowing me to get right in the enemy's face and let him know, 'you don't scare me devil!'

3/01 *(Word about Man with the Legion)*
I was working at my computer when a ferocious demonic spirit appeared. A new person began watching me by camera. The spirit seemed to be part human and part dog or wolf. I could not tell. I asked the Lord who it was. He replied, *'__the man in the tombs.__'* [4] I responded, 'come again? I did not understand you.' The Lord said, *'__it's the man in the tombs. Legion.__'* I asked the Lord what He wanted me to do. He replied, *'__ignore him.__'* The Lord then explained that this man did not choose his twisted world. Someone else did this to him. The Lord wants to save him and use him. Before our conversation ended, the Lord gave me one more zinger, *'__he won't be satisfied just watching you. He will try to touch you.__'* I said nothing. I just thought to myself, 'why can't I just have normal assignments like everyone else I know?' The Lord subtly reminded me of my being on enemy turf to fulfill His purpose.

3/01 The Lord told me to start prayer groups with East side churches. He said, *'__go from house to house daily.__'*[5] I met Dee at PSRC. We set up an altar and benches at my condo.

Weekly Prayer Schedule:

Monday	Condo
Tuesday	PSRC
Wednesday	All night prayer at condo or Dee's
Thursday	ACC
Friday	AGF
Saturday	Condo (mornings) HIF (evenings)

We began a telephone prayer line and worked on creating a prayer room at Dee's apartment complex.

3/01 The food bank in Columbus offered me the Assistant Director's job. The Lord told me to turn it down and remain in Cleveland.

3/01/01 *(Word of the Lord Concerning Teaching)*
The Lord told me to **'*FEED MY SHEEP.*'** He gave me the outline for
a discipleship training program. I began training on various topics,
including intercession and telephone prayer.

March-May 2001   There was much intensive prayer, study and
writing. I began another teaching program on the Kingdom of God.

5/01 *(Word about Investigators)*
The Lord showed investigators watching me. I am not sure if they
were the same ones from Columbus. They were not really watching
me. The Lord showed them watching the men that were watching me.
They were staked out at an apartment complex across the street from
me. Someone was also attempting e-mail surveillance at office. After
analyzing the hit patterns on our network, we assumed the perpetrators
were from the government.

5/01 *(Command to Speak to the Camera)*
It was my routine Wednesday all night prayer. Things were going well
until about 10 p.m. My neighbor was watching me pray by camera
and decided to join me. There were about six people all together in one
apartment. While I was praying in tongues to praise music, they
decided to have an orgy. The Lord showed me that they all had a doll
that represented Paula and began doing perverted sexual things with
the dolls while I prayed. They decided to make Paula part of their
little party. The Lord told me to keep praying and ignore them.

5/01 *(Speak to the Camera, Continued)*

At about 2 a.m., the Lord showed me the location of a camera near where I was praying. He said, *'**speak to the camera.**'* I responded in tongues, and the camera went dead. Then I heard the neighbor banging on the walls and swearing like an idiot. He could no longer see me. Then the camera came back on again. I continued to pray without ceasing. At about 4 a.m., the Lord again said, *'**speak to the camera.**'* Again, I obeyed and the camera broke.

At 6 a.m. the command was repeated. This time the camera never came back on. I immediately got dressed and left the apartment. As I left, a car drove up and I saw the neighbor speaking to someone downstairs. The Lord let me know that they were going to upgrade the equipment to follow me by satellite. And, within about 30 minutes that is exactly what happened. I had no fear, but I knew that whoever was following me was relentless and the Lord was allowing them to go as far as they wanted. But the Lord had another plot waiting for them. Men arrogantly use technology and think it makes them powerful. They forget that God is the creator of all things. Technology was God's idea, not man's. God sees all and will give men the just reward for their deeds. And, judgment is just around the corner.

5/01 *(Seeing the Fruits of Our Labor)*

Supernatural results were flowing out of my teachings. The Lord was showing His Hand mightily. People were coming into their callings and the gifts were flowing. One person asked, 'why is it that I did not see angels until you showed up.' It always amazes me when those I teach began to bloom in their gifts. It's like watching a baby walk for the first time. They are nervous on one hand, but when it's over they are proud that they actually heard and obeyed. One woman boldly prophesied to her pastor after church.

5/01 *(Continued)*
This woman was so blown away by the experience that she apologized for speaking so boldly to the pastor. The Lord gave her a word of encouragement for the man. He looked at her strangely because she is very shy and no one realized that she had a speaking gift. Another in the group had prayed for years that the Lord would wake her and use her to be a watchman for her church and city. When I became ill, the Lord told me to ask her to pray for my healing. The woman began crying and said that the previous night the Lord showed my face to her in the spirit. She woke up and immediately fell on her knees. She said that there was fire coming out of her belly. She was honored that God called her to pray for me.

As a teacher my greatest frustration is disciplining those whose pastors don't teach the basics of how to operate in the things of God. I was given several people who have been in leadership over ten years. They knew how to operate in the church, but were very lazy, choosing to be spoon-fed the word rather than digging in and studying on their own. They thought I was too tough. My constant prayer is to impart a passion for the word of God to all those I teach. When these students obeyed the Word, they began to see the fruits of their labor. This motivated them to abide in the Word and the Lord manifested Himself to them even more.

April-June 2001 *(Provisions Supplied By The Spirit)*
As a demonstration to my students, the Holy Spirit supplied supernatural provisions for all to see. The Lord periodically asked me what I wanted to eat. I'd tell Him and He would say, *'**go to Dee's cabinets**.'* This happened at least a dozen times.

April-June 2001 *(Provision, Continued)*
It became a running joke that the Holy Ghost was stocking Dee's cabinets with whatever Paula requested. Dee was not working. She definitely was not shopping, but whatever I asked for I always found in her cabinets. One day the Lord showed me that Dee was complaining about not having any money. The Lord sent me to her house. She opened the door and I walked straight into her living room to a very large jar in the corner of the room.

When I picked up the jar, Dee let me know there were only pennies in the jar. The Holy Spirit told me that there were bills inside of the jar. Dee began to argue that the jar was only used for pennies. I told her that the Lord sent me and He would not lie about the bills. As I turned the jar sideways, there were numerous folded bills. There were one dollar and five dollar bills throughout the jar. Dee swore that she did not know where they came from.

As I pulled out the bills, I told her they came from the same place the food came from. I let her know that the food did not just appear in her cabinets all those weeks for nothing. The Lord was demonstrating His way of providing when we trust in Him. Jesus fed the 5000 and the 4000 (Mark 6:44; 8:9). Money appeared in the mouth of a fish (Matthew 17:27). Is there anything too hard for God? We have been faithfully praying and taking care of God's business. He automatically takes care of our needs when we seek first His kingdom.

6/01 *(Word about Prayers Being Answered)*

The Lord wanted to demonstrate His power again for my students and intercessors. He told me that whatever we asked for in prayer, He would grant to us. The Lord told me to go to Gwen McCurry's meeting in July and there would be a public confirmation that our prayers were answered. I had everyone call people they knew and collect as many prayer requests as they could. I asked for their most desperate and difficult requests. We read them in our sessions and kept them before the Lord knowing that they would be answered. The Lord had me call someone I vaguely knew and ask, 'what do you want from God more than anything?' This woman said she had just asked the Lord in prayer to send her someone that could stand in agreement for her difficult request. I was not only in agreement with her, but asked her to come to Gwen's meeting for the confirmation. To my surprise, this woman said that Gwen was her spiritual mother for many years. They had been out of touch and she wanted to see her again.

6/01 *(Word of the Lord Concerning Army)*

The Word of the Lord came to me saying, '**_I am sending you an army able to call bombs out of the sky._**' I understood this to mean powerful intercessors. My prayer group at my home church in LA also called bombs out of the sky.

6/01

We prepared to open a prayer room in July and I got a sense in prayer that a major disaster was to occur. The Lord had us praying for food shortage solutions and told me that I needed a warehouse for food. My assumption was a natural disaster. I obtained a geological map of the Midwest and began praying for earthquakes faults, etc.

6/01 The Lord led us into strong prophetic prayer for the city and the nation.

June-July 2001 I began classes with Gwen McCurry. They had a community outreach center. I assumed this was where God wanted me. He confirmed my attendance for service.

7/01 *(Word about Prayers Confirmed)*
The Lord spoke through Elder McCurry about our prayer efforts. She said that we boldly asked for things that would have scared most people of faith, and all that we asked would be done. The woman I encouraged to come to the service also got confirmation of what we agreed to in prayer. After service, she looked at me stunned and said, 'you have crazy faith. I've never met anyone quite like you.' We both laughed and cried at the wondrous thing the Lord did that afternoon.

For weeks that followed, the praise reports flowed. Cancers were gone. People got delivered from crack in an instant and began serving God. Children were coming home and getting saved. Marriages were mended. Men and women were changing careers and began serving God full-time. It was a glorious time of praising God for answered prayer. In hindsight, the Lord had to demonstrate His goodness then, so that during the bad times we would not forget that He hears our prayers. Danger was still on the horizon.

7/01 *(Word of the Lord Concerning War)*
The Lord told us to *'**prepare for war.**'* We were not sure what
and where He meant, but we began praying intensely for our
country and started stocking up on can goods for distribution.
Another prophecy came forth from Elder Gwen's service about
war and cleanup we would be expected to do in Cleveland.

7/01/2001 There were intense days of prayer for the city and
nation. We put together more prayer teams.

8/2001 The prayer room opened in August at Dee's apartment
complex. The first overnight prayer session was scheduled Friday
September 7th.

8/01 A spiritual shift occurred taking us to new levels of
darkness. It was mid afternoon when the shift occurred. I saw a
dark spiritual blind cover our country as though we were being
eclipsed by evil.

9/07/01 We were directed by the Holy Spirit to pray 7 p.m. to 7 a.m.
for our nation. We were putting together a checklist of things to have
during war. Several people showed up for prayer, most left by 9 p.m. I
remained in the prayer room alone praying for the nation until
Saturday 7 a.m.

9/8/01 That evening at HIF prophecy came forth alerting us of a
*'**shaking**'* of our country. Intense praise and prayer was made on
behalf of the nation.

9/10/01   An evening prophecy at ACC came concerning *__shaking__* and tragedy in the US. No details were given. We were told not to fear, but to keep praising. Our protection was in our praise.

9/11/01   By 7 a.m.-8:30 a.m. we finished our war prep list and morning prayer session with intercessors.

9/11/01   When I arrived at the office 8:30-8:45 a.m., I was asked what I was up to. I said 'preparing for war.' Everyone looked at me shocked and asked if I heard the news. The television was on in the conference room replaying the attack on the World Trade Center. I knew it was not an accident. As we spoke, the second tower was hit. The FBI investigators grounded two planes in Cleveland. Mayor White told the press of a 2 a.m. warning from the government about a possible terrorist attack.

9/14/01   (Word of the Lord Concerning Persecution)
The Lord told me to *__prepare the people for persecution__* like in other countries. I contacted Voice of the Martyrs (VOM) [6] by Internet and ordered materials on worldwide persecution. We used prayer requests of VOM for the prayer room intercession.

9/14/01   *(Vision about City Occupied by Arab Troops)*
This afternoon at work, I went into prayer, led by the unction of the Holy Spirit. I saw a US city occupied by Arab troops. Complete occupation! I did not know what city the Arabs took. I continued in prayer for our leaders, country and military until the Lord released me.

September–October 2001   There were many low flying planes over Cleveland. We also saw rocket launchers flying over the city. Prayer was made without ceasing. My spirit was in constant prayer even while asleep.

9/30/01 *(Vision about Food Warehouse)*
The Lord showed me a warehouse. He explained that I would be getting food to distribute around the country.

10/02/01 *(Supernatural Occurrence at the Office)*
I ran water in the kitchen sink to wash my hands. As the water warmed up, I placed my hand into the water. The healing power of God began to flow from my hand. When I removed my hand from the water it stopped. When I put my hand back into the water, the healing power flowed again. Then I asked the Lord what was going on. He said that there was something harmful in the water. He said that the enemy would poison the water and I need only to know that I could drink any deadly thing and it will not harm me according to Mark 16:18.

The Lord then explained that when the children of Israel left Egypt the waters were bitter (poisoned) at Marah (Exodus 15:23-25). He gave them a tree and told Moses to cast its branch into the waters. Then the water became sweet (healed). He told me that I also had a tree. A branch from the root of Jesse (Isaiah 11:1), named Jesus. In His name is the healing power to make the bitter waters sweet. There is no need to fear poisoned water.

10/01 *(Word about Cave People)*

The Lord spoke to me in prayer about calling out the cave people; those that live in perpetual darkness and never see the light of day. These included the deceived and deluded, the mentally ill, demon possessed and witches. The Lord is calling them to Himself and out of the dark places where they have chosen to hide. Then the Lord spoke, *'this is your ministry. I have given these to you.'*

10/01 *(Vision about Witches Being Translated)*

The Lord gave me a vision on two separate occasions. He showed a group of evil witches watching and following me. Then one day they came to my house to kill me. When I made my way home, they were waiting with baseball bats and other weapons. They were angry because none of their spells stopped me from doing the will of God. These people hated me with a passion and decided to take me out. The first vision ended with them descending upon me to beat me up. Then the vision replayed again almost exactly the same with one exception. It continued past where the first vision ended. When the witches descended upon me, the Lord let them touch me. Then the most amazing thing happened, they all fell to the ground: slain in the spirit. When they got up off the ground, they had been translated from the kingdom of darkness into the kingdom of God. It reminded me of what happened to Paul on the road to Damascus (Acts 9:1-6). I remember the reactions of a couple of the witches. There was this older black man who started saying, 'I've never felt love like this. It's so powerful. I can't believe I spent all those years holding on to hate when I could have been in this kind of love.'

10/01 (*Vision about Witches, Continued*)
Then there was this white woman who had such joy that she could not stop crying and thanking God. He confirmed for her what she always knew as a child: God was love. The others were in shocked of what happened. None could deny that they had met up with a force that was bigger than anything they had ever encountered. I remember telling them that they could never go back to the old way of living. Some of them knew immediately what God wanted to do in their lives. He told them on the spot. None could keep quiet about this miracle. The Lord showed me that they told everybody about what He had done for them.

10/01 (*Prayer and Fasting Against Sexual Predators*)
The Lord sent to me several women of God who were bound sexually to married pastors. The Lord had us fast and pray for a day to break these bonds. The women were released at 9 p.m. But the Lord did not release me until about midnight. At about 12:30 I lay my head down to rest and the spirit that I broke off the women came back angrily to harass me. He had the nerve to ask me, *'who do you think you are coming into my territory and breaking a stronghold I have had on these churches for years?'* I didn't even bother to answer. I told the Holy Spirit, it was up to Him to fight this one, I was going to sleep, and so I did. The Holy Spirit in me spent some part of the night beating the tar out of that devil. But, my sleep was sweet.

September-October 2001   There were many visions of unidentified low flying planes hovering over the city's eastside. The visions showed military planes in formation and enemy bombs filling the sky. There was much carnage. People were running scared in the visions. Seeing enemy planes in visions and then hearing the low flying planes outside was at times unnerving.

10/01 *(The Call to Pray)*
The Lord told me to call the Trinity Broadcasting Network (TBN) [7] and make a prayer request concerning trouble in Cleveland. When I spoke to a prayer partner, she said she did not believe me and refused to pray for me. Instead, she told me to pray and she would stand in agreement with me. As I began to pray the Spirit of the Lord moved upon her and the prayer partner began crying. When I finished praying, she apologized, and said that Cleveland was her hometown and her family was there. The Spirit of the Lord told her to pray and cover her family in Cleveland with the Blood of Jesus.

10/01 *(Word about Teaching on Sunday Mornings)*
The Lord informed me that the Pastor was going to ask me to teach Bible Study on Sunday mornings. It was required for the leadership to meet for Bible study and prayer before the morning service. I was hesitant about the assignment because I was not sure the early morning group would be ready for my style of teaching. Occasionally I taught on Monday nights if Elder Gwen was absent, but that was different. The Monday night crowd was more progressive in things of the spirit and I have even shaken a few of them a time or two.

I have had people run out of my prayer meetings because things got too hot in the spirit. One gentleman referred my prophetic style, to a nuclear warhead with pinpoint accuracy. Was this quiet, religious Sunday morning crowd ready for Paula, fueled by the Holy Ghost? Ready or not, we were coming. The Lord told me to accept the position, and then watch Him take over. I knew that was exactly what He meant, and I was a bit concerned.

10/01/01 *(Vision of Millionaires Giving Money)*
I was in a conference room, probably in Los Angeles, with many multimillionaires. They were giving me checks for the relief effort.

10/08/01 *(Vision of Air Bombings)*
I saw more planes overhead in formation shooting at the people below. This vision repeated throughout the week.

10/10/01 *(Dream about Underground People)*
I was underground leading hundreds of people (who lived underground) to the surface. We came to the surface of the earth to hundreds of planes overhead. The planes never saw us. The people were under my covering. They also had no fear of the warplanes.

10/11/01 *(Vision of the Lord's Table)*
During praise and worship at ACC, we had a visitation from God. He showed a table. The Lord was seated at the head. I was seated next to Him. The angels served me from His Table. The angels also fed me.

10/12/01 *(Vision of Burning Buildings and Kids Playing)*
We were at a church meeting. In the background children were playing under crystal blue skies and beautiful clouds. They were wearing coats outside. They seemed happy. In the background of the children playing were buildings on fire. No one seemed to be affected.

10/15/01 *(Vision of Army Jeep)*
I was being driven around in an army jeep wearing a suit made of army fatigue pattern.

10/29/01 *(Vision of Black School Buses)*
I saw black school buses filled with Arabs dressed in black. The school buses had red arrowheads on the sides. I saw this vision two days in a row.

11/1/01 *(Vision of Gunmen in Truck Beds)*
I saw a long covered flatbed truck driving down Superior Street in East Cleveland. Men came from under the cover of the truck bed and started shooting down people on the street.

11/18/01 *(Vision of Black Bus Caravan)*
I saw another black bus caravan, this time containing only woman and children, all Arab, all dressed in black mourning clothes. This time the caravan had an escort. Six white men on motorcycles led the caravan. They looked like BIG TIME bikers. They wore turbans made from the confederate flag.

11/2001 *(Sunday Morning is Ablaze with the Word)*
The Lord took over every Sunday morning. My plan was to teach a chapter and verse study of the Gospels. I prepared every week, but there were things coming cut of my mouth that I had never heard before. I knew things were going well, when the Pastor jumped up and shouted, 'I never heard that before, but I know the Holy Ghost is speaking.' He later told me that his teenage son was fired up to get to church just to hear what was coming out of Sister Paula's mouth. This kid would literally sit on the edge of his seat with his Bible and his mouth open.

11/2001 *(Continued)*

The early morning session was growing larger as people brought their family and friends to hear the message. Sometimes they were not so enthusiastic because the Lord would be up close and personal in their business. By 6 p.m. every Sunday evening, my phone would ring off the hook with people confessing to something they heard me say that morning. One of the assistant pastors even jumped up during one session screaming in amazement, 'how did you know? How did you know? That is exactly what is going on.' She began publicly confessing a hidden sin before the congregation. Whenever something like this happens, I take the time to deal with the person publicly so that all can learn and partake in deliverance that goes forth. It's amazing to see people confessing to each other and bringing so much healing for all. I also take them to the Word so that they know that what we are doing is Biblical. For lengthier subjects, I even prepare additional written materials on the topic with Biblical references and make it available on the next Sunday.

11/01 *(One Leader's Attack on My Teaching)*

One of the pastoral staff became angry that the pastor let me teach and not her. She began on a personal crusade to destroy Paula. It did not work. This woman accused me of being a fraud. She said that I was pretending to be nobody while all along; I had a Doctorate of Divinity. This woman declared that she would expose me to the entire Cleveland community. I told her there was nothing to expose, and although I did not have a D.D., I received her words as a prophecy of things to come. The Lord told me I had to go back to school. When I explained that it was the Holy Spirit doing the teaching, she did not believe me. In her mind, no one could teach the way I do without a D.D.

11/22/01 *(Vision of Blood on the Capitol Dome)*

It was Thanksgiving morning at about 2:00 a.m. The Lord startled me out of a deep sleep by showing the United States Capitol Building with blood oozing from the dome. Then blood began to pour. He said, *'The American people will be held hostage.'* I began to pray and the Lord stopped me. He said there was nothing I could do to stop it. He blamed it on our government practices of many years.

11/28/01 *(Vision of Shoot out At Grocery Store)*

I saw Anita, Marcus and Rico shopping at Tops grocery store. A shoot out began. Anita took Rico and ran to the checkout. Marcus ran in the opposite direction when he saw an injured Arab soldier lying on the floor after being shot. Compassion came upon Marcus and he walked toward the soldier with his hand reaching to touch the wounded man. The Lord carried me by the Spirit to remove him from the store. I took him outside to Anita. Anita said, 'I didn't know you were shopping here too.' I walked back in the store and the Spirit of the Lord carried me by the spirit back to my original location.

12/01/01 *(Dream of Plane Crashing Into Building)*

I was conducting a meeting on the top floor of a building, not sure where, maybe LA or Chicago. The building was all glass. The conference room was full. I was standing at the head of the table speaking when suddenly an airplane came crashing into the window with the intent of killing us. As the plane hit the building, the window did not shatter. Instead, the window became like melted plastic. It bowed inward and wrapped itself around the nose of the plane. The side of the wall where the impact occurred went back into position; however the nose of plane was stuck in the glass. The glass had hardened around the plane and it could not move. The petrified pilot remained in the cockpit. We simply changed conference rooms and continued our meeting.

12/2001 (*Word about Doing Altar Calls for Leaders*)
The Lord told me to begin holding altar calls for the leaders. He said that some leaders committed to the ministry but never committed to Jesus Christ. Others left their first love and the Lord was calling them to repent. I got a confirmation of the Lord's Word later that day from the mother of the church. She and I agreed in prayer that the leaders turn to God and get saved. I gave the altar calls after each teaching. No leaders ever came forth publicly, but the Lord said some were turning back to Him.

12/5/01 (*Word about War Supplies and President Bush*)
The Spirit of the Lord came upon me, I said, 'God's people will have food and supplies for the country. God's people will be used by the government to help end the war.' After I spoke these words, the Lord then said to me, *'**Prepare to meet President Bush.**'*

12/09/01 (*Vision of a Warrior*)
I was fighting in a war wearing a warrior headband and Rambo[8] type attire.

12/12/01 (*A Night Vision of The Lord Shaking the Earth*)
I saw the Hand of the Lord hovering over the entire earth. He picked up the entire planet earth and began shaking it. I heard the voices of demons crying in horror, 'have mercy on me!' The Lord ignored their cries and the horror continued. I was awaken by the terrible shaking and the screams. I could still hear and feel the horror so intensely that I went to the window to see if there were indeed people in the streets crying out to God for mercy. There were none.

12/20/01 *(Judgment against Evil Shepherds)*
The Lord spoke to me about His judgment against the shepherds that have not taken care of His flock. Then I found myself in the spirit prophesying before a congregation. There were many leaders present when I spoke and the Lord spoke judgment on evil shepherds (Ezekiel 34:1-16). I remember several immediate reactions by the leaders. One bishop began searching his heart and repenting before the Lord. Another bishop was so blown away by the prophecy that he kept saying to the Lord, 'you didn't tell me you were going to do this. I've never seen anything like this before. I have never seen anything like this.' There was another minister who was not in attendance, but I heard her reaction. She was watching me speak by television and laughing hysterically. She said to the Lord, 'thank you Lord. It's about time we have someone that will tell the truth about what's going on.'

There was another female minister in attendance that was not moved by the Word of the Lord. She just sat with a jealous look on her face. She tried to rally the other leaders against me. She commanded, 'you get rid of her now!' As she spoke, a demon was beginning to manifest. While this was going on, the Lord told me to break the bondages off the congregation who were bound by works of these evil leaders. The people ran forward and many were on their knees crying out to God. They were all set free. By this time, the female minister had gotten the evil leaders upset enough that we had to get out of there. The vision ended.

12/01 *(Sunday Morning Manifestations of the Spirit)*

As the teachings continued, the Spirit of the Lord began to hover over us each week. There was a constant glory cloud in our midst. A woman walked in off the street. She said she was on her way to the liquor store but something pulled her into the church. This woman swore that she felt angels bringing her into the church. She sat in the back of the sanctuary and wept. In another service, deliverance came forth such that demons were manifesting in the saints in the midst of the congregation. Even the pastoral assistant began growling in the spirit while I was praying. When I finished and took my seat next to her, the fire of God surge from my body in her direction. This woman along with others ran out of the church in fear. The Lord was dealing with His people in a dramatic way and everybody knew it.

12/22/01 *(Vision of Judgment of a Pastor)*

The Lord took me by the spirit to a church to speak to a Man of God, possibly a pastor. The Lord had me speak a Word of Judgment to compel him to repent. He rebuked me and asked, 'Do you know who I am?' Then he began describing all the churches he started, all the books he had written, and how important a man he was. The judgment was calling for him to repent for the crimes he committed against the people of God. He refused to heed the Word of the Lord. I then spoke by the Spirit of the Lord, 'Because you will not repent, this day your soul will be required of you.' The Man of God dropped dead in the midst of his congregation, and in front of his small children who began crying in horror.

12/01 *(Judgment against Sexual Predators)*

The Lord showed me in prayer that there are many bishops and leaders having sex with men and women who have trusted them. They come hurting and in need of help, and leaders use and abuse them. God is very angry. He called it spiritual incest. Those that don't repent and get help, the Lord will destroy from the face of the earth.

12/01 *(Word about Sexual Perversion in Leaders)*

While praying in the spirit, the Lord showed a group of homosexual men, all pastors and leaders hiding a life of sexual perversion. Some of these men are abusing the women in the church and stalking them. The Lord showed that some pastors placed cameras in the women's bathroom stalls and then used the tapes for folly. God said He was sending me to their churches to call them out.

12/01 *(Perversion and Homosexuality in the Church)*

The Lord explained that sexual perversion in the church would not be easily broken. He took me to Judges Chapters 19 and 20. It tells a gruesome story of a sex crime and murder among God's people. A man refused to have sex with evil men and they instead, gang raped the man's wife, killed her and left her body on the doorstep. In his grief, the man cut his wife's body into twelve pieces and sent her to each of the Twelve Tribes of Israel, demanding that they do something about the evil among their brothers. The Tribe of Benjamin refused to listen and went to war with their brothers defending the lewd acts done in their city. The battle was fierce. It took much prayer, fasting, and loss of life (on both sides) in three battles before Benjamin was defeated. Victory came because the tribes banded together under God to get the evil from among their people. The church speaks boldly against homosexuality and sexual sin of strangers, yet we don't deal with the sexual sin inside of God's House.

12/01 *(Perversion and Homosexuality in the Church, Cont.)*
God knows that there are homosexuals and others who don't want His will for their lives, but He is more concerned about those doing the same or even worse deeds and calling themselves Christians. We, the family of God, know God has house rules that we all must follow. But we cannot enforce those same rules upon others who are not in our household. This is where the church has gone wrong. My parents had rules in their house that I had to abide by if I wanted to stay in that house. And, if my friends came over to visit, the house rules applied to them as well, but when they left my house, they could do whatever they wanted; it was between them, God and their parents. The Lord showed me that the church won't even enforce the house rules upon those who are in the House of God. They ignore the sexual perversion among the brethren. We know of men who publically preach against sexual sin and homosexuality, yet in private are practicing the very thing they preach against. Some are bound to this evil and wish to be free; others use their preaching as a diversionary tactic to prey upon their congregations. For the church to battle with sinners outside the house but not deal with the sinners inside the house, is hypocritical!

In this Bible story, God knew the people living among His people were lewd, but He did not intervene until they hurt His people, and until the brethren went to God for justice. And so it is in our day as well. Do whatever you want in your own house, but if you try to prey on God's people with your lewdness, His rules apply and you will be destroyed. The Lord made it clear that the Body of Christ will not be free of perversion until we all band together under God's Word and vow to fight to free our brothers. And when the world sees us help our brothers to be free, then they will trust us to help them get free. This is the love of God that the world is waiting to see; that
we give our lives for our family and friends.

THE WAR JOURNAL
YEAR 2002: *The Enemy Exposed*
And God's Plan Revealed

THE WAR JOURNAL
YEAR 2002: *The Enemy Exposed And God's Plan Revealed*

1/1/02   This first week was filled with more visions of planes overhead and bombing from the sky.

1/09/02 *(Vision of Chinese and Russian Bomber Airplanes)*
There were more bombs and planes in this vision. Their nation's flag identified the planes. There were about 30-40 planes from various nations of the world. I clearly recognized the flags of China and the Russia, and I sensed North Korea was involved as well.

1/14/02 *(Visitation for Protection by Angels)*
I was awaken by an extremely bright light, and the power of God filled my bedroom. There was something going on in the house; danger of some sort. I heard footsteps rapidly leaving from the first floor of the house. I then heard a car speed out of the driveway. The Lord spoke to me and said that just like the angels protected me from danger that night, the same would be done during war. He said that even if the enemy breaks down the door to hurt others in the house, they would not come near me. He said the angels would protect me and would not let anyone come near me.

2/02 *(Vision about an Exploded Building)*
I rescued a woman who was trapped under a portion of an exploded building. The sidewalk had been ripped open. I could not reach her. From a distance I looked her in the eyes and told her to grab my hand. When she reached toward me, I flew in mid air and took her hand. I noticed that her body was severed in half at the waist, but she did not know. The bottom half of her body miraculously reattached itself when she grabbed my hand.

2/02 *(Vision to Alert of Nuclear Attack)*
The Lord said *'**prepare for nuclear attack.**'* He showed me two flags, China and Russia, along with ground troops (looked like Arabs) dressed in green fatigues and carrying guns.

2/02 *(Word of the Lord about War)*
I spoke utterances by the Spirit as the unction came upon me. He spoke about *'**war beginning on March 15th**.'* Not sure where the war was to occur in USA or elsewhere. I also spoke in tongues to the Lord.

2/02 *(Vision of Food Warehouse)*
The Lord showed me a warehouse full of food. A Word came to Elder McCurry confirming a warehouse coming to me for food.

2/02 *(Vision of Open Heavens)*
I saw the windows of heaven open. Tons of gold coins poured from the skies in buckets.

2/02 *(Vision of Gold Coins from Heaven)*
I saw planes opening their cargo doors and pouring out buckets of gold coins on me.

2/02 *(Vision of Food Donations)*
I was invited to get food from manufacturers; no one else I knew was allowed to come. They let me pick from the best they had. I could order cases to distribute. They wanted me to sample all of their foods. Roger and Willie watched from a distance.

3/02 *(Vision of Detonated Nuclear Bombs and Hussein)*
The Lord awakened me by saying, ***'Prepare for Nuclear War.'*** I then saw seven (7) nuclear bombs. The Lord said at least 2 were detonated. He told me to speak and pray for failure. Five (5) of the bombs were destined for the US; the other two (2) for US allies. The Lord showed me the face of Saddam Hussein and said he was behind the planned bomb attacks.

3/02 *(Word of the Lord Concerning Book)*
The Lord spoke concerning the book and class. He said, ***'write it and they will come.'***

3/02 *(Vision of a New House)*
The Lord took me by the spirit to a house that someone gave to me. It was new and furnished. My family came to visit me. Carrie was in the driveway with a new van.

3/02 *(Vision of Food in Kitchen)*
I went into the kitchen of the new house. It had a huge empty refrigerator. I made a list of what groceries to buy. When I opened the refrigerator door again, and the food I wanted appeared. Then I wanted a hamburger. I opened the once empty freezer and there was a case of ground round patties, chicken breast and steaks. They just appeared out of nowhere. All the food appeared in large quantities.

3/02 *(Vision of Abundance in My Refrigerator)*
I had so much food in my huge refrigerator that I was feeding people from my house. They were lined up at my refrigerator and the food kept multiplying. It never ran out.

4/02 *(Vision of Bombs Obeying the Word)*
I was rescuing people on the street. I spoke to a bomb and it changed direction. It did not come near me. Other bombs also disappeared. Gas stations and businesses were on fire everywhere.

4/02 *(A Visitation of the Unknown Kind)*
I was sleeping at my brother's house downstairs under the skylight. All of a sudden, a bright light appears. The dogs began barking. There was some kind of probing coming from the light. There was no evidence of human life or demonic force. It was probing and then it disappeared. The next day I told my brother what happened. The Spirit of the Lord spoke saying, *'**get ready, it's time.**'* What that meant we did not know.

4/02 *(An Angelic Visitation for Protection)*
Gina and I were shopping. When we left the market on Detroit Avenue and walked to the butcher shop, danger was in the air and the angels immediately covered us. The glory of God was very heavy. We left there and went to the supermarket on Dennison and the same thing happened. The glory of God was so heavy that we could hardly stand up. My body started transforming (my spirit man took over my body). This was the case for the next two days in a row.

4/02 *(Another Visitation for Protection)*
The glory of God was very heavy. Angelic protection was everywhere, but the heaviest on the Westside of Cleveland.

4/02 *(Vision of Rescue at a School)*
I moved children from school to their homes while planes were bombing from the air. I did so, only when the Lord said I could take the kids out in safety. When He gave me the go ahead, I led them home. Those that I led made it home safely, but when we got to one house, babies had been killed while playing outside. They had no warning before the bombing started.

5/02 *(Vision of a Rescue Mission and Tidal Wave)*
While sitting in a friend's car, the Spirit of the Lord took me by the spirit to a school, possibly in Santa Barbara. It was a high school or college located on the cliffs over-looking the ocean. I went specifically to prophesy to a young black woman called of God during this time. I spoke to her about God's call on her life. She began to prophesy about disaster and told everyone to go below to a lower level. Many ignored her. I looked out of the window for bomber planes, when I noticed a tidal wave coming toward the school. I urged many to go below. The tidal wave struck and the school was destroyed, all, except where we were on the lower level.

5/02 *(Vision of Trouble for an Office)*
Some people were angry with Joe. They were plotting to kill him and destroy his office. They came in the office, with major weapons, prepared to kill Joe and blame it on the Arabs.

5/02 *(Vision of Protection During War)*
The Lord showed me running to and fro without incident and taking care of Kingdom business while war was going on. There seemed to be a bubble of protection all around me. I was totally covered.

5/02 *(Vision of Sniper Fire)*
There were armed men, dressed in army camouflage, sitting in trees and shooting people in the residential neighborhoods.

5/02 *(Vision of Bombs on Jeeps)*
The Arabs were going up and down neighborhoods, randomly bombing homes in residential areas. The weapons were hand-held missiles being fired from jeeps.

5/02 *(Vision of Poisoned Water and Saddam Hussein)*
The Spirit of the Lord led me to pray for protection of the nation: that no weapon formed against Cleveland and the US will prosper; that poison in the water supply and food will not prosper. The Lord showed Saddam Hussein, again indicating his plan to poison our country's water supply.

5/02 *(Word of the Lord Concerning Open Heavens)*
The Word of the Lord came to me saying, '***the heavens are open.***' This was an answer to my prayer for opens heavens over Cleveland so that we will be free to move by the Spirit of the Lord during war.

5/02 *(Word of the Lord about Media Confusion)*
The Lord said that the US would be taken by surprise. There are many distractions: 1) blaming the president for the prior knowledge of 911. 2) CIA preparing people for bombing attacks. The Arabs intend on launching nuclear weapons. They are listening to our media confusion and will go opposite of what the media and government think.

5/02 *(Word of the Lord about Allies)*
The Lord spoke to me *'Alliance with France and Germany.'*
Not sure what He meant. I assumed they were US allies, but
nothing else was given.

5/02 *(Word of the Lord Concerning Army Surplus)*
The Lord said that the Arabs would go to army surplus stores to get
US Army attire. Their intent is to fool the public and slaughter many
in this deception.

5/02 *(Word of the Lord to Prepare Journal)*
The Lord said, *'Prepare a War Journal for the President.'* The
purpose is to show that God is tracking the enemy in war.

5/02 *(Note about the City of Cleveland)*
The city is preparing emergency evacuation procedures. There have
been more bomb scares and planes investigated. People don't seem to
be alarmed.

5/02 Much prayer was directed for Cleveland. There is a spiritual
conspiracy against the city. No one seems to care that it is a troubled
and cursed city.

5/02 *(Dream about Hurling Bus Obeying Word)*
I was in a huge glass building, probably a hotel or airport (not sure). It
had an atrium lobby. There was an explosion nearby and debris was
flying everywhere. A Metro bus was hurled into the air. It was
headed for the atrium. I yelled for everyone to move away from the
atrium. We all began running. I picked up someone's child and also
began running. Then I perceived in my spirit that the entire building
would collapse if the bus hit the atrium.

5/02 *(Continued)*

I turned around with the child still in my arms, and pointed at the bus and yelled, 'NO.' The hurling bus immediately turned right side up and landed on its wheels just outside the door of the building. No one was hurt and there was no further damage.

Many of the people, after hearing me yell and seeing the results, turned to me and asked, 'what did you say?' They were shocked and amazed. They wanted to know how I stopped that bus. I began to preach the Kingdom of God and the power of Jesus Christ. Some believed while others walked away in disbelief. No one, however, could deny that they had witnessed firsthand, something that was beyond all human abilities.

6/02 *(Dream of Bombs Exploding)*

Bombs were exploding all day and all night. In one dream I was given the location of bombs that were not yet detonated. Authorities defused many bombs as God led His people to find them.

6/02 *(Dream of Crusade)*

I was singing in a worldwide crusade. As the Glory of God increased, I began dancing feverously on stage until I was elevated into mid air. My feet never touched the ground. The Glory increased more, and I began dancing over the heads of those in the congregation. No one seemed to be moved by what I was doing because they all were caught up in the Spirit.

6/02 *(Vision and Translation into Heaven)*
In the midst of my morning prayer, I was taken up to heaven. I began to shout, 'Sing Unto the Lord a New Song. Sing unto the Lord All the Earth!' All of a sudden, I saw a bright light and heard the angels singing a song over and over. The Lord showed me sheet music and a song written on it. He told me to write down the song. It would call His Glory into the midst of the gross darkness. The Lord then took me to Psalm 96 to read about His Glory and His Judgment.

6/02 *(God's Command to Obey)*
During noon prayer the Lord commanded me to mobilize His troops. I cried out by the spirit, 'OBEY GOD!' I repeated this over and over until His Spirit released me.

6/02 *(Prophecy Concerning New Move of God)*
'This coming move of God is His Grand Finale before Jesus comes;
Fire in the Sky and Earth; Fireworks. It's the time of God's justice;
good and bad rewarded for their persistence.'

6/02 *(Personal Word to Me from The Lord)*
'**_Do not walk around the neighborhood._**' Danger is lurking and I am the target. The Lord keeps showing armed camouflaged men.

6/02 *(Vision of Troop Inspections)*
I was getting off of a military or government jet. I was inspecting the troops. I was wearing an Air Force General's uniform, highly decorated with honors.

6/02 The Lord led me in prayer for our nations' leaders several days in a row intensely. I prayed specifically for President Bush, Vice President Cheney, Secretary of State Colin Powell and Senator Richard Gephardt (D, IL).

6/02 *(Dream of Pastor's Office during War)*
Bombs are flying about and Art and Larry are terrified. Art is concerned about dying and starts remembering all the evil things he has done. He can't bring himself to repent because he is caught up in fear. At the same time he believes Pastor Randy will tell him if he is in trouble with God.

Pastor Randy is hearing from God, but a suicide spirit is on him. He hopes Art is killed. Randy also wants to die rather than fight. A bomb is coming straight at the office, Randy sits looking at it coming toward him and waiting for it to strike. He has no will to live. Art wills to live, but knows he can't continue in his sin. Larry on the other hand, is losing his mind. He was sneakily sitting in a closet eating a scoop of ice cream because there is a food shortage. There are only two packages of hot dogs in the refrigerator. Both men were afraid of the war. Larry kept telling Art to 'call Paula', so he could get right with God. Art even went and bought the Bible on tape hoping to find a solution. The Word of the Lord came to me saying that Pastor Randy will be held responsible for Art and Larry's salvation.

6/02 *(Repeated Visions of the Dead in the Streets)*
There were many visions of dead people lying in the streets of residential areas. Some people were running for help to what they assumed to be US soldiers. They were not our soldiers, but Arabs dressed in army fatigues deceiving those in need. These evil men shot down the innocent people who were seeking help.

6/02 *(Vision of Woman Killed in Her Home)*
I saw a woman's face. She was an attractive 50+-year-old Latino woman. Then I saw this same woman standing in a room. She was wearing a navy sweatshirt with a red embroidered heart on the front. She had a coffee cup in her hand. Upon hearing some noise outdoors, she walked to her back door. When she opened the screen door, four armed men disguised in US military attire, pushed the woman inside of her home, and open fired with many rounds of ammunition.

7/02 *(Repeated Visions of Terror)*
Arabs were pulling people out of their homes and began executing them in the streets.

7/02 *(Repeated Visions of Terror)*
There were people, who had been outdoors fitness walking unaware of danger, lying dead in the streets.

7/02 *(Dream about LA Bus Bomber)*
I saw two non-Arab people driving a white station wagon. The woman was Black with long braids and the man was possibly a Latino. Their car stopped along a bus stop during morning or mid-morning rush hour. They opened the car door and placed a bomb under a Metro bus without being noticed. I drove up with another person, and pulled the bus over.

I got on the bus and announced that a bomb could go off any moment, and told the people to hurry and get off. Most of them yelled at me because I was making them late. A few got off the bus. The bus made a right turn around the corner. Just as it went out of sight, there was an explosion and debris was flying everywhere.

7/02 *(Vision of Mountain Being Moved)*

I saw a mountain that was moving. There were men climbing up the mountain as it moved. These men were so frightened that they climbed faster and higher hoping it would keep the mountain from moving. These men frantically hid in mountain caves and prayed that the rocks would fall on them.[12] They did not want to experience the wrath of God. The Lord showed the base of the mountain. It was being moved by a hand full of God's people who were at the base of the mountain moving it by His Spirit. The mountain not only moved, but it rotated and shook. It did not remain.

7/02 *(Vision during Prayer-Slaying the Bear)*

I entered into a kingdom fortress. As I went to close the huge wooden gates to the kingdom, a large bear pushed open one of the gates and it fell on me. I got up to push the bear out and attempted to close the gate and the bear pushed it down again. I then called on the Lord to send the angels and before I could finish calling, legions of angels came and knocked the bear down. His head was caught between the gates. He fell and was badly injured. I was standing over the bear with a sword in my hand. I cut off the bear's head and paraded it around the kingdom on the tip of my sword. The angels pushed the bear's body outside the kingdom and safely secured the gates to the kingdom.

7/02 *(Dream of Arab Shoot Out in Street)*
A large Arab army was marching down a wide street in LA. They overtook a boulevard the size of Vermont Avenue. They had tanks, trucks and men on foot marching through the streets killing everyone in sight. A little kid was shot down in front of me. I picked him up and rocked him in my arms crying to the Lord to wake him up. 'Make an open show of the devil right here and now', I cried. The voice of the Lord answered, and commanded me to, *'**wake them all.**'* Immediately I shouted for them to get up. All the dead arose to their feet and began walking toward the Arab troops with fierceness. The Arabs retreated and ran in fear. Some began to shoot, but when the bullets did not hit anyone, the enemy ran in fear.

7/15/02 *(Dream of Black Man's Hand)*
I kept seeing a black man's hands beckoning me to come. I asked the Lord to tell me who it was. I saw the hand again and this time a face appeared, it was Dr. Price. The Lord told me to go to LA.

7/17/02 The Lord was downloading instructions about LA to my spirit. Dr. Price was mentioned more than once. He has something to do with my assignment. The Lord gave me no details in my understanding.

7/20/02 *(Vision of Las Vegas Destruction)*
While at HIF between 9-10 p.m., the Lord gave me a vision during praise and worship. I saw the city of Las Vegas. The strip and downtown went up in a huge explosion. The enemy troops detonated the city from the mountain regions surrounding the city.

7/21/02 *(A Vision at the Word Church)*
While kneeling in prayer at the altar, the Lord appeared to me with open arms. He let me know that my work in Cleveland was complete for now. He appeared a second time and declared victory over the enemy in that city.

7/22/02 *(A Vision of Hired Killers)*

During 5 a.m. prayer, the Spirit took me up to a park (possibly somewhere in Southern California). While walking through the park, I saw eight to ten armed men wearing fatigues. Their faces were covered with ski masks. I noticed that they were not shooting down everybody in sight like the Arabs did in previous visions and dreams. These gunmen passed by many Americans as though they were looking for someone specific. I walked out of a park shed and actually ran into one of the gunmen. He did not react to my presence because he could not see me. I was hidden under of the protection of God's angels.' The men went into an open area where several people were eating. They open fired on a man and his family then fled. As the gunmen fled, I noticed that one of them was an affluent white woman whose French manicured fingernails were exposed while she held her weapon.

Then the Lord took me from the park and suddenly I was driving down a street. I drove past a particular house, with an expensive red truck parked on the lawn, right up against the front door of the house. There were several people unloading crates from the truck. Some were carrying silver weapons cases. Then the Lord showed a young woman standing on the bed of the truck. He showed her hands. These were the same hands I had seen holding a weapon earlier at the park. The young woman was very attractive, with perfect makeup and preppy cut blond hair. She was wearing large diamond studded earrings. The ringleader of the group was a white male with chiseled athletic features. He had dark brown hair worn in a close cut preppy style. The group was neatly dressed. The Lord said these were the gunmen I saw in the park. They were former college students with a grudge against a professor. They decided to kill him and let authorities blame the Arabs. The Lord also said there was money involved in this killing. A jealous colleague of the professor arranged for the weapons and disguise.

7/23/02 *(Vision of Plane Crash at Refinery)*

During my morning prayer, the Spirit of the Lord constrained me from praying by telling me to *'Watch!'* He then showed me a small private plane flying toward a silo at a manufacturer's plant. It was a refinery of some kind, possibly an oil refinery. The Lord showed me the corporate logo; it looked like the letter "X" overlaid on either a letter "B" or an "E." When I attempted to pray to stop the plane from crashing into the silo, the Spirit of the Lord constrained me again. He told me to watch what was to occur next. The plane hit the silo causing a major explosion. After the explosion, some unknown particles were released into the atmosphere. It was my sense that these were chemical or biological weapons that had been aboard the plane. It was definitely the impact of the plane crash that caused the particles to be unleashed. After the release of the unknown particles, armed ground troops came from every direction and descended on the city. The Lord said there was nothing that could be done to stop this incident from occurring.

7/24/02 *(Dream of Separation)*

I was in Cleveland trying to talk one team member into obeying God. She refused. She and another person were going to sit around and do nothing. They both wanted to die and not fight. I asked her what she wanted me to do with her books I borrowed. She said, 'keep them as a memory of me when I'm gone.' I then realized that I might never see her alive again. The power of God fell on me as if to comfort my pain of separation. Very sad music also began playing as the Spirit of the Lord told me to leave. He said there was nothing I could do to save her. I could see the storm of the war approaching the shores of Lake Erie. I loaded my car and headed for Michigan as led by the Lord. On my way, I unleashed a dog that was tied to a post. It was left to die in the storm. I put it in the car and took it with me.

7/24/02 Immediately after the dream of separation, I packed up all my belongings. I drove three hours to my parent's home in Michigan where I placed my things in storage. I returned to Cleveland before dark. From that moment on, I awaited the final go ahead from the Lord to leave for Los Angeles.

7/24/02 There have been no new significant visions or dreams from the Lord concerning the war in America, just some repeated visions of warplanes, explosions and chemical weapons, as well as miraculous moves of God to counteract these catastrophes.

7/25/02 I was awakened by the Spirit of the Lord at 4:30 a.m. and told to **'*Go to LA, Now!*'** I was told to report to Dr. Price by Sunday morning 7/28. I immediately got up, showered, and packed my car. I left my home by 6:30 a.m. Left Cleveland for LA around 8:30 a.m. after wrapping up any business in the city, servicing my car, and saying goodbye to my family and friends in the city.

7/25/02 I arrived in Michigan at 12:30 p.m. to say final goodbyes to my parents, and headed to Los Angeles at 4:00 p.m.

7/28/02 I arrived in LA about 12:30 a.m. after driving non-stop from Michigan. I rested in a hotel for a few hours before heading to the 9 a.m. church service. I spoke with Dr. Price immediately after service. Our conversation was brief. I explained that the Lord told me to report to him that morning, but I was unclear about my purpose for being there. I told Dr. Price that the Lord had called me to prepare the people of God for war. I also mentioned that the Lord had me to preparing a document for President Bush concerning war in America. He and Dr. Betty agreed to stand in agreement that God would reveal my purpose for returning to Crenshaw Christian Center.

7/29/02 I spent a couple of days at Prayer Mountain. I sought the Lord about my purpose in coming to Los Angeles. He said there was information I needed to give to Dr. Price concerning my work in Ohio. The Lord told me to write a report summarizing my work.

7/31/02 I spent much time in Bible study and intercession at the Crenshaw Christian Center.

8/06/02 I went back to Prayer Mountain for further instructions on what to write in the report. I could find no peace in prayer and inquired of the Lord what to do. He commanded me to leave the mountain and lock myself in the hotel for four days and write. I quickly obeyed.

8/07/02 I still had no idea of how or what to write, but the minute I sat down to write, the Spirit of the Lord began to dictate the details of the report. I spent the next four days writing continuously as the Spirit of the Lord led me. I wrote whatever He spoke to my spirit. He entitled the report, *'**The Ohio Project.**'*

8/11/02 The Lord told me to give Dr. Price the summary of my assignment concerning war in the US after Bible Study on next Tuesday night.

8/13/02 The finished report was given to Dr. Price after Bible Study.

8/14/02 The Lord told me to finish the War Journal for the President, and give a copy to Dr. Price.

8/18/02 The handwritten journal was completed by 10 p.m.

8/19/02 I began finishing touches on the book and video training program.

8/25/02 A copy of the handwritten journal was given to Dr. Price.

8/30/02 The Spirit of the Lord told me to type the journal and give a copy to Dr. Price.

9/10/02 A typewritten copy of the journal was completed, and a copy was given to Dr. Price.

9/26/02 Final edit completed.

9/29/02 Two copies of the copy protected final edit were given to Dr. Price. The Spirit of the Lord told me to include an extra copy for Dr. Price to give to Bishop Clarence McClendon. He also told me to give Dr. Price the first couple of chapters of the new training book.

9/29/02 *(The Devil's Threat Part I)*
After speaking with Dr. Price, the Holy Spirit told me to get back to the hotel as soon as possible. Trouble was brewing. When I walked into the hotel room, the borrowed computer and my disks for the books were missing. A minister, from whom I borrowed the computer, talked the hotel manager into helping her gain entry to my room. She said that the Holy Spirit told her to break into the room. This minister's pastor spoke with me about the minister's jealousy over the Word the Lord gave me for the nation. I never told them that I was writing, the Lord revealed it to them. They also believed that I could help them train their leaders for the next move of God. Unfortunately, they asked me in the presence of the other minister,
who responded with a jealous fit of rage.

09/30/02 *(Word Concerning a Place to Stay)*

A member of my church came by the hotel and we prayed all night to God despite the jealous minister's several attempts to break into the room again. The Lord did not tell me to leave; instead He said that two pastors would pay my hotel bill and help me find a place to stay. By 10 a.m. the jealous minister told the manager to throw me out of the hotel and refuse to let me come back. At noon, the owner of the hotel asked me to leave. They let me store my bags at the front desk, until I was able to find someone to help me find another place. Later that evening I met two pastors at a church that the Lord told to put me up in another hotel. One of the pastors recommended that while I was waiting on God and writing, it would be best for me to call the Department of Public and Social Services (DPSS), AKA welfare office, for assistance in finding an interim place to stay.

10/01/02 *(The Devil's Threat Part 2)*

After a restful night and prayer, the Lord confirmed that I was still in His perfect will and told me to go to DPSS. At 5 p.m., after hours of waiting, I was told to return the following morning in order to get help with a place to stay. I left DPSS and walked to church where I prayed until 7:30 p.m. At about 7 p.m., several people boldly walked into the church and sat directly behind me. Somehow, they were made aware of what I was writing. They were told that my only reason for being there was to take another minister's position. They informed me that nothing would happen at their church unless the other minister spoke. I responded by the Spirit, 'she is only a woman, but I guarantee you that nothing will happen unless God speaks.' The people got up and left the church.

10/01/02 *(The Devil's Threat Parts 3&4)*

After service, the Lord told me to stay before Him all night long in prayer. Several of us were in the prayer until 11 p.m. There was such a sweet spirit in the room. The Lord was moving upon all of us. At about midnight, four people stormed in the room binding the devil and shouting in the spirit. The Lord told me not to move, but to stay in His Spirit. Then a woman stood at the podium and began binding up anyone that would dare come to their church spreading rumors of war. She quoted some of the things that I had shared with no one but her pastor. After about an hour, she and the others nervously left the church. The Lord said they were not upset because of what He gave me to speak. They were upset because they were the leaders of Crenshaw, and the Word was given to me. Finally at 3 a.m., a female barged in asking, 'aren't you done praying yet?' I responded, 'When the Lord releases me, I will leave.' At 6:30 a.m. the Lord told me to leave. I went to the rest room, threw water on my face, got breakfast and headed back to DPSS.

10/02/02 *(Breaking Strongholds in Skid Row)*

DPSS assigned me 'homeless' status and sent me to the Panama Hotel in Skid Row. The Lord told me He wanted to show me where His heart was. The people in Skid Row are the lost and forgotten of our society. The Lord said He needed me down there to break His people out. He said some of His most powerful leaders were down there hurting and without hope. My assignment was to resurrect that hope and break them free. I fasted and prayed intensely.

10/02/02 *(Skid Row, Continued)*

The Lord showed me the bondage that grips people when they are under DPSS. It has become a spiritual stronghold on many families. He showed me what it was trying to do to me just because I was taking assistance and labeled homeless. He had me speak to this devil and break them all out. The Lord also had me walking the streets at 5 a.m. and praying in the spirit. It was such a freeing experience. Nowhere have I been so free to pray and travail aloud in the streets. Nobody cared that I was talking to God out loud because so many insane people were speaking to the demons every day. They were more afraid of me because they did not understand what I was saying.

The Lord also had me laying hands and prophesying to His people down there. One day the Lord turned a help line into a prayer line. They were coming from everywhere. The people were hungry for God, but they don't trust outsiders and they don't trust church people. These people on the street could spot a hypocrite easier than the average Christian can. When I gained their trust, they watched my back.

The Lord also had several Crenshaw pastors also watching my back. I would check in with them from time to time. Each of them admitted that the Lord has been dealing with them about outreach to the homeless and specifically Skid Row. One pastor said they needed me down there so I could help them understand how they can help. I later asked the Lord why I was chosen for this assignment. He said that no one from Crenshaw would come. They were all too afraid of losing their positions and concerned about what people would say if they spent time down there.

10/02/02 *(Another Mantle from Dr. Price)*

Dr. Price was not at Bible Study last night. It was rumored that he was on vacation. I was awaken at around 6:30 a.m. Dr. Fred and Dr. Betty were praying for me. Then Drs. I.V. and Bridget Hilliard began praying for me. I could sense all four praying for me at the same time. Then a very heavy mantle fell upon me. The Lord did not identify what the mantle was, so I just thanked Him. It was a relief to know that my spiritual parents and friends were supporting my assignment.

10/15/02 *(Vision of Rap and Hip Hop)*

I was awaken at 2 a.m. with a rap beat in my head. I don't care for rap music, but my spirit was rapping the Word and I heard everything. It was so clear that I got my pad and wrote what I was hearing. When I finished writings, another rap song came across my spirit. I wrote that one down as well. I fell back asleep with this music in my head. About two hours later I awoke to a vision of my dancing on the streets with a crowd watching. I was doing moves that weren't humanly possible. Then I heard these kids saying, 'Man, she dances like Michael.' This one thing I knew, that it wasn't Paula dancing, it was the Holy Ghost in Paula that was dancing.

After these visions, I had to ask the Lord what He was doing to me. He explained that there was a generation that I had to reach and He put their style of music and dance in my spirit. He said it was not about what I liked. It was about reaching the young people with the gospel in a way they could understand.

10/15/02 *(Rap and Hip Hop, Continued)*
A month later the Lord would demonstrate the gift of rapping that He put in me. I was on a part-time job with a few Latino and Filipino teen gangsters. I needed them to get something for me and their rap music was so loud they never heard my request. In my frustration, I went to the back of the store and with an awesome beat; I began rapping at them about what I needed. They were stunned at first and then broke out in laughter at someone as straight as I looked who could out rhyme them in rap. From that moment on they thought I was cool and some began talking about God and asking about things they heard about Jesus.

10/22/02 *(Breaking More Enemy Strongholds)*
I stayed with the sisters of Good Shepherd. The first thing the Lord had me do was to break the stronghold of the Catholic Church off of the sisters and the women in the house. There was much prayer for the city and the nation. I met several women who the Lord sent to Crenshaw. They all ended up homeless, and in the same house. One of the women shared with me a project the Lord wanted her to do in LA for homeless women and children. That's why she came to LA. She and the others were ousted from Crenshaw and were made to feel unwelcome, particularly among the intercessors. Most had been thrown out of the prayer room just like they tried to do to me. The Lord showed us working together blazing a trail of light through Skid Row. We were doing exactly what He said do in the way He said do it. I remember hearing comments of unbelief from social service agencies and homeless experts. They could not believe how our efforts were miraculously transforming lives. It was the power of God that was moving through people's lives.

10/22/02 *(Enemy Strongholds, Continued)*

The people on the street were not only getting delivered from the lowest hell on earth, but they were rising to positions of leadership and authority. They were following the leading of the Spirit of God and carrying out all that He had originally put in their hearts to do. Not only did the Lord show a band of light tearing through the darkness, but also it had other bands of light spinning off in the same direction and with equal force. All of this, coming from several women He called **'*Jacob's Daughters.*'**

10/30/02 *(Vision about Chemical Weapons in LA)*

I was walking outdoors in an area near Hollywood when I noticed a small plane flying overhead. An object appeared to drop from the plane. While still in mid-air, a greenish yellow powdery substance was coming from the object that was dropped from the plane. The object fell to the ground a distance from where I was standing. The powdery substance covered the atmosphere and people fell dead everywhere I could see. There were only a couple of people still standing, everywhere the substance was blown. I asked the Lord why very few people were still standing. He said those standing knew Him personally and believed His Word. The wind blew the substance in my direction, and more people fell dead. I saw Jenny walking toward me, panicking because people were falling near her. The substance was beginning to affect Jenny and I brought her into the house. She wanted to know why I was not affected. I explained to her what the Lord told me. Jenny said, 'but why is it hurting me, I'm saved?' I asked how she knew she was saved and Jenny responded, 'I've been in the church all my life. I was a member of the choir. I was an usher. I believe in God.' I responded, 'something is obviously not right between you and God because you are dying.'

10/30/02 *(Chemical Weapons, Continued)*

Jenny began to be prideful about her salvation asking, 'why do I need to repent, I am already saved? I responded harshly, 'you're the one dying, not me. If you want to live then you are going to have to repent. You don't have time to waste.' Her breath was beginning to cut off when she humbled herself and repented. Immediately Jenny's breath strengthened and she sat up saying,' this thing is real. God is really real!' We both began to cry tears of joy. Several days later, the Lord told me to share this vision with Jenny. She knew that war was coming. As a career military officer retired, she had a sense of danger that was to come. When it came to her salvation, Jenny listened and said thank you. She knew that God was calling her to be accountable for her backslidden state. Jenny thanked me for telling her about the vision and simply walked away pondering what she had just heard.

10/02 *(Preparing for War in Los Angeles)*

I met people that God was calling into new gospel ministries. Most knew about the war to come. The Lord had set up command posts throughout the city with His warriors ready to take action at the slightest sign of danger. Many were working independent of local churches because their leaders were not hearing what God was saying about repentance and preparation for war in America. The Lord gave me a Word for some of them to go back to their churches and wait on God to release them into their ministries.

10/02 *(Word about Prophet's Judgment)*

The Lord had me praying for a particular prophet. As I was praying in the spirit, the Lord had my spirit speak to her spirit saying, *'your soul will be required of you.'* This woman had been judged guilty for willful rebellion against God. She had been responsible for drawing God's people away from Him and to herself, leading many into rebellion against God.

11/02/02 *(Word about Book Copyright)*
The Lord told me to get two *'**clean copies**'* of the Journal. I was instructed to register with the copyright office and to get an ISBN[13]. Two weeks later my father sent money. Immediately I prepared the paperwork and registered the copy. I then began researching ISBN.

11/02 *(Vision about Food Poisoning)*
The Lord showed me that our country's vegetation was being tampered with even now. He gave no specific locations, but only showed several people poisoning the ground and crops across the US.

11/02 *(Word about War Relief)*
The Lord gave me instruction about starting a relief organization. He explained its organizational structure and purposes. I was instructed to write down these details for execution at a later date.

12/02 *(Word about the War Journal Book)*
The Lord showed me the layout of the book entitled *War Journal*. He told me that it was not just a report for President Bush, but a full-length book to be published and available to the public. The book would be dedicated to the President and would call forth those that see like Ezekiel and speak like Elijah.

THE WAR JOURNAL

YEAR 2003: *The Storm Is Coming!*

THE WAR JOURNAL
YEAR 2003: *The Storm Is Coming!*

January –February 2003 *(Revelation about the Book)*
The Lord gave an outline and detail for <u>The War Journal</u> book. There was much writing completed during this time. I also got direction to start a publishing company.

2/03 *(Confirmation about War)*
The Lord told me to take a specific bus downtown. When I reached Seventh Street, a woman I recognized from Skid Row got on the same bus. I remember her telling me that the Lord gave her a Word about war in our country. She shared the message with her bishop, who shared it with his friend, who also happened to be a bishop. The woman said that both of the men ridiculed her. She left church and separated herself from God's people. Later, the woman ended up homeless in Skid Row. It had been months since I had last seen her. She never knew that I also had received a Word about war. The Lord told me to go speak to her on the bus. The Lord wanted to reassure her that the bishop had come around to believing what she had told him years ago. She smiled and said that she had just asked the Lord about the same thing that morning. She thanked me for relaying the answer to her prayer. I got off the bus and headed home.

2/03 *(The Call to Take the City)*
I was attending an evening service when the Spirit of the Lord told me to, **'*Take the City.*'** I had been praying heavily for LA and the upcoming war. When this command came, it sounded audibly throughout my being. It rang in my ears and my heart. I said, 'yes, Lord, I will take the city.' I was pumped about the command from God although I had no earthly idea what it meant. I knew whatever was coming would be good and beneficial for His kingdom.

February - March 2003 *(Birth of the Publishing Company)*

With the Lord's help, I began all the paperwork to create the company. The Lord talked to me about all that He has given me to do. He said just like the heavens and earth began with the spoken word, so it will be with what He gave me. It all begins with what will be published through this company; the Word about War and other writings He had given me. All of the other companies will flow from what the company publishes (the Word) and all it will produce a harvest in the earth.

3/17/03 *(America at War in Iraq)*

A warning of declaration of war was given to Saddam Hussein on March 17.[11] At that time evacuation began in Iraq. March 21, America went to war. This war came just as the Lord said in the prophecy of February 2002.

3/03 *(The Voicing of Evil Prayers)*

I was awakened from sleep by the voice (in the spirit) of a prophet I knew. Her pastor made her aware of the Word the Lord gave me about war, and she became jealous. She believed the word, and because she knew she could not keep it from coming to pass, her prayer was that no man of God would believe a word I said. She prayed that they would ridicule me and ignore the Word. I was disturbed to learn that she would intentionally risk the lives of God's people in order to save her position. I rebuked the devil that was using this woman of God, and prayed that the people of God would have eyes to see the signs of the times.

3/03 *(God's Command to Take a Job)*

Several job opportunities were presented to me, but I declined because the Lord told me to write the book. I got a second interview for one job and the Lord told me to go. When the offer was made, the Lord told me to take the job. I was concerned because He had just given me volumes to write and time was of the essence. I did not understand how I would be able to take on a full time job and finish writing. The Lord told me to take the job and break the back of the devil that was trying to destroy my God given call. He said that several people were praying in agreement that I would become destitute and not able to complete my assignment. By taking the job, their evil plans would be destroyed. I obeyed God and took the job, but my heart was grieved about not being able to finish writing.

March-April 2003

There was much prayer for the troops and government leaders. Prayer was also constantly made on the behalf of the victims in the war with Iraq.

4/03 *(Last Visit to Prayer Room)*

The Lord sent me to prayer and Bible Study at Crenshaw. After about a half hour in the prayer room, I felt a tap on my shoulder. I looked up and smiled at the prayer leader and put my head back down and continued in prayer. A couple of moments later someone hit my shoulder. I looked up and it was the same woman. She wanted to start an argument while I was praying. She asked what I was doing there. I responded, 'praying, like everybody else is doing.' I put my head back down to continue.

4/03 *(Prayer Room, Continued)*

The woman became angry and asked, 'so, did you get the position you wanted here at Crenshaw?' I responded, 'I don't know what you're talking about.' She said, 'we know why you came, but your plan didn't work.' This time I became irritated with her persistent ignorance and said, 'I never came here for a position, I already have one.' Once more I continued to pray. This time, she tapped me again and just stared at me. I asked, 'why are you staring at me?' With a dumbfounded look on her face she replied 'you look good.' 'I don't understand, you really look good,' she said. 'Why should that surprise you?' I responded. 'When I obey God, no matter what the circumstances, He always blesses me and takes care of me.' She got up and left out of the prayer room. After the woman left, the Lord revealed that this was one of the people praying against me and hoping I would be destroyed.

After leaving the prayer room, the Lord sent me to Bible Study. Immediately after the service, I started for the door. The Spirit of the Lord restrained me from leaving the room and told me to go speak to the pastor. The pastor asked me why I came back to the church when God closed that door. Then he asked if I was offended that they rejected me. I told this pastor the same thing the Lord told me. When they rejected me, they rejected Him because He sent me. I let the pastor know that I was deeply saddened because the blessings God had intended for them would go to another. I mentioned the tremendous reception from those outside of the church because they clearly heard God confirm things they already knew. Yet, the church rejected the message because of jealousy.

4/03 *(Prayer Room, Continued)*
Much favor was being showered upon my life because of my obedience to God. The pastor said my situation sounded a lot like Joseph's (Genesis 41:25-40). He then spoke by the spirit and said 'that's exactly who you are, a modern day Joseph. I might as well call you Josephine.'

When I left, there was sadness in my heart for my church. I asked the Lord how He felt I performed in this assignment, before I could finish asking Him, He responded, 'well done.' Then I asked what would happen to the church because they rejected the message. The Lord responded, *'they will perish.'* After He spoke, my heart became heavy and I wept for their souls. The Lord told me it was time to move on to the next assignment.

4/03 *(Prayer for New Employer)*
The Lord revealed great darkness hovering over my new employer. There is a curse on the company that was very obvious. Several employees mentioned the evil they sensed and blamed it on the clients. Lord revealed that it was coming from the employer. They were oppressing people to the point that some committed suicide. Others made evil threats against the company. In my prayers, I saw nothing but death and destruction coming to this place. It was a prime target for terrorist activity. The Lord said I was there because of a specific work my boss had to perform for God.

4/03 *(Dream about the Judgment of a Prophet)*
I was attending worship services at a specific church. A visiting bishop called a prophet before the congregation. The bishop then called me before the congregation. He began to prophesy to the prophet about her ministry.

4/03 *(Judgment, Continued)*

When the bishop finished, the unction came upon me to speak. The Lord put a word of judgment in my mouth against the prophet for having led multitudes of God's people astray. He told her to repent, or her soul would be required of her that day. The prophet attempted to rebuke me but the Lord struck her down to her knees, clinching her chest. The prophet refused to repent and attempted further to attack me in spite of what the Lord was doing to her. Then five of her leaders came forward in anger and began threatening me with rebuke for killing her. The Lord struck them all down, yet none would repent. As powerful and renowned as this prophet and her leaders were none of them recognized the Spirit of the Lord when His glory caused judgment to fall upon them.

4/03 *(Word about Happy Babies)*

One day I began to notice that there were babies everywhere. There were similarities among happy babies that fascinated me. Happy babies were sitting in strollers with a bottle in one hand and the other hand on their toes kicking their legs up and down. Some were singing and making happy jabbering sounds. Others leaned in a casual secure manner observing the rest of the world with a sense of wonderment. They stared at the birds. They stared at the sky. Happy babies seemed not to have a care in the world. No matter what was going on or where they were, as long as they were safe in the arms or care of that loving parent, the happy baby was secure and carefree. Then the Lord asked me, *'**Paula, can you be happy and carefree like a baby and let Your Father take care of your needs?**'*

206

4/03 *(Happy Babies, Continued)*
The Lord has always taken care of me and He will continue to do so. He cares for me like any father would who loves his child. I thanked Him for His love, smiled and said, 'yes.' Now when I see happy babies I am reminded of how I trust God to provide and care for me. I see myself safely tucked under His loving wings. My desire is to spend more time staring at the sky, watching the birds, kicking up my heels and singing praises to Him.

5/03 *(Word Concerning Money)*
The Lord told me that my money was coming soon. He appointed one bank as the place of first deposit. The Lord told me to have my payroll check automatically deposited there as well. He said it was a lot of money and it would take weeks to clear the bank. Once the check cleared, He told me to open several bank accounts to handle it all. He specified which banks to use. I was told to transfer a few millions to each of the war relief organizations He wants me to start. He also told me to draw up the initial budget for the publishing company that would include two fulltime employees on payroll. He told me to get a line of credit, and look for a house and office space. The Lord showed me staying on my job until the accounts were established and everything was in place for me to immediately work on the book fulltime. He also had me prepare to distribute the $18 million to those on my ledger.

6/03 *(Word about Moving)*
The Lord told me to prepare to move. He told me what gifts to give the Kawada staff when I leave. He told me that I would leave my job soon as well.

6/03 *(Vision about Book Giveaways)*
In a vision, the Lord showed me giving away copies of books to specific people and organizations. I wrote their names and the number of copies in my ledger.

6/03 *(Vision about Visit with Bush)*
I was at the president's home in Texas discussing my book. He was very interested in what God had to say. Condoleezza Rice was also there listening to every word. I am not sure she believed, but she was very attentive.

6/03 *(Word about my Handwritten Journal)*
The Lord reminded me that I would need to surrender my handwritten journal to the government. He said they would also want to know who received copies of the book. When I asked why they needed the handwritten copy, the Lord said they would perform a handwriting analysis to determine if I am mentally stable. I was amused at His answer.

7/03 *(Vision about President at the Office)*
In another vision, the president made a surprise visit to my job. He wanted to personally apologize to my employer for my being late. He let them know that I should be excused because we were discussing issues vital to the safety of the nation. My employer bent over backwards to entertain the president. They even offered him a tour of the grounds and wanted to take pictures.

7/03 *(Vision about TV Job)*
I had a brief vision about a television analyst job. Several news networks called on me to discuss terrorism and the war. My only expertise was what I knew God was saying. I was impressed that these news people were very interested because it was obvious that no one else knew what was going on in the country. They were trying to find comfort and solutions for the citizens of our country.

8/03 *(More TV Visions)*
I found myself on several television interview programs. The viewers and the television hosts were desperately seeking God. One particular show stopped when the interviewer asked me, 'what must I do to be saved?' The production crew began weeping and the host was on his knees sobbing and crying out to God.

8/03 *(Vision about Actors Learning About Jesus)*
In a brief vision there were actors who were talking about how my teaching changed how they viewed Christianity and Jesus. They were excited about reading the Bible for themselves and learning how relevant it was for today.

8/03 *(Word about Governor's Recall Election)*
The time had come to determine the next governor of California. The race seemed almost like a sideshow. I began to jest about Arnold Schwarzenegger when the Spirit of the Lord convicted me. I quickly repented and asked the Lord to explain. He told me know that Arnold was His choice for governor. Then the Lord showed His hand on President Bush and on Arnold. I saw the Lord put them both in office. He said it was because of the war to come that these were selected.

8/03 *(Governor's Recall Election, Continued)*
He chose men that would be moved to follow His Will for the sake of His people. The Lord also said that Maria Shriver had a heart for the people. She would show much compassion and effort to bring the state of California and the nation together during the time of war. There will be a strong partnership between Bush and Schwarzenegger that will benefit the state and the nation.

9/03 *(Vision about Praise Service with Actors)*
I was conducting a praise service in a classroom with entertainers and actors. They were off the hook with enthusiasm for God. This was like the latest fad thing in Hollywood. They enjoyed being in the presence of God and loved sharing the Gospel with their friends. I had a brief message about discipling others. They were so excited that they all got up and began cheering like a team ready to win a game, and headed for the door. They nearly knocked me over. I had to stand on a desk and scream to get them to settle down.

9/03 *(Dream about an Actor Hating Jesus)*
In this dream, we were living in a posh home surrounded by movie stars and actors. The neighbors harassed us almost every day. They resented us talking about Jesus and what He was doing in our lives. Some even grew to hate Jesus and they blamed Him for their impoverished state. They had homes that could not be maintained because they had no money. My next-door neighbor, a famous actress, wondered into my yard and ended up at my kitchen door. I happened to see her wandering with dirty clothes in her hand and invited her to come in and sit down. She was distraught, bewildered and tired of us talking about Jesus. She said it was unfair that Jesus would make us rich and make them poor.

9/03 *(Dream about an Actor Hating Jesus, Cont.)*
This woman said that she did not know how to be poor. They had little food, no work and no money. She said all she had was grief and John Murphy's dirty underwear. Murphy (not his real name) is a very famous actor. She asked, 'how are we supposed to make it?' 'How can you say Jesus loves us when He is hurting us?' I replied, 'You can have Him too, if you want Him?' 'I can?' she asked. I explained that Jesus blesses anyone who will turn to Him and give his or her life to Him. She begged me to show her how to do that. She got saved at my kitchen table and began praising Him uncontrollably.

9/03 *(The Spirit of the Lord Influencing Industry)*
The Lord is raising up what He calls *'**giant slayers,**'* just like David. Believers equipped to take over industries formerly held by the enemies of God. I was called a giant slayer, and given ideas to revolutionize several industries, including, music, movies, television, books, fashion and witty inventions. The purpose of the wealth is to finance the work of God's Kingdom.

9/03 *(Vision about a Check For Price)*
In a vision, the Lord showed me standing before the Crenshaw congregation giving Dr. Price a $1.5 million check. What was interesting about this vision was Dr. Price's reaction when he got the check. He was happy to receive it, but while I was talking, he read the inscription: 'And the multitude of them that believed were of one heart and of one soul: neither said any of them that ought of the thing, which he possessed, was his own and with great power gave the apostles witness of the resurrection of the Lord Jesus: and GREAT GRACE was upon them all. Neither was there any among them that lacked (Acts 4:32-34).' The inscription reminded Dr. Price of what the Lord put in his heart to do, and the congregation voted it down.

10/03 *(The Lord's Choice for Governor Won)*
Arnold Schwarzenegger won the governor's election[12] and will take office in November of this year.

10/03 *(Vision about Racism Prohibiting Wealth)*
In a vision, I was going wherever the Lord told me to distribute money to His people. I went to a cafeteria where He directed me to look for such a person. The Lord gave me no information about the person. I just waited for Him to say *'**this is the one.**'* While waiting, I decided to get something to eat. Two older white women were looking at our table and the one became angry just looking at me. I was not dressed fancy, just my jeans and a shirt.

After a while, the two white women took up their trays and started for the door. The one was still glaring at me in anger. She came over and threw her tray on the end of my table, as if to hit me with it. The woman then walked quickly for the door. Her friend turned around to see if I was coming after them. At the same time, the Lord spoke, *'**she's the one.**'* I then looked at the friend and motioned with my finger that they both come back to where the incident occurred. The friend pulled on the angry woman and made her stop walking. By this time I was standing next to her. The angry woman turned to me with hatred in her eyes. Before she could open her mouth, the spirit of the Lord spoke through me telling her to repent. The woman immediately fell to her knees saying, 'Lord forgive me.' She knew the voice of God. This was a woman of prayer.

10/03 *(Racism versus Wealth, Continued)*

The Lord had me tell her that I was carrying the answer to her prayer, but because of her evil heart, I could not give it to her. Her racism blocked her blessing from God. This woman was truly remorseful. After seeing her change of heart, I prayed with her that God swiftly give the answer to her prayers. I knew in my heart she had changed.

10/03 *(Dream about Judgment on Evil Leaders)*

The Lord showed auditoriums filled with people and the power of God was flowing. He also showed several different men and women in the pulpit. The Lord showed their black and evil hearts. The Lord told me that they don't believe the word they preach. They hate Him and the people of God. Some resented the fact that God blessed the people and not them. Others had unanswered prayers and hated it when God answered the prayers of the people. The Lord said that he was going to remove these leaders because their evil was affecting the people of God. The power of God flowed because the people had a need, and began pulling on the anointing of God. But, because the vessels were not clean, the people did not get what they needed from God. Instead, the people were also becoming hardened against God. They began to question how there could be a great anointing and no change? The people began to doubt God and His word because of these leaders.

11/03 *(Word about Buildings in Carson)*

The Spirit of the Lord showed me two building He said were in Carson, California. The one building had a specific address. The other was identified by type and location. The Lord said I would acquire the buildings as part of the war relief effort. No other details were given.

11/03 *(Vision and Word about the Storm Coming)*
The holidays were coming and I had desired to spend time with friends in the city. I asked the Lord's permission. He responded with a very disturbing dream. In this dream I was with a friend of mine and we had just walked out of the house to go shopping. I personally hate shopping, but needed to buy a pair of boots to wear back East, so I agreed to go with her. My friend began to irritate me because she wanted to go from store to store refusing to go where I could get boots. Then the Lord spoke, **'<u>Paula, the storm is coming.</u>'** I turned to my friend and said, 'the storm is coming.' She cut me off and said, 'I know, I know', but refused to stop shopping. Then I repeated what the Lord said, 'the storm is coming. We need to go for shelter.'

I started to take the car keys from her to drive home. The friend snatched the keys out of my hand and said angrily, 'I know. I know', but she still would not stop. Then I looked up and the storm was right upon us. It was only when she saw the storm that she stopped, got into the car and gave me the keys to drive, but it was too late. Our only place of shelter was the house where we were staying, but when we went back and opened the door, there was a solid brick wall behind the door preventing us from reentering the house. Then I looked behind us and saw a very wide and dark funnel cloud. It was so ferocious that twisters were spawning in every direction from the main funnel cloud.

11/03 *(Vision about the Storm, Continued)*
Together it seemed that the twisters and main funnel measured the entire length of a major city. In the distance, I also saw my cousin on a rock outside waiting for the storm to kill her, and now I was bound to be killed by the same storm because I chose to hang with someone pretending to know the truth. As I saw the storm coming closer, I saw my entire purpose and call flash before my eyes. I became remorseful about the souls lost and the leaders I would betray if I failed to carry out my assignment. The Lord again told me, ***'Paula, I don't want you running around, because the storm is coming.'*** It took nothing more to convince me that my purpose and call would only be carried out by my obedience to God's every command. I could not let friends; family, any detractors or distractions cause me to forfeit my purpose in God. I quickly dismissed all holiday plans and spent time fasting and in prayer before the Lord.

12/03 I was in prayer and fasting for the nation two weeks before Christmas.

12/15/03 *(Vision about Hussein Underground)*
At 4 a.m., Monday, I was praying in the spirit when the Lord gave me a vision about Saddam Hussein in some underground location. He was in a tailored suit (not military), standing behind his desk in a very nice office somewhere underground. A man wearing all white is standing in front of the desk. His headdress and clothing were white. Saddam Hussein handed the man a white overstuffed letter-sized envelope. They shook hands and the vision ended with the Lord telling me to turn on the television. When I turned it on, CNN[13] was showing the capture of Saddam Hussein. I was not convinced it was Him because of the vision I had moments before.

12/03 *(The Meaning of the Storm)*
The Lord indicated that the vision of funnel and twisters was a hyperbole: a metaphor for the destruction and confusion coming to our nation. I prayed to understand more about the conditions that led to the funnels appearance. The following passage in Proverbs spoke directly to my spirit.

Wisdom crieth without; she uttereth her voice in the streets:
She crieth in the chief place of concourse, in the openings of the gates:
In the city she uttereth her words saying, how long, ye simple ones,
will ye love simplicity? And scorners delight in their scorning,
and fools hate knowledge? Turn you at my reproof:
Behold I will pour out my spirit unto you,
I will make known my words unto you.
Because I have called, and ye refused;
I have stretched out my hand, and no man regarded;
But ye have set at nought all my counsel, and
would none of my reproof:
I also will laugh at your calamity; I will mock when your fear cometh;
When your fear cometh as desolation, and your destruction cometh as
a whirlwind; when distress and anguish cometh upon you.
Then shall they call upon me, but I will not answer;
They shall seek me early, but they shall not find me;
For that they hated knowledge, and did not choose the fear of the
Lord:
They would none of my counsel: they despised all my reproof.
Therefore they shall eat the fruit of their own way,
and be filled with their own devices.
For the turning away of the simple shall slay them,
and the prosperity of fools shall destroy them.
But whoso hearkeneth unto me shall dwell safely,
and shall be quiet from fear of evil.

Proverbs 1:20-33(KJV)

THE WAR JOURNAL

YEAR 2004: *The Year Of Completion*

THE WAR JOURNAL
YEAR 2004: *The Year Of Completion*

1/04   I began the New Year with much fasting and prayer for the coming storm and for the safety of our nation.

1/04 *(Prayer against Amalek in the Church)*
For a couple of days the Holy Spirit had me pray intensely against the spirit of Amalek that exists in the church. The Amalekites illegally dwelt in the land that God promised to the Children of Israel (Number 13:28-29). The Lord told His chosen people to take the land, but they had to destroy the illegal inhabitants in order to possess it. The Lord made it very clear to me that there are Amalekites squatting on property, marriages, ministries and other entitlements of those chosen to inherit the promise. To possess the land, we have to cast this devil out!!

1/13/04   *(Preaching About Demons in the Church)*
In a dream I was preaching to a large crowd about how demons are allowed to work through Christians. The Spirit of the Lord was adamant about His people choosing His way and not their own way. Their way often leads to demonic activity. God's people are deceived into believing that they can do whatever they please once they are saved. Jesus is the way, but we must choose to obey Him and walk as He walked. And if we disobey, we will perish and the wrath of God will abide upon us forever (John 3:36). The person that says he has fellowship with God and walks in darkness is a liar. But, if we walk in the light as He is in the light, then we have fellowship with Him and the blood of Jesus cleanses us from sin (I John 1:6-7). In this dream, the Lord had me quote John 3:16 and emphasizing that Jesus came that those who believe should not perish. He then said that it does not mean that they could not perish.

2/04 *(Prayer against Lust Demons in the Church)*
The Lord had me praying for many who are bound by demons of lust. They are trying to resist the devil, but have not submitted (obeyed) the Word of God. They meditate on lustful thoughts and not the Word. They approach lust with fear and not with faith. Their house is divided because the flesh and the spirit are warring against each other. Their house is divided, and the strongman (the Spirit of the Lord) is bound, and the flesh is possessed (controlled and influenced) and defeated by these demons. They are trying to defeat a spiritual enemy with the arm of the flesh. This battle can only be won by submitting to God, in fasting, prayer and the Word.

2/04 *(Prayer of Deliverance from False Prophets)*
The Lord woke me up with intense prayers of deliverance for His people from false prophets. They have spread evil seeds among the congregation, and have turned the people away from God and to themselves. He told me that there are many calling himself or herself prophet (or prophetess) and the Lord never called them, man did. They are suffering from low self-esteem and rejection but are using God as a platform from which to make a name for themselves. They are gathering to themselves ignorant followers who have ears tingling to hear their false words. These are professing God, but are in willful rebellion against Him. They are the blind leaders of the blind and all will very soon fall into the ditch. If these people do not repent, they will die says the Lord. God needs His people to return to hearing His Word. It is the only place of safety when war comes. Those that hear God and obey His Voice will live.

2/04 *(Visitation to Hell)*

The Lord took me by the Spirit into what felt like a rapid downward spiral into the center of the earth. I immediately knew where I was when I landed. I was in hell. There was no visible fire nor did I hear weeping and gnashing of teeth, but I knew in my spirit that this was indeed hell. This was a unique place in hell. The Lord said it was the place where the familiar spirits lure people into hell. This place was a surreal replica of earth. There were people walking on streets and doing seemingly normal activities, but I knew these people were dead. I even saw a couple of people that looked like people I knew had been dead for years. They looked somewhat real, but I could sense demons. When I looked at these people again, the demons revealed themselves. One of the demons waved at me with a sheepishly grin on his face. They knew that I could not be fooled by their masquerade.

The Lord explained that demons use a person's own emotional state or hidden evil desire (lust) to seduce them into hell. This deception is highly effective on people who are led by their feelings. These feelings are so natural (familiar and comfortable) for these people that they never suspect that they are entertaining demons.

For example, someone having a loved one to die, could, because of grief or an emotional longing, conjure up demons from hell who masquerade as the dead loved one. Or, one in ministry having a strong desire to make a name for himself could, because of pride and self-deception, conjure up demons to provide exactly what he desires. God is a loving father. He wants us to cast our cares and anxieties on Him (I Peter 5:7). But, people, who persist in keeping company with demons and justify their actions; will follow those demons straight to hell. It's like the Bible says, there is a way that seems right to a man, but the end of which leads to death (Proverbs 14:12).

3/2004 *(Disobedience Blocks Blessings of Wealth)*

The Lord had me mentor a young woman He was calling into the ministry. I spent several months teaching her and praying with her. The Lord told me to take her with me in my ministry. And so I did. The Lord showed her great things about wealth, inventions and other great things He had for her. The Lord even showed her the man He chose for her husband.

One day in prayer the Lord told me to speak to her spirit saying, 'that man is not your husband.' I had no idea what was going on until I spoke with her later that day. She had met a man who according to her was, 'fine.' He just happened to be married, but that did not stop her from dating him. She even told him to divorce his wife and come with us into my ministry. She did not repent because she said, 'you don't understand. I have feelings.'

It was not my plan to stand in agreement with this woman's adulterous affair. In her opinion, if God gave her a word, it was going to happen no matter what she did. The Lord spoke by His Spirit and said this woman let the lust of other things choke the word and it would not come to pass in her life. Here was a word about millions of dollars, a husband, and inventions that would not be fruitful; because this woman exalted her emotional and sexual needs above obedience to God's word. There are others like this woman who want the blessings without being obedient to God. They want the spoils without fighting the good fight of faith. Many Christians will be disappointed when the wealth transfer occurs and they realize that only a few are qualified to receive.

4/04 *(Word of the Lord Concerning Books)*
The Lord told me to **'*continue writing.*'** And so I did.

5/04 *(Vision about My Assignment Revealed At Work)*
The Lord showed me standing at my desk at work talking to my co-workers. They were talking to me and looking up at me in amazement. They were excited to know that my assignment was military, and some were dumbfounded.

5/19/04 *(Prayer to Break Curse of Rebellion off Church)*
The Lord had me pray to break the curse of rebellion off the church. He says the church is playing the harlot. She has committed to God with her mouth but her heart is far from Him. In her heart the church has broken covenant and is committing spiritual adultery by serving other gods. Her idolatry has made God jealous and he will punish those that don't repent. They must return to God and love Him with all their heart, with all their soul and with their entire mind.

5/04 *(Dream of Preaching about Purpose in Christ)*
The Lord showed me a bull's eye on a dartboard, saying that His people have missed the mark. The life of Jesus was the mark we were supposed to hit, but most of the church is out of God's will and purpose for their lives. Then I found myself before a large congregation teaching about pursuing God's purpose for our lives. It is the Father's will that we know Him and obey Him. Jesus said he would cast out those who never took the time to ask Him what they were to do. Jesus knew specifics. Paul knew specifics. So did the Apostles. The Lord said that they knew specifics because they <u>knew</u> God. They spoke with Him and obeyed His voice.

6/04 *(Prayer against Eli and His Evil Sons)*
In prayer the Lord gave me a vision of particular bishop who had brought up many ministers. The Lord called five of them out by name. One of whom was female. The Lord charged all of them of having sex with people from various congregations. They were infecting the church with widespread homosexuality, adultery and perversion. Then the Lord showed me that the female minister had intentionally broken up several marriages in order to take the men for herself. Then the Lord showed me a young man in his shower crying out to God in agony. This same female minister had claimed him as her husband in the spirit and tormented him day and night with her sexual demons. The Lord called the bishop out and made him punish his evil sons. He was embarrassed, but the man punished these ministers by the method the Lord commanded. The Lord kept me in prayer over several days for this vision.

6/04 *(Prayer against False Prophets in the Church)*
The Spirit of the Lord came very heavy upon me in prayer as the Lord spoke about His punishment to come for the false prophets. He showed me a woman who claimed to be a prophet, who often says, 'the Lord said', when the Lord has not spoken. She prophesies evil over ministers and prays against the leaders of the church. The Lord spoke to me, *'let her prayer be sin.'* And then in an instant I saw her death. In my haste, I responded, 'Lord spare her life and move her to repent.' I began praying in the spirit for her soul. When I finished, those words the Lord spoke burned in my heart. I knew I had read those words somewhere in the Bible.

6/04 *(False Prophet, Continued)*
Psalm 109:7-8 reads, 'when he is judged let him be found guilty, and let his prayer become sin.' 'Let his days be few and let another take his office.' Then I knew that the Lord's judgment of death was certain for this prophet. I repented for stepping in the Lord's way of judging this woman. For the next hour the Lord led me to read how He dealt with the false prophets throughout the Bible. Death was always the judgment on false prophets, and so it was to be in this case.

7/04 *(Vision about Bethel Leader)*
In a vision the Lord took me to a leader that I knew. He had me tell her to prepare the people at Bethel for war. I pleaded with her to make the people aware so they can prepare themselves. Her response was a polite, 'no.' She said that they were planning to do something else instead. This woman, like other leaders, was convinced that war would not happen in America. Although the Lord sent me to them they rejected the word and felt no reason to prepare.

7/04 *(Word at Convention)*
I was attending the Bible convention when the Lord spoke a word to my spirit. He said, *'release the power to believe all things.'* I replied, 'thank you Lord, I release the power to believe all things, for with you all things are possible.'

7/04   *(Prayer for Political Issues)*
There was much prayer for our nation on political issues:
- •Same Sex Marriage
- •Stem Cell Research
- •Terrorism
- •The economy

In my spirit I knew that the Lord is not pleased with where America is heading. It is as if He is letting us hang ourselves. I prayed heavily to wake up the church to pray and stand on God's word concerning our nation. We are the only hope for America.

7/04   *(Prayer for John Kerry)*
I pray often for the president and nation's leaders, but the Lord kept bringing up Democratic Presidential candidate, John Kerry. I was given no information concerning what the prayer was for, I just prayed in the spirit until released. This prayer went on for two days.

7/26/04 *(Prayer against Evil Church Rulers)*
The Lord had me praying for evil church leaders to repent. It was a very intense time in prayer. I sensed that there was some urgency to my prayer because the wrath of God could be felt as I prayed.

8/04 *(Prayer for Our Nation's Safety)*
The Lord told me not to put stock into the newspapers or television coverage of political matters. Our country is still in danger regardless of what they say. He had me pray heavily for our safety.

8/04 *(A Personal Reflection on the Times)*
This month was very good for me in many ways. I strongly sense that the word of the Lord will soon come to pass. It seems like a season of completion of all things promised. I also see it in my family. The family gathered several times this month for happy occasions. I see so many promises coming to pass for those I love. It is only a matter of time that they come for me as well. Be it unto me Lord, according to your word.

8/04 *(Oral Roberts Prophecy on Television)*
Dr. Oral Roberts appeared on television talking about his vision from God. He called it a wakeup call for America that the whole world will see. What he was given is consistent with what the Lord gave me. I will continue to meditate on this Word from God.

August-September 2004 *(Intense Bible Study)*
There was a need for more spiritual cleansing from the Word. I realize that my system is naturally accustomed to feeding on large volumes of the Word in addition to listening to my gospel tapes overnight. When I write, more time is spent praying in the spirit and studying only what pertains to my writing. Sometimes I need more. There has been much oppression from the enemy around me zapping the Word right out of my system. A supernatural healing and refreshing was evident in my soul and spirit after these studies.

9/04 *(Sensing a Season of Change)*
There has been somewhat of a spiritual change all around me. Masako and Akiko are leaving at the end of October. The woman around the corner is also leaving this month. The Lord has used these women mightily over the past year.

9/04 *(Season of Change, Continued)*
God used them to sustain me supernaturally. Now they are leaving. I also need to get away in prayer. I asked the Lord to go to Prayer Mountain for a couple of days to better hear Him. There is an added sense of darkness on the streets of LA; a hostility among the people. I know that it is spiritual. My request to go to Prayer Mountain was denied so, I stayed in town shut down in prayer and waited for further instruction.

9/04 *(Revelation of Evil Men in My Life)*
The Lord ministered to me about my disappointment with the men in my life who attempted to break my spirit and bind me from obeying God. They criticized my strength and abused me. They attempted to dominate me in order to exalt their manhood. They hurled insults by labeling me 'bold and radical.' I remember asking the Lord what he thought of me. The Lord responded by saying, *'**bold and radical.**'* He then paused and I was speechless. The Lord then continued, *'**just like I made you.**'* I laughed. The Lord continued by saying that He made me bold and radical because of what He called me to do. He wanted to do a quick work in the earth and needed someone bold enough to step out and obey regardless of what man thinks.

9/04 *(Prayer for Forgiveness)*
The Lord let me know that I had a particular hatred for men who use women and prey upon them sexually. There are men all around me that constantly meditate on rape and murder and twisted sexual perversion of women. They hate women and this preoccupation with sexual things provides a way to retaliate against the women who hurt them.

9/04 *(Forgiveness, Continued)*

They don't desire sex. They desire violence. Having been victimized repeatedly by men of this sort, I have little patience or understanding. In my opinion, people who hurt innocent women and children are just plain evil. These are not men, but vulgar animals.

The Lord showed me my heart and told me to let the hatred go. It was not easy, but I had to let the hatred go because it was a weight on my soul. What kept me bound was the idea of the premeditation of violence against women and children. A man does not accidentally rape his victim. He stalks her over a period of time. He talks to her by chat room on the Internet. He is someone familiar who smiles and waves at a distance. The eminent victim is unaware of the snare that is being set for them. People who prey on others are vile and wicked. I release them to the Lord and let Him recompense the wicked for their deeds. My soul is free.

9/04 *(Office Confrontation about Bush)*

A co-worker approached me with anger about the upcoming election. He said he wanted Bush out of office because it's not appropriate for the President to be talking openly about Jesus. The man continued by saying we need to stick to separation between church and state. I told him that there was no such thing in our constitution and the man looked shocked. I told him that what people referred to as separation between church and state was a legal interpretation made by judges, but was never stated or implied by our forefathers. I also informed him that our nation had strong Christian roots and that even our laws were biblically inspired, as were our national songs. Yet now we want nothing to do with God.

9/04 *(Bush, Continued)*

The co-worker said America didn't need God anymore. He said, 'we have evolved.' I gave this man an example he could clearly understand. I told him it's like his being born and raised Latino (which he was), but once he achieved great things, not only pretended not to be Latino, but also denounced his strong Latino upbringing and traditions claiming that he had evolved. I told him that was exactly what America was trying to do with God. The man paused and turned away saying, it's not the same thing.' He walked away, but I could tell by the look on his face that the message got through. As minorities in America we all know someone who achieved greatness and then forgot they were once one of us. We consider this kind of person a traitor. Just imagine how God feels about America.

9/04 *(Another Bush-whacker At the Office)*

I received another surprise visit by a co-worker who hated Bush. He also felt it inappropriate for a Christian President to impose his values on the nation. This person was upset about what happened in Florida and felt that as a black woman I also should be upset about what happened in the 2000 election. I told him that it was an unfortunate turn of events, but it is the responsibility of the people in Florida to clean up their messes. I never talk about religion or politics unless someone asks me a question, but it was amazing that two people sought me out to air their opinions.

9/03/04 *(The Day I Met Moses)*

I was doing errands one evening when the Lord told me to get something for dinner at a Chinese restaurant along the way. I was not hungry, but I got take out and headed home. While waiting for the bus, I saw a very unusual man standing at a distance across the street. At a glance, he reminded me of the character Moses in the Ten Commandments.[14] This man was wearing a very strange outfit and the way the wind was blowing he looked like Moses. The Lord said, *'**give the food to him.**'* I said, ok and waited for him to cross the street, but the man was nowhere to be found. My bus came and I got on board.

Before the bus took off, this man boarded. I remembered what the Lord said about the food, but waited for the opportune moment to approach him. I watched as this man greeted people who got on the bus. He was very intelligent and distinguished, yet he was dressed like Moses and had a staff. As we continued on the bus ride, this man began eating a melted Hershey bar. He was obviously hungry and I wanted to give him my food. As he arose to depart the bus, I went up to him and said, 'I bought this for my dinner, but I really want to give it to you.' He took the food and said, 'God bless you. What's your name?' When I told him, he said, 'I will pray for you Paula.' As he spoke the anointing of God was all over him. I was almost in tears when I thanked him and went back to my seat. Before I sat down, I turned and asked, 'what is your name?' He responded proudly, 'my name is Moses.'

As the bus took off, I could barely hold back the tears. I just gave this man food and yet I felt that he did more for me when he said he'd pray for me. The Lord said this man was one of the chosen and faithful. Then, I was reminded of how God chooses the foolish things of this world to confound the wise. The foolishness of God is wiser than men.

9/26/04 *(Prayer for Clarity on Oral Roberts Prophecy)*
While sleeping, I began praying in the spirit. My spirit was quite disturbed because I saw men in ministry running wild with speculation about Oral Roberts' prophecy about America. I saw Oral Roberts and Kenneth Copeland, but the confused leaders were not identified. These men were not seeking God, but rather letting their imaginations fill in the blanks about what was going to happen to the country. I continued to pray that leaders would seek God and not jump to conclusions and create mass hysteria. I also gained more understanding as to why the Lord had me reveal my prophecies to specific people at this time. If God's people are reacting to a vague prophecy how much more will they react to the detail God has given me? When I woke that morning Kenneth Copeland was airing a special[1] on Dr. Robert's prophecy and its interpretation.

9/27/04 *(Word about Landslide)*
I awaken praying in the spirit for John Kerry. Then the Lord flashed President Bush before my eyes. I prayed for him also. Then the Lord said, *'landslide.'* I then realized that I had heard this in passing a couple of weeks ago and did not pay attention. This was the second time the Lord said to me, *'landslide.'* I assumed this had something to do with the election, but I was not sure who was elected in a landslide. I thanked the Lord and repeated what He said. I also told the Lord that regardless of who is elected, I would continue to prepare this prophecy for President Bush as planned.

9/30/04 *(Revisiting the Storm)*

The Lord put the vision of the storm heavy on my spirit. I prayed and meditated on what He had previously told me. There was a sense of urgency in preparing His people for the storm. I continued to pray in the spirit until released.

10/03/04 *(Prayer for Promises of God)*

Since the Lord began speaking to me about millions of dollars coming to me, the enemy has constantly attacked my finances. I cried out to the Lord to bring forth His Word in my finances and to take away the reproach of what the enemy has tried to do to me. The Holy Spirit spoke Psalm 138:8 to my spirit saying, *'**The Lord will perfect that which concerns me.**'* Immediately the Lord flashed before my spirit all the dangerous situations He took from me over the past ten years. I knew in my spirit that if He took me from the many death plots, healing my finances was a walk in the park. I knew that the hard things were behind me. If the Lord hovered over my finances before, He will complete that which He started in that area of my life. Much joy and peace filled my soul as the Lord responded to my cry.

10/05/04 *(God Seeking to Bestow Inheritance)*

I was asleep and dreamt that I was teaching before a congregation. All I remembered saying was, 'for the gifts and callings of God are without repentance (Romans 11:29).' That morning when I woke, I prayed the Lord to reveal what I was teaching. The Lord said that He was seeking ones who were worthy to receive the promises of Abraham, Isaac and Jacob. He is searching for all who will obey Him. He is searching through all the families of the nations of the world for that one person who will seek Him and obey. God has a promise to fulfill and will not rest until His Word accomplishes what it was sent to do in the earth.

10/05/04 *(Inheritance, Continued)*
God has for Himself a remnant of the nations of the world who will indeed obey and obtain the inheritance. He is calling them forth to make them known as the true sons of God.

10/06/04 *(Heavy Burden for Nation and Election)*
The Lord reminded me that when He showed the blood of Americans (11/01), it was flowing from the Capitol Building and not from the White House. He told me in 2001 that war was coming because of how our government does business. The Lord revealed to me that the Capitol Building houses the Congress and Senate (the Legislative Branch). They make the rules by which the US conducts business at home and abroad. They now blame the President for war in Iraq, but the Lord blames those on Capitol Hill and their conduct for the war that is coming to America. No matter who is President, Capitol Hill and its corruption must be corrected. The Lord said there is too much political control and manipulation on Capitol Hill.

10/10/04 *(A Special Prayer for President Bush)*
As I was praying in the spirit for President Bush, the Holy Spirit spoke, **_'the king's heart is in the hand of the Lord.'_** I searched for this verse in the Bible. Proverbs 21:1 reads, 'the king's heart is in the hand of the Lord. As the rivers of water, He turns it as He wills.' The Holy Spirit led me to pray that President Bush be strengthened as the Hand of the Lord His God is upon Him (Ezra 7:28), and God's ear is attentive to the prayer of His servant (Bush) and to the prayer of His servants who desire to fear God's name and prosper (Nehemiah 1:11). I also prayed that President Bush draws even closer to the Lord and that the Lord reveal His specific will by visions and dreams to the president and all those in authority who have ears to hear and eyes to see God's truth for the sake of the people of our nation.

10/18/04 *(Prayer for John Kerry)*
The Lord brought Kerry before me two days in a row. He said something about ***'trouble brewing.'*** I prayed in the spirit until released. Later the Lord said something about Kerry's house being divided about his running for president. There was also something mentioned about his wife. I continued to pray until released.

10/18/04 *(Seed Sown for the Election)*
I prayed in the spirit and filled out my absentee ballot for the election. I sowed it as a seed for all things the Lord prophesied about America and His Hand being on our nation. I sowed it as righteous seed looking for a harvest of more righteous seed coming forth to vote according to God's will.

10/24/04 *(Prayer of Deliverance for Female Hostages)*
Late in the evening, the Lord led me to pray for deliverance for women who survived various hostage circumstances. Some were political hostages. Others were hostages of war, or were taken hostage by stalkers and extortionists. Regardless of the circumstance, each woman was held against her will, physically and mentally brutalized by her captives until she gave up the will to fight. As I prayed, I began to understand that this deliverance was also for me.

The body easily heals itself, but sometimes the mental scars and images linger deep in our subconscious. I know that only the Lord is able to plunge into the depth of our soul and shed light into our deepest darkness. For each woman I prayed that every evil seed be destroyed; every evil tree be uprooted with its fruit and be cast into the fire; that there be restoration of all things; and that the peace of God rule in each woman's heart and mind.

10/25/04 *(The Fate of the Carnal Christian)*

During my 2 a.m. prayer, I had my Bible CD playing. I heard the Matthew 16:23 passage in which Jesus rebukes Peter saying, 'get thee behind me Satan, you are an <u>offence to me</u>.' When I heard those words, the Holy Spirit took me to Matthew 13:41 where Jesus said that <u>He would cast out of the kingdom, all things that offend</u>. Then the Holy Spirit explained that this has to be because the carnal man is God's enemy and cannot be part of the kingdom. Instead, the carnal man (one who offends Jesus) will be cast into hellfire if the offense is not corrected (Matthew 18:7-9).

10/25/04 *(Word about Bush and Schwarzenegger)*

CNN[16] News had coverage of Governor Schwarzenegger campaigning with President Bush. The Holy Spirit reminded me of the vision where the Lord showed His Hand putting both men in office and declaring the strong partnership ordained by God for the upcoming war.

10/27/04 *(Prayer for Leaders with Integrity)*

I was praying for John Kerry and the Lord said he was popular because he represents America's way of living: not committed to any particular issue; wavering with the winds of popularity; no integrity. He said that Bush is hated because he is a man of integrity and will not bow to popular opinion. In our time of war, the Lord says we need a man who will stand firm and take a stand.

He says that Americans believe there are no absolutes. That's why they can say they are Christian yet vote against Christ publicly. They want God's protection and blessings yet they don't want His rules of operation that qualify them. America needs to grow up. She cannot have it both ways. She will pay for her harlotry with God and her fickleness on issues that affect God's people.

10/28/04 *(Abortion—The Death of God's Seed)*

I was awaken early with the Lord speaking about humans shedding blood of another. He said that if human blood is shed, another's blood is required for atonement (Genesis 9:6). The Lord then said that America has killed babies and if they do not repent and accept Jesus, their own lives will be required of them.

The Lord continued to say that there are many more abortionists within the church than outside the church. These are those that took God's spiritual seed and killed it. Because a life was taken, one will also be required in the spirit if Christians do not repent. Jesus said He would cast out those He never knew (Matthew 7:21-23). God's people intentionally choose their own way and abort God's. This is a more prevalent and serious offense against God. He said that the world is expected to kill babies. They don't know God. The church is called to know God, yet has the boldness to kill His spiritual babies and keep those fathered by Satan.

The Lord told me that all of the miscarriages I had were due to sexual sins of my father's fathers. I was cursed because my father's birthed the evil seed and aborted God's seed. These were men of God who chose Satan's way. The evil seed was passed through the generations as a curse. It yielded abortions and miscarriages (inadvertent abortions) in both the natural and spirit. I was the product of the curse, yet I was called for the blessing (Galatians 3:29). When I repented for the sins of the fathers, and my sin, I was free to experience the blessing and carry out God's seed for my family and me; to inherit the kingdom that was prepared for me before the foundation of the world (Matthew 25:34).

10/28/04 *(Vision of Dad in the Army)*
The Lord showed several visions of my dad wearing a military uniform and awaiting his orders from the Lord. Seeing this warmed my heart for it was an answer to my prayers. Dad has been diligently seeking the Lord for his assignment during this season.

10/31/04 *(Word about Commercialism in Church)*
In a dream the Lord showed books and various Christian products displaying the faces of their authors. He said these people were using the name of Jesus to distribute their wares. They are serving up spiritual junk food that will not feed the hungry soul, but will line the minister's pockets with cash. Their commercialism is causing the world to blaspheme the name of God. These leaders are not preparing the people and turning them to God. They are leading them into deception, and judgment is here! The Lord then spoke another word about His people. He said they have heaped up for themselves leaders who entertain. Therefore His people are not equipped for the day of calamity, which is soon approaching. These leaders have shut up the kingdom of heaven against men. They neither go in themselves nor allow God's people to enter in (Matthew 23:13).

10/31/04 *(Prayer for Ignorance of Blacks in the Church)*
After the Lord gave me the dream and the word, my spirit was grieved because the leaders He showed were black. I saw them extorting other black people who should have known better. The scenario I saw in the spirit was like the 'house niggers' during slavery times. The 'house niggers' tapped danced and smiled and did whatever the master told them in order to enjoy better conditions than the slaves that worked the fields. What I saw in the spirit were dancing fools who were not even in the house, but on the back porch trying to get in. There were church leaders standing inside the porch doors blocking the entrance to the house (kingdom) and telling the people what was supposedly going on in the house.

10/31/04 *(Ignorance of Blacks, Continued)*
The believers were satisfied with dancing on the back porch because it was still better than working the fields. It never dawned on them that those same leaders, who were blocking the door, were so busy keeping them out, that they themselves had not been inside the house nor had they seen the master.

As I prayed the Lord showed me that these believers will not obtain things of God because they have their sights on leaders and not on Jesus. When they hear the Lord speak, the leaders tell them that the opposite is true so as to keep the people from God's best. What is worse, the believers back down and disobey God because Bishop so and so or preacher such and such told them they weren't hearing God. God is angry that these believers fear man and not Him. But, time is near when all will fear Him or die.

11/01/04 *(Prayer for Presidential Election)*
I was awaken during my sleep praying for President Bush and the nation. I felt very good about Bush in the election. He was strong!! I did sense terror lurking behind the scenes. I cried out in the spirit for God's watchmen to sit on the city walls and watch for danger. I prayed for safety and peace at the polls. That seemed to be the major concern in the spirit realm. I was awaken two or three more times praying against danger and terror plots against our nation.

11/01/04 *(Another Call to Take the City)*

I had a late afternoon appointment in Hollywood. As I was walking down the street, I passed several buildings that represented the occult. When I passed by those same buildings while heading home, the Holy Spirit spoke the same words I heard in February of 2003, *'**Take the City.**'* Just as before, those words rang in my ears and my spirit with great intensity. I continued walking and declared, 'Lord, I will take the city for the Kingdom.'

11/01/04 *(Prayers for Healing)*

The Holy Spirit specifically directed my evening prayers for healing for two people. One was my step mom; the other was for John Kerry's wife. My step mom needed physical healing while recuperating from surgery. John Kerry's wife needed emotional healing from the lost of her first husband. I prayed for both women throughout the night until the Holy Spirit released me.

11/02/04 *(Election Day)*

I woke up at 4 a.m. listening to my Bible CDs. The spiritual atmosphere was clear. There was nothing in my spirit that needed immediate attention. So, I did my normal prayers and went to the track to work out for a bit. I spent the entire day working on this book and listening to tapes. It was my plan to stay away from all media hype and concentrate on the Word I am preparing for the nation.

11/03/04 *(President Bush's Historic Victory)*

The spiritual airwaves were somewhat clear at 4 a.m. The Holy Spirit told me to stay in prayer until 7 a.m. During prayer I was told to make certain errands for the day.

11/03/04 *(Bush Victory, Continued)*

I was leaving at about 8 a.m. and decided to turn on CNN[17] to get election results. They were announcing that Kerry was conceding. I shouted for the victory. The Lord said that His hand put Bush in office but it did not dawn on me until that moment that this was the landslide He spoke about twice. The Lord showed Himself strong on the behalf of the president.

11/03/04 *(God's Kingdom Has Come Upon America)*

The Holy Spirit reminded me of the passage of scripture in Luke 11:20 where Jesus made a powerful statement. He said, 'If I with the finger of God cast out devils, no doubt the kingdom of God is come upon you.' Just by obeying the spirit of God, Jesus evoked the power of the kingdom in a situation. The Lord told me years ago, that when I obeyed His Spirit concerning a situation, my obedience would cause the kingdom to rule in that situation. His kingdom rule means that natural laws no longer apply in that situation.

When the Lord gave me the Word about Schwarzenegger and Bush, it was my duty to vote according to God's will. I cast my vote under the direction of the Holy Spirit. My ballot was sown as a righteous seed looking for a harvest of more righteous seeds seeking the will of God for our nation. President Bush prevailed because of faithful believers praying and voting for the will of God to overtake our nation. Now the Kingdom of God has a pathway to rule our nation once again.

11/03/04 *(God's Kingdom, Continued)*
I am extremely encouraged about the future of America. With our nation's leaders put in position by the Hand of the Lord, and the believers diligently seeking the face of God, the heavens will be open over America no matter what evils await us. It will become even more evident to the world that indeed the Kingdom of God has come to America.

11/04/04 *(Meeting a False Prophet)*
I had to take a bus to the other side of town to run an errand. The Lord told me to take my journal to do some editing while I took the long ride. The drive was wonderful and I got much done. About three blocks from my stop a black woman with an accent sat down next to me. She noticed my journal and began to talk. She asked whom I voted for. I told her the person the Lord told me to vote for. She replied, 'so you voted for Kerry.' 'No', I replied. 'I voted for George Bush because the Hand of the Lord is on him and on our nation.' The woman went berserk. She claimed to have visions and dreams from God. When I asked her how the Lord told her about Bush, she spoke about a vision, I knew was demonic from the start.

This woman claimed that God appeared in a vision, as a frog and told her that George Bush was the antichrist. I asked the woman who was her Lord. I asked her to name him by name. She did not. Then she had the audacity to lecture me about making sure my visions and dreams lined up with the Bible. I cut her off and asked where the frog appears as a messenger of God in the Bible. She refused to answer me. I asked who her pastor was. The Holy Spirit let me know she had none. I was reminded of the number of people I have met who think they know God because they go into the spiritual realm. They don't know the Bible, but are convoluted in their understanding.

11/05/04 *(Word about Preparing Ohio)*
While asleep, the Lord spoke to my spirit to speak to the state of Ohio. I felt eminent danger for that state and the Lord was calling all His glory into place. He told me to, *'declare that His glory reign over Ohio.'* I spoke and declared that the glory of God would reign over Ohio. Then I spoke in tongues preparing the people of God for what was to come. As I prayed, the Lord reminded me of all the signs of danger He spoke of for Ohio. Some saw what looked like a nuclear blast. Others saw a storm. I specifically saw a storm coming off of Lake Erie that would devastate the entire state.

11/06/04 *(Declaration from the Lord)*
I woke to the following words flowing out of my spirit, *'**The righteous seed has prevailed and will manifest God's glory in the earth. God's glory will manifest in all the earth to the glory of God the Father!**'*

11/06/04 The remainder of the month prayer was made to destroy evil in the church. This day, I heard a command in the spirit *'**Lock and Load!!! Destroy the Enemies of God!!!**'*

11/07/04 *(More Prayer for Ohio)*
The Lord had me again praying for those in Ohio. I was specifically praying for the intercessors; the prayer warriors. Some will be martyred for the gospel.

11/10/04 *(Scripture for Day)*
While in prayer, I heard the words of Haggai 2:7 in my spirit, *'**I will shake all nations and the desire of all nations shall come: and I will fill this house with glory, saith the Lord of Hosts.**'*

11/16/04 *(Prayer to Purge the Church)*
The Lord showed many pastors and leaders boldly and routinely participating in sexual immorality and blaspheming the name of God. The heart of God was so grieved that my spirit cried, 'Father, purge your house, for your name's sake. Your people have become a reproach among men.'

11/17/04 *(The Lord Proclaims A Salvation Miracle)*
The Word of the Lord came to me saying, *'**The dog has been saved.**'* I knew that He meant that the same dog that I untied and took with me to California was now saved. In the spirit, I heard 'How can a dog be saved?' The Lord reminded me that salvation is about the heart of man turning to God. All that is required is for a man to hear the Word and believe what he hears and act out on that Word. Salvation is not a decision of the mind; it is a decision of the heart to believe.

11/19/04 *(Prayer for those Oppressed by Evil Men)*
Around 2 am while praying, I saw the Lord's Hand defend the oppressed and set them free from all hurt, harm and danger. But, I saw church leaders living with demons because they did not want to be free. They were too prideful to receive from God. Then the Lord showed demoniacs everywhere being set free forever!!! They were so excited about what God did that they told it everywhere they went.

11/19/04 *(Oppression, Continued)*
After this intercession, the Lord gave me a vision about believers denying the spirit and trusting the flesh. I heard someone ask if whether something was real, or was it just in the spirit. The Lord was grieved by this question. But I attempted to show how the things of the spirit are more real than what we can see with our own eyes. We are told to walk by faith and not by sight (II Corinthians 5:7), yet many believers do not obey. This will prove detrimental during war. Many will be defeated by what they see and will have no faith in God.

11/26/04 *(Vision of Bastards in the Faith)*
The Lord had me praying for the Body of Christ to repent and turn back to God. He showed a vision of a woman I had working with me in ministry. She left out of rebellion. The Lord showed that she wanted to come back, but not to help me. Her deceptive heart devised a plan to come back to prove something to me. The Lord said that if she came back, she would do her will and deliberately overturn all He told me to do. He said that like many Christians, they are deceived by their own ambitions and have no awareness, or any desire for His truth.

12/06/04 *(Destroying Kingdom Stumbling Blocks)*
He will destroy immoral leaders and troublemakers calling them stumbling blocks to the congregation. God will destroy those who say, 'we will not have this man (Jesus) reign over us' (Luke 19:14, 27). They will be cast out of the kingdom even though they call Him Lord (Matthew 7:23). The Lord had me praying continually for the church to repent and prepare for war. The church refuses to realize the power of repentance in the kingdom. The glory of God will destroy all uncleanness, but when we repent, He will cleanse us. Once cleansed, God again can protect us.

12/12/04 *(Prayer for the Judases)*
The Lord placed in my spirit a word for the Judases in the faith. Because they betrayed Jesus, they will be replaced in ministry and another will take their place. These evildoers refuse to repent and therefore must be replaced. Like Judas, they had obtained a part of Jesus' ministry, but they lost their office (Acts 1:17-25).

12/23/06 *(Prayer to Release Shackles)*
The Lord showed a specific leader who was in severe bondage. He was tied to a woman calling herself a prophetess of God. This woman fed this man with lies and kept him from doing God's will. The man knew he was in bondage, but was not able to lose himself from this evil woman's grip.

12/26/04 *(A Child like Faith in God)*
The Lord spoke to my heart about the importance of His people having a child like faith (Matthew 18:3-4). God's desire is for His people to return to a child like faith, by being quiet before Him and believing His every word. God said He wants us to obey without questioning Him. He said that a child who trusts a parent would value that parent's word more than life itself. He reminded me of children saying, "My mommy said . . ." or "My daddy said . . ." The word a loving parent is the gospel to a young child's trusting ears. That child will seek to obey and please the parent. A child does not try to figure out the parent's motives nor does he or she try to outwit the parent. He simply hears, believes and obeys whatever the parent says. This child trusts that the parent loves him and will do him no harm. God wants us to trust that He love us, by obeying whatever He says knowing that He has provided good and not evil for us (Jeremiah 29:11).

12/31/04 *(A Word about Running to Win)*
The Lord reminded me that we are all called to do a work on earth according to His plan. When are born again, we have positioned ourselves to fulfill His purpose. By seeking God, we will find our purpose In Him, as revealed by the Holy Spirit (I Corinthians 2:9-10).

God said that we are in a race, not simply to compete, but to finish and obtain an imperishable crown (I Corinthians 9:24-27). He requires that we lay aside everything that would disqualify us from successfully completing our race (Hebrews 12:1). Our focus should be on Jesus and His example, and not on other ministers. We may emulate their faith and dedication only as they emulate Jesus. Jesus only acted as God directed Him. The Lord said that men do their own thing and disqualify themselves in the sin of disobedience. He said never forget that it is Jesus who alone is the author of our race (Hebrews 12:2-3). He determined before the foundation of the world, our lane and purpose in which we are called to run (II Timothy 4:7-8).

We cannot win without Jesus' direction. We win only if we run in our assigned lane, follow God's rules, and compete to the end (II Timothy 2:5).

THE WAR JOURNAL

YEAR 2005: *The Glory Is Here!*

1/01/05 As usual, I begin another year fasting and praying for the nation. I was particularly interested in what the Lord had to say about the tsunami that hit Southeast Asia on Christmas day. He gave me no warning nor did He prompt me to pray against the storm. And even now, the Lord is not speaking. In my heart, I know that God's judgment was executed.

1/02/05 *(The Purpose for the Glory Manifested)*
The Lord spoke to my spirit about what happened when He struck Saul with blindness. Saul was intent on destroying the church and persecuting Christians, when a bright light from heaven knocked him from his horse and left him blind. Saul was struck down and his eyes were open as he was turned from darkness to light (Acts 26:14-18). God did not strike Saul to kill him; He struck Saul so that he would be a minister and witness of Jesus Christ. The purpose of the light of God's glory is not to destroy men, but to move them off their paths of destruction onto the path of light. In truth, Saul deserved death, but God chose to redeem Saul and make him valuable to the kingdom. When the glory strikes and we turn back to God, He will forgive us and give us an inheritance in the kingdom.

1/08/05 *(Prayer for Tsunami Victims)*
I began to pray for the victims of the tsunami when the Lord halted my spirit. He told me that our time was coming. The Lord told me to pray for American eyes to be opened. I prayed fervently that Americans would turn back to God.

1/09/05 *(Enduring Persecution)*

I experienced unusual persecution by a neighbor, and I asked the Lord why He chose suffering as a manner for Christians. I asked why one who loves God should be led like a sheep to the slaughter. The Lord spoke to my spirit about being like my Master who was led like a sheep to the slaughter. He said, *'It is what it is.'* I expected more of an explanation, but received what I was told and moved on.

1/10/05 *(Another Vision Warning of War)*

The Lord showed in a vision, a woman who knows that war is coming; yet she is deliberately teaching the opposite. The Lord had me speak to their spirits. These people refused the truth and began to laugh at me. Several ministers also laughed at me and called me crazy. I remain unmovable because the Lord would not let me walk away from this warning of war, even if I wanted to.

1/14/05 *(Prayer about Adultery of the Church)*

During prayer time, the Lord spoke about the adulterous heart of the church. They have forgotten God and don't understand that He sees their hearts and evil desires. It is what is in the heart that defiles them (Mark 7:20-23). The Lord will destroy them because their evil heart is set against God.

1/15/05 *(Prayer of a Heart Desiring God)*

The Lord told me that He is looking for hearts that truly want what He wants; hearts that desire to obey, honor and please God. Christians have learned to confess with their mouths and hold evil desires in their hearts, whether good or evil. They believe that it is God's job to give them the desires of their hearts. The Lord reminded me of what happened with me. I went after the Lord with all my heart and asked what He had for me.

1/15/05 *(Desiring God, Continued)*

The Lord poured Himself out on me and gave me more than I could ever ask. When He spoke, His desires burned in my heart and took control of my reins. God has been in the driver's seat of my life ever since. The plans I had for myself were minor compared to where the Lord wanted to take me. Even now, He has me doing things that I would have never imagined doing. Now, I am curious as to what else God has for me. Following God had been the best adventure of my life. I don't make any plans of my own; I ask God what the plan is for my life, and obey His instructions.

1/17/05 *(Prayer for Jeffrey)*

I woke up with heavy prayer in my heart for my son Jeffrey. The Lord did not speak anything, so I just prayed until the heaviness lifted.

1/22/05 *(Vision of the Secret Place)*

While sleeping, I saw an abused little girl asking me to take her to God's secret place. She wanted to hide some place where the enemy could not get to her. God answered her prayer. Her parents were evil and hurt her many times. I took her and asked the Lord to hide her from danger. I asked that he protect all those who were being abused. God protected them all.

1/23/05 *(Word about Enemy Giving Up)*

The Lord gave me words of comfort concerning my son. He said that his father couldn't continue to fight against me: it's too costly for him. None of his plans are working. He has made the choice to give up and leave me alone. I asked about Jeffery's freedom. The Lord said that he is hesitant, but he has agreed to let Jeffrey go as well.

2/7/05 *(Word about Eternal Life)*

In my prayer time the Lord took me to Mark 10:17-30, when Jesus was asked what we must do to inherit eternal life. He reminded me that not only did Jesus tell the young man that he must follow the commandments, but he must be also willing to give up his attachment to things on this earth. The disciples were so shocked by Jesus' answer that they asked, "Who then can be saved?" Jesus said that it is impossible for men to save themselves. But with God, all things are possible. If we do things God's way, in the world to come we will have eternal life.

2/14/05 *(Word about Living in Him)*

I heard in my spirit the words Jesus spoke, "the prince of this world is coming and has nothing in me (John 14:30)." Satan was about to use men to crucify Jesus. Jesus did not deserve death, but would be killed for no fault of His own. Devil could find no fault in Jesus. Then the Spirit of the Lord said, *'**In Him there is no darkness, and the wicked one touches us not** (I John 5:18).'* When we walk in the Light as Jesus is in the Light, then the blood of Jesus cleanses us from all sin (I John 1:7). The devil will find nothing in us that can destroy us, as long as we are operating In Jesus. If the devil still attacks us, he does so for righteousness sake, and our reward will be great in heaven (Matthew 5:11-12).

2/26/05 *(Intense Prayer for Leaders)*

The Lord said that many leaders are in bondage and severely off course from God's plan. He had me praying for the deliverance of leaders. Intense travail went forth for God's people who were being abuse by these misguided leaders.

3/2/05 *(Prayer against Brute Beasts)*

The Holy Spirit pronounced a curse on evil ones who continue to pervert God's ways and defile God's people. He called them Brute Beasts who relentlessly do evil and have no desire to do God's will. God will not forget their evil or that of their fathers. He will turn them over to ultimate destruction and an eternity in hell. In their time of terror these people will cry out to God, but He will not answer.

3/3/05 *(Word Concerning Stalkers)*

The Holy Spirit told me to read Psalm 124 as an answer concerning the men who are stalking me. He said that what the enemy meant for evil, God has turned for good. The Lord has not given me over as prey. My soul escaped and the snare is broken because I have escaped.

3/29/05 *(Word about Kingdom Traitors)*

The Lord said that there are too many people coming into the kingdom and pledging allegiance to Jesus, then working in opposition to God's will. These are traitors. They will be tried for treason. The only sentence for treason is death. King Jesus will cast them out of His kingdom and they will perish. These traitors operate like demons in the kingdom. They believe the word and tremble, but won't obey (James 2:19).

3/30/05 *(How Traitors Defile the Body of Christ)*

We who are in Christ are one body and one flesh with God. We are called the Body of Christ and members of one another. And adulterer in the body is like a cancerous cell that must be eradicated if the body is to live healthy. Even the mafia and gang bangers kill their traitors. But evil flourishes in most churches. If the existing church does not purge its cancer of sin, the Lord will destroy it and raise up another. And, we will see it happen in our lifetime.

3/30/05 *(Overnight Prayer for Healing)*
I was led by the Lord to pray all night for healing and deliverance for several people in dire need.

4/1/05 *(Intense Prayer for Leaders)*
The Lord led me to another overnight prayer session. Intense prayer for leaders to be healed, delivered and positioned for the upcoming season.

4/3/05 *(More Intense Prayer)*
I was led into prayer from 2am until about 6am for leaders. I had intense prayer for Pastor Argie. Then I was translated into a room with Dr. Betty, and Pastor Argie. Dr. Betty was talking to us both and downloading information to our spirits. I could not understand her words, but I knew God was doing something big. Dr. Fred was in another room close by. I never saw him, but I knew he was there, but doing something else.

4/9/05 *(Vision of Arab Executions)*
While in early morning prayer, I saw Arab military men wearing green suited uniforms and red berets. They were executing their own people by gunfire. Then I saw their leader: a man lying in state after his death. He was dressed in a white headdress and white caftan. He was a dark man with a beard. I don't recall ever seeing this man before, but I know he was their political leader. A military man wearing a red beret kissed the face of the dead man.

4/13/05 *(Prayer of Safety for Governor)*
The Lord awakened me with orders to cover Governor Schwarzenegger's back. I saw a man with a weapon following the Governor in order to assassinate him. God had me stop the death plot.

4/19/05 *(Word of God's Vengeance)*
The Lord spoke of terror and death over the men that are following me. He spoke of an execution. God said that they have defied Him and there is no forgiveness in them. He said they are arrogant in their sin and another man will arrogantly slay them.

4/29/05 *(Word about Destruction of Evil Men)*
It's not God's desire that any man be destroyed, yet those who continue to ignore Him; those who have pleasure thinking and doing evil, will be destroyed. Now is the time of God's vengeance on evil. He will show no mercy. *'**They have been warned. The time is now!**'*

5/1/05 *(Warning About War)*
The Lord declared to my spirit, *'**Prepare for war!**'* No other utterances came forth. I responded by praying in the spirit and waiting for further instruction.

5/18/05 *(Another Warning About War)*
The Lord again, said, *'**Prepare for war!**'* He also had me praying for our part in preparing for War. I saw President Bush, and I getting ready for war. There were other terrorist attacks that shook things up in the country—Los Angeles is a target. The Lord also had me pray for Mayor Villaraigosa. He is not equipped for the job according to God. He will faint when war strikes LA.

5/21/05 *(Intense Prayer for War Preparation)*
The Lord led me in strong intercession concerning war that is soon coming. No details given at this time. I prayed until the Spirit released me.

5/23/05 *(The Aroma of Death)*
This morning's prayer was again focused on war. When I finished praying, there was a smell of death in the air. I could smell dead rotting bodies. There was a smell of masses of dead bodies. The sense of war was all around me. We have no escape from what is to come.

6/5/05 *(Instructions for Relief Organizations)*
The Lord told me to write business plans for nonprofit organizations. He said that the attorney would need the detail in order to set up the organizations legally.

6/6/05 *(Teaching of End of World)*
The Lord spoke to me about putting this book into Bible perspective. He told me to parallel the events in the journal with events in the Bible.

6/17/05 *(End of World Teaching Continues)*
The Lord instructed me to create a timeline of end time events. I incorporated the events mentioned in this book with the events from the Bible. I also created a time line of events in American History and great moves of God. This project took weeks to complete, but the research was very informative.

6/29/05 *(Prayer for the Nations)*
The Lord declared, *'**It's here!**'* He spoke about dangers in the world and told me to prepare for an emergency.

6/30/05 *(Vision about Woman in the Window)*
This was another time of prayer for the nations of the world. After prayer, the Lord took me by the spirit to a place in Europe. I saw a black woman standing in a large upstairs window of a beautiful old mansion. The woman was very dominant in stature. She was wearing a fine tailored suit and standing in a beautifully tapestried private room. The terrain looked like somewhere in England, France or Germany, but the Holy Spirit said *'**Germany.**'* There was a single road leading from this mansion across the countryside wooded areas. There was one car on the road driving away from the mansion. The car was an older model Rolls Royce convertible. Inside the car were four white elderly gentlemen out on a joy ride. The woman was looking out of a huge window that ran the entire length of the castle-like walls. She was listening to God and watching as a distant evil heads their way. The men laughed carefree in the car, unaware of danger. There was another window in the same room. It was a smaller window located next to the larger one where the woman stood. I walked into the room and stood in the other window and listened to what the woman was hearing. Then I heard the voice of the Lord say, *'**It is Here!**'*

7/04/05 *(Word at Copeland Convention)*
I spent the Fourth of July at the Copeland Convention in Anaheim. The Lord commanded me to, *'**Believe the Impossible!**'*

7/08/05 *(Word about Increase)*
The theme in prayer this morning was overwhelming increase. The Lord said that He would increase me more and more, me and my children.

7/20/05 *(God's Perspective on Warfare)*
This day the enemy is stirred up in every direction. If felt like I was a moving target. There was so much noise in the spirit that all I could do was shout, "shut up devil." All I wanted was peace and quietness, when the Lord said, *'**Life is Good!**'* He emphasized the word, 'good.' I laughed so hard that I could no longer hear the demonic noise.

8/1-31/05 *(Extended Teaching on End Times Completed)*
My faith has been increased tremendously after putting together a time line paralleling American History with great moves of God's Spirit. I also finished a timeline of end time events and highlighted things that appear in this book. My conclusion is that God has orchestrated things to His glory on earth.

During times of turmoil, the glory was always revealed to bring America out of trouble. Then we had period of prosperity and forgot God again, until the next problem occurred. Our country's relationship with God looks much like that of the Children of Israel in the Bible who in prosperous times would forget God. God would punish them until they cried out to Him. God always sent a deliverer to bring them out of trouble. Forty or fifty years would pass and the Children of Israel would once again forget God, and the whole scenario would repeat itself (Judges Chapters 1-6).

One thing that the Lord made clear to me is that the season of His glory will be the final event before Jesus comes.

8/1-17/05 *(Bible Teaching Theme)*

In going through my journals, I noticed that the Lord had me studying about the faith of Abraham. This topic came up on various days in many ways; from seeking God's wisdom, being strong in faith, leaving family for God, and walking in forgiveness and avoiding strife. The Lord let me know that the blessings I have inherited are of faithful Abraham. By following the voice of God, I have obtained the promise to inherit the world (Romans 4:13).

8/26/05 *(Overnight Prayer to Break Bondages)*

The Lord led me in a prayer for deliverance all night long. He brought people before my spirit and had me break the bondages that were holding them. He gave me Acts 16:25-26 to stand on while I prayed. It reads, *'And at midnight Paul and Silas prayed, and sang praises unto God: and the prisoners heard them. And suddenly there was a great earthquake, so that the foundations of the prison were shaken: and immediately all the doors were opened and every one's bands were loosed.'*

8/30/05 *(Word about the Prince of Peace)*

The Spirit of the Lord brought the words of Isaiah 9:6-7 to my spirit by saying, ***'Jesus is the Prince of Shalom, and the increase of His Shalom shall have no end.'*** Shalom[18] is the Hebrew word for completeness or peace. Jesus brings us back to a covenant of peace with God. When we let the Spirit of the Lord govern our lives, we will be changed from glory to glory until we are completely transformed into the image of Jesus (II Corinthians 3:17-18); who is our peace.

9/1-30/05 *(More Christian History Studies)*
Most of my spare time on evenings and weekends was spent in the
Central Library in downtown Los Angeles. This was a time of very
few revelations about war and the upcoming glory. It was a period of
study of history of God's glory around the world. The more text books
and biographies I read, the more questions I had about why God's
people never consistently called the glory into manifestation. It
seemed that persecution or pressure from outside sources caused
certain individuals or groups to move the Hand of God against the
enemy that was causing pressure, and the glory showed up. And, the
same is about to happen again in America and around the world.

9/11/05 *(Word about Spiritual Integrity)*
After finishing prayer one morning, the Holy Spirit said, *'**The Lord
Our God is One Lord.**'* He said that the Father, Son and Holy Ghost
are three distinct persons, but they are in one accord. They will never
speak against, or act against one another. They govern as One Lord.
The Spirit said that is why we must love God with all our heart, and all
our soul, and all of our mind and all our strength (Deuteronomy 6:4-5).
We must have complete unity within ourselves and with God. If our
spirit is one with God, then our soul, mind, and strength must be
brought in line with the spirit. When our mind, soul, and spirit are
divided against God, then we will not be able to stand against the devil
and his devices (Matthew 12:25). But if we keep the word in our
mouths, and meditate on the word day and night, and make a
conscience choice to obey the word, then we will be prosperous and
successful in everything we do (Joshua 1:8).

10/2/05 *(God's Perfection versus Man's Pride)*
The Lord talked about how the coming season of glory would produce similar results like Adam had in Eden. I asked the Lord how man could do evil after being created perfect and given much wealth and wisdom. Then the Lord brought to my mind the perfection of Lucifer, yet iniquity was found in him. Lucifer had more wisdom than Daniel and nothing was hid from him. With wisdom and understanding Lucifer increased in strength and riches illegally (Ezekiel 28:3-4, 15-17). Then there was Adam and Eve who had all the wealth, beauty, and wisdom and knowledge of God in the Garden of Eden; yet, they desired their own thing and part from God. Proverbs 4:5 says to get wisdom and above all understand, and do not turn away from the words of God. Psalm 119:9 says that if a person wants to keep his path clean (honest) before God, then he must take heed to God's word. Then I totally understood why the Lord warned the Children of Israel not to say that it was by their power that they got great wealth. God told them to remember that it was He who gave them power to get wealth to establish His covenant, and if they forgot this fact, they would surely perish (Deuteronomy 8:18-19). My heart was humbled by these words from the Lord.

10/2-18/05 *(A Word on Uncleanness in the Church)*
The Lord gave me a series of teachings on walking in spiritual integrity. He said that in the upcoming season of His glory, He is sending, *'Holy Terror'* on His enemies. The Lord is sending death and destruction to all those who are unclean in thought and deed, and to those who are defiling His Body with their filthiness.

10/22/05 *(Judgment for the Secrets of the Heart)*
The Lord told me that there are many in the churches that do not believe that God sees the things they do in secret. They sin because they think no one sees and no one knows. But, God knows everything and sees everything. The Holy Spirit said, *'**God knows all. He knows the secrets of men's hearts. He will reward man based on the secret and seen things that he does or thinks.**'*

11/1-30/05 *(Various Teachings and Writings)*
This was a month of heavy writing on the subject holiness. There are at least one dozen teachings given between November and December, in addition to writings to complete this book and the business plans.

11/5/05 *(Who Will Be With Jesus?)*
I asked how to teach men to follow Jesus' example and obey God. Many claim to serve God, but do their own thing. The Spirit of the Lord spoke, *'**If any man serve me, let him follow me and where I am there shall also my servant be (John 12:26).**'* Then He reminded of Jesus' words saying, *'**If any man follow me, let him deny himself, take up his cross and follow me (Mark 8:34).**'* Then in Matthew 7:21 Jesus said that no can come into the kingdom having done their will and not that of God the Father. Bottom line: Do like Jesus did and you will have what Jesus has, and be where Jesus is.

11/11/05 *(Word on God's Kingdom Plan)*

I woke up hearing the Spirit of the Lord talking about God's upcoming plan on earth. He said, God was raising the **_Kingdom Dynasty on Earth._** He urged me to fervently seek the kingdom plan with all my heart, mind, soul and strength.

12/1-31/05 *(Month of Kingdom Teachings)*

When the Lord spoke about Kingdom Dynasty, He flooded me with teachings throughout the Bible about the purpose and plan for the kingdom on earth. God stressed the absolute plan for Jesus to be ruler and King over His people. It was interesting to review the Kingdom Manifest; meaning who's in,[α] who's out,[β] and who thinks they are in and who will be cast out.[∞] If we are to remain in the kingdom, we must be loyal subjects of our King. He also emphasized that there is punishment for those not wanting Jesus to rule over them. This month was filled with intense and constant kingdom lessons flooding my spirit. I was so fired up by what the Lord was saying; that a new song came up out of my spirit about the kingdom. This song flooded my spirit for hours.

THE WAR JOURNAL

YEAR 2006: *Possessing The Land*

THE WAR JOURNAL
YEAR 2006: *Possessing The Land*

1/1/06 *(Word about War)*
The only word I heard from God on New Year's Day was, 'War *is Here.*' I prayed in the spirit and remained quiet before the Lord to see if anything else was forth coming.

1/2/06 *(Vision about God's Vengeance)*
Jesus and I were destroying every demonic force and principality in His way. Jesus handed me the spiritual weapons and I did the destruction. We destroyed every enemy of God. None was left breathing. It was brutal and complete. No evil was spared.

Jesus was not angry; He was just fulfilling God's Word, rapidly, swiftly and powerfully. Whatever the Word required, was what happened, whether it be good or bad. He was no respecter of persons. It was all about the Word: whatever reward or punishment was stated was the thing that came to pass immediately. I heard these words in my spirit, *'For these be the days of vengeance that all things which are written may be filled.'*

1/4/06 *(Kingdom Dynasty Revisited)*
The Lord said this was the year for my part in the dynasty to manifest on earth. God spoke to me in detail about all He ordained me to do for the kingdom. The Lord reiterated the point that what He has shown me is just the tip of the iceberg, and He has shown me much more than I can comprehend even now. He quoted this scripture to me, *'For if we died with Him we shall also live with Him. If we endure (suffer) we shall also reign with Him (II Timothy 2:11-12).'*

269

1/4/06 *(Dynasty, Continued)*

I have a big promise from God and was made aware that there are giants possessing the land. The Lord called me His giant slayer, equipped to take down anyone and anything that gets in the way of God's will. He said that He has specifically trained me for this time and season. All the blows I took in my life that were meant to kill me, only made me more determined to overcome and glorify God. Goliath is coming, but I have my staff, slingshot and five smooth stones ready to take off his head.

1/6/06 *(Teaching on Wholeness)*

The Lord taught me years ago to listen to the Word on tape to combat tiredness, demonic attacks, and to heal my body. I have had many miracles happen just with tapes and CD's ministering to my total being. Often ministers will tell people to be healed in their bodies from the top of their head to the soles of their feet. This is fine for some people, but in other cases healing is not a physical, but an emotional and/or a spiritual need. There even could be someone in need of healing a broken relationship or healing a sick financial position. The Lord responded by telling me to minister healing wholly, spirit, soul and body. He reminded me of II Thessalonians 5:23 that reads, *'__the very God of Peace (Wholeness) sanctify you wholly,..and your whole spirit, soul and body be preserved blameless unto the coming of our Lord Jesus Christ.__'* God will sanctify our whole beings and everything that concerns us. This is completeness according to the Word of God.

1/14/06 *(Another Word about Who Is in the Kingdom)*
The Lord continued His talk about who is in the kingdom, who is not, and who will be cast out. He said that there are some who just make it into the kingdom; others achieve high status within the kingdom. What we achieve in the kingdom is dependent upon our obedience to the Word. The highest rewards are to those who remain faithful and obedient under extreme persecution and death. According to your faith, so it will be unto you. Those with little faith will be rewarded little. Those with so great faith will be rewarded greatly. Some will have faith enough to get into the door of the kingdom, but not enough faith to achieve great things for God.

1/28/06 *(Word about Shield of Faith)*
January was a great month for revelation and warfare. I got hit from so many angles from the enemy that I had to go to God and see if there was anything I was doing wrong. He responded by saying that I had, ***'fortified shields of faith.'*** One thing I know about my armor. I never take it off, and the enemy is always trying to hack through it, to no avail.

2/2/06 *(Spiritual Warning of Danger in Family)*
I got this knowing in my spirit that death was visiting my family. I also knew that it involved one of my siblings. Immediately I prayed in the spirit for God's wisdom. Nothing came forth. I just prayed until the spirit released me.

2/13/06 *(The Violent Take it By Force)*
The Kingdom of Heaven is suffering violence and the violent take it by force (Matthew 11:12). The heavenly violence occurs because of the word. Satan does not want the word of God to come to pass in the earth. He wages war against all of us who have faith in the word.

God gives us a word of promise; He will fulfill His promise, if we don't give up. Satan's job is to do everything in his power to make us forfeit the word. He can't' take it from us. He can't prevent the word from coming to pass. All the devil can do is get us to stop believing God and give up the fight of faith. But, we will reap, if we do not faint.

2/19/06 *(Word about Darkness Fleeing)*
This prophetic word came out of my spirit after prayer saying, *'**The Light will destroy the darkness completely. Just like switching on a light in a dark room, all darkness will flee. Jesus Christ will eradicate all darkness in the world. He is the Light of the world.***'

2/23/06 *(Plague of Death Coming)*
The Lord said that He was sending a *'**death plague**'* to America to destroy those who have tried to hurt and enslave God's people. They have exalted their many gods and refuse to bow to Almighty God. America continues to persecute and make light of those who serve Him. God will prove His strength against this nation. God will demonstrate who among people belongs to Him and who the pretenders are. He will spare no one. All will die. Every house will feel the pain of despair except those who serve Him and those who have the Blood Jesus covering them and their households.

2/24/06 *(Call to Overnight Prayer)*
While at work, the Lord gave me a heavy burden for prayer. I knew that this could keep me shut in for the weekend. I prayed in the spirit over night. No information was given me in my understanding.

2/25/06 *(Burden Not Lifted)*
Early this morning Mom calls and I tell her that I am staying in because I need to hear from God what is going on. I stayed in prayer until about 2 or 3 pm. The Lord released me to run some errands for a couple of hours. Before the evening ended, I got a call from my sister saying my nephew had been shot to death.

I was not immediately moved by the news of my nephew's death until I got some answers from God. I was ready to raise his body but the Lord said no. He said that the young man was better off where he was. That is all the Lord would say. Then I realized that the sense I had about death in my family involving one of my siblings had finally manifested. My heart immediately turned to God, asking the Holy Spirit to direct my prayer for my family and friends during this shared sorrow.

3/1-15/06 This time was spent with family. Most of my prayer and prophetic words were strictly for comfort and edification of certain people greatly affected my nephews' death.

3/20/06 *(Kingdom Teaching Continues)*
The Lord reminded me that every time a person obeys His Word, it causes the kingdom to manifest in that circumstance. He said that signs and wonders follow the obedience to the word.

3/20/06 *(Kingdom, Continued)*
Jesus did and said whatever the Father desired. He declared, *'If I with the finger of God, cast out devils, no doubt the Kingdom of God is come upon you (Luke 11:20).'* It was the finger of God that caused all the plagues to fall on Egypt (Exodus 8:19). This was a demonstration that God's power was supreme over all the gods of Egypt. Likewise, in the upcoming season of glory, God will show His power to the world.

3/24/06 *(The Lord Declares Increase)*
The Lord said that He would increase more and more, me and my children (Psalm 115:14).

4/9/06 *(Word about God's Vengeance)*
The Bible says that if we do things God's way we will have life and blessing, but it we do things against God; we will have death and cursing in our lives (Deuteronomy 30:19). This is the season of God's vengeance. He will pay each man according to what he does. God will not be mocked. He will bring about the blessing and the curse upon all those who have sown seeds for such.

4/13/06 *(Prayer for Immigrants)*
The heart of God is grieved by the historical treatment of the Native Americans and immigrants in this nation. He said that He would avenge the innocent blood that cries from the dust of our land. The Lord will restore everything that was stolen from these people.

4/13/06 *(Word about the Mayor)*

The current mayor of Los Angeles is not God's choice to direct the people of this city. The Lord said he is very political and does not care about the people. He will sell them out for a position; in fact, he already has sold them out.

4/13/06 *(Word about Husbands Blaming Wives)*

The Lord had me praying for marriages. He said that men, who are disobedient to God and blame their wives, have committed the same sin that Adam did. These are not godly men. These are men who won't take responsibility for their own actions.

4/13/06 *(Why God Chose King David)*

The Lord showed me that David was an imperfect man. God said that David would fulfill all His will (Acts 13:22). When God's will was complete, David desired to do even more. He wanted to build God a house (II Samuel 7:1-6). God appreciated David's zeal to please Him. David always desired to do above what God required. This is also how God operates. He desires to do exceedingly abundantly above all we ask or thing (Ephesians 3:20). This is also what God desires of us. God wants us to obey Him whole-heartedly so that He can bless us abundantly. After all, God did not withhold His Son; and He will not withhold any good thing from those who obey Him (Psalm 84:11). He will restore us to Eden and bless us with Abraham's blessings. Because He goes over and above, God expects us to give and to love over and above. The son must be like the Father.

4/13/06 *(My Heart's Victory Cry)*

My heart began crying out to God, "Thy kingdom has come. They will is done!!!"

4/14/06 *(God's Warning to Evil Men)*
The following prophecy came out of my spirit, *'__The plans of God will__ __go forth without hindrance. Those who interfere will be destroyed,__ __says the Lord. My servants who choose to obey will destroy you and__ __Satan will laugh at your demise. I am God, Yeah Almighty God and__ __will continue to reign. My kingdom is here. You will be destroyed.__ __You who continue to disobey and harm my servants. You will not go__ __unpunished. You will reap what you have sown.'__*

4/15/06 *(Song of God's Glory)*
'__We declare the Glory of God in the earth. His glory is here and His__ __justice will be seen in all the earth. Men will fear. Yeah men will__ __have great fear. For the Lord Almighty reigns now and forever.__ __Hallelujah!'__

'__God's Justice! God's Justice is here!! Evil is overturned. The__ __righteous will be blessed. Distress for the wicked!! God will reward__ __every man on this earth at this time. No one will go unpunished.'__

4/15/06 *(Dreams of God's Glory)*
All night long, I saw glimpses of God's Glory in the earth. There was much death, destruction and pain all about, but for the righteous there was peace and unspeakable joy. We saw the God of the Bible do what we always read about. He showed Himself strong!! Then I saw myself preaching in stadiums around the world: Multitudes and multitudes standing in line for days to hear from God. I saw several co-workers in the meetings. They were amazed that such miracles could happen through the hands of someone they knew. God was really praised in their eyes. He became BIG in their eyes.

4/15/06 *(More Dreams of Glory)*
The power of God swept through the stadiums at lightning speed. The Lord reminded of someone prophesying that my meetings will be bigger than other meetings. My spirit responded, of course the meetings will be bigger because God is bigger than mere men. I vowed years ago that I would not interfere with God's power in the earth. I would let Him come in a meeting and take complete control. People did not come because of me; they came because God showed up. It wasn't controlled or contrived and the people knew it. They wanted more of God.

4/21/06 *(Who is the Glorious Church?)*
During this season of glory, the Lord will reveal His glorious church (Ephesians 5:25-27). He told me years ago, *'**Anyone can be saved, but I am coming back for a glorious church.**'* He made it clear that His Glorious Church was filled with believers who obey only His command, regardless of the situation. These are the true sons of God.

4/30/06 *(Command to Possess the Land)*
The Lord again gave me the command, *'**Take the City!**'* This time He had me study the commands He gave to Moses and Joshua about possessing the land. God told them to utterly destroy the enemies of God. They were commanded to destroy all that breathed (Deuteronomy 20:16-17; Joshua 10:40). He told them to destroy the city, the people, their possessions, and animals. In some cases, they burnt the cities to the ground (Joshua 6:24; 7:25; 11:13). Joshua even stopped the sun from going down just so he could kill the last man (Joshua 10:12-14). The Lord commanded me three (3) separate times to take the city. We will reestablish God's Kingdom dynasty in Los Angeles, California, in the United States, and in the world, in Jesus' Name!

5/06/06 *(Command to Spare Not)*
The Word of the Lord came concerning my finances. He told me to, **'*Spare Not!*'** My rent was about to increase 22% and the Lord told me to pay the increase. I always sow my extra money into other ministries, but the Lord said that if I paid the increased rent, I would also be sowing into the kingdom. He said that if I helped the owner pay off his building, I would receive a harvest of buildings I need for my businesses.

5/14/06 (Word about Increase)
The Lord reminded me day and night that He is increasing me more and more. He told me to go grocery shopping. While I waited at the bus stop, He reminded me again about increase. My spirit leaped for joy and would not stop. I knew that God was supernaturally multiplying my finances. He told me to lay hands on my money and command it to increase. As soon as I opened my mouth the anointing was released and I started praising God even more! The Lord then told me to sow seed into several other people's lives and release the same increase on them! Hallelujah!!

5/15/06 (Hallelujah It's Increase Day!!)
Today is my 22% increase in rent. The Lord said that the money was invested into the kingdom before the payroll check was cut. I released it by faith when I received His Word about the purpose of the increase for my buildings. When it came time for me to pay, the manager was not available to take payment. I was not allowed to leave payment, no one on staff was authorized to take my payment, and the management was nowhere to be found. How dare that devil interfere with my increase from God! Truth be told, the managers did not show up because several tenants had threatened to report them for an illegal rent increase.

5/15/06 *(Increase Day, Continued)*
I did not care if it was illegal for the landlord to charge so much. I just wanted to obey God. I called my office and informed them that I needed to wait until I could pay rent and then I would report for work. At noon, the management still did not show. I left a written letter informing them of my intent to resign for another year at the increase rent. I requested that they give me instructions as to how I could make my payment. They responded the next day and my increase was manifested both in the spirit and in the earth.

6/01/06 (Standing on the Word for Increase)
The Lord kept me meditating on the word about increase. He had me sow gift sets of CD's to both of my brothers and my father for Father's day. I sent out the cards and gifts today rather than waiting like I usually do. I again thanked God for giving seed to sow and bread to eat, and thanked Him for increasing my seed sown.

6/06/06 *(Increase Is Here!!)*
My office manager informed me that a person from our department left unexpectedly and I would have to do overtime until they find a replacement. The extra one (1) hour overtime was to start the next day until further notice. I thanked God for the increase, but I did not expect to work more hours for it. Nevertheless, the increase is now here!

6/09/06 (Satan Attempts to Halt Increase)
I went to the bank to cash my paycheck like I often do at lunchtime. I went to the same teller I see every other week, but this time something was wrong.

6/09/06 *(Satan's Attempts, Continued)*
She went to see her manager and I asked what was wrong. They said they could not cash the check without my presenting a second photo id. I did not happen to have another id on me at the time. When I asked what had changed, the teller was embarrassed but said that was what the manager was requiring of me. Then I heard a black man yell at another teller about the same thing. The devil was at work that day, but he would not keep me from sowing my increase into the lives of others. On Saturday, I went to another location and the check was cashed without a problem.

7/4/06 (Fourth of July Solitude)
I would normally spend 4th of July at the Copeland Convention in Anaheim, but the Lord told me to conserve my energy and stay home. I was disappointed, but the Lord was directing my steps for His good, and mine.

7/07/06 (All the Increase is in Hand!!)
I cashed my check at the same teller, and I did not need a second photo id to cash my check. Imagine that! The anointing was flowing from my hand to the teller as she gave me the money. God is so good! That afternoon I called the bookseller and asked if the CD was still available. They could not find it, but the Lord said it was set-aside for me. He told me to just go there. After work I arrived at the bookstore cashier and asked for the CD reserved under my name. She found it after a brief look at what was reserved. God knew it was there all the time. On my way home, I knew that God ordained all I had done and things could not have failed.

7/15-30/06 *(Back To Writing This Book)*

This was a productive month for writing. I finished two whole chapters and started research for another. It's coming together just like the Lord planned.

7/25/06 *(Creating Memorial Stones)*

I was reading the book of Joshua and noticed that God had His people keep memorial stones (Joshua 4:6-7). They were told to remember how the Lord brought them across the Jordan River on dry land to possess the Promised Land. The stones would remind them when they were taking the land, that God went before them and dried up the Jordan, just like He parted the Red Sea under Moses' leadership (Exodus 14:21-31). Moses was dead, but God's promise was to be fulfilled under Joshua's leadership. It came up in my spirit that before I possess the land, I too would create memorial stones to remember how God brought me through what appeared to be insurmountable circumstances.

I took an ornate basket and put on the inside lid, 'I will remember the works of the Lord (Psalm 77:11).' I also used other scriptures on the lid: 'But you shall remember well, what the Lord your God did...so shall the Lord your God do.' (Deuteronomy 7:18-19); and 'Is anything too hard for God (Genesis 18:14)?' I created color cardboard stones. On each stone I mentioned a great work of God in my life and in the lives of those who I have touched. My faith was increased significantly after reviewing what God has done. I am fully persuaded that whatever God wants me to do, will be done within His power.

8/9/06 *(Walking in the Faith of Abraham)*
The Lord spoke to me about walking in the faith of Abraham. He reminded me of how when He told me to leave my family and go to Los Angeles. I picked up and went, having never seen LA. I just obeyed. God reminded of how I offered my son Jeffrey, like Abraham offered up Isaac, and God knew that I would do whatever He asked. He said that what made Abraham's faith significant was that he heard and obeyed the voice of God. The Lord told me that all Abraham had only a voice to follow. God said do something, and Abraham did whatever God said. Abraham was called the friend of God (James 2:23). This is what God requires of us today.

Many Christians will read the Bible, but have no idea what it means to follow the voice of God. The Lord told me that the Bible was never meant to be a substitute for man listening and following His voice. It was provide for our doctrine and instruction (II Timothy 3:15-17), but it was also provided so that we could understand and recognize the voice of God when He manifests Himself to us. The Lord recalled when Jesus told the Pharisees that they searched the scriptures because they thought that by doing so they would have eternal life (John 5:37-40), yet they refused to come to Him to receive that life. Our salvation is not in the Bible scriptures. Our salvation is in the person of Jesus Christ. We must know God (via Jesus), and follow His voice in order to have eternal life (John 17:3; 10:9). There are churches filled with people who have never met and nor surrendered to Jesus, so how can they be expected to walk in the faith of Abraham?

8/15/06 *(The Importance of Obeying God)*
The Lord spoke to me about the power of obeying His word. He spoke about how I broke the back of the devil each time I did what He told me to do. God said that when we obey, His will has absolute power over sin and Satan. He said we don't need to know how it works; we just need to obey. So, anytime we do something that is in disobedience to the Bible, or to His word spoken to our spirits, we open the door for the enemy to take us out. Ephesians 6:10-17 tells us that the Word of God is our armor. So, when we disobey that word, we have deliberately taken off the armor that was meant to protect our vital parts. I John 5:18 says that whoever is born of God does not practice sin, but he keeps himself attached to God's word (our armor) and that wicked one touches him not.

8/30/06 *(God's Will for Man on Earth)*
The Lord told me that the Bible is His written Will and Testament. There is an earthly and heavenly inheritance available under the terms of this will, but one must qualify in order to receive an inheritance. God is desperately seeking those who will read the will, obey the terms, and make themselves eligible to receive the inheritance. When Adam lost his inheritance, God found Noah to be next in line. Then there was Abraham, Isaac and Jacob. After Adam, none of these men could in themselves receive all the inheritance until Jesus came. Only Jesus was qualified to receive all that Adam lost on earth and share it with joint heirs who will also hear and obey God.

9/05/06 *(Possessing the Land)*
The Lord gave me another command to, ***'Take the City!'*** I asked that He give me specific orders on what I should do. I simply replied, "I will take Los Angeles for the kingdom, in Jesus' Name." I also went back to Joshua's battles and what he did when God told him to take the cities.

9/13/06 *(Waiting on God's Next Instruction)*
I was still waiting for the Lord to give detailed instruction about taking the city. The Holy Spirit told me to read Psalm 32 for my answer. The verse that spoke to my heart reads, *'I will instruct you and teach you in the way you shall go: I will guide you with my eye (Psalm 32:8).'*

9/15/06 *(I Believe the Impossible)*
I was praying in my sleep unaware of what was going on when the Holy Spirit spoke, ***'All things are possible to him that believes (Mark 9:23).'*** I responded, "Lord I believe, help my unbelief." I immediately got up looked for this scripture and others in the Bible about believing the impossible. I started praying that I believed the impossible and had absolute faith in God. This prayer was feeding my spirit to overflow.

At lunchtime I went to the bank to cash my check and behind the teller station was an easel. The words on the easel brought me to tears, it read, 'All things are possible to those that believe. So with faith our goals are met.' My spirit went into overload and the anointing of God fell so heavy on me that I wanted to sit down in order to keep from falling down. I knew that God was doing something; I just did not know what.

9/18/06 *(Another Command to Possess the Land)*
During prayer, the Lord shouted these words to my spirit, '*Take the City, Take the State, Take the Nation, Take the World!! Utterly destroy the enemies of the kingdom—leave none breathing. Break down their altars. Tear up their groves. Burn their idols. Do not marry them. Do not covenant with them. Utterly destroy them that you may live peaceable in the land that I promised to give you!*' I agreed to do all that the Lord commanded, in the Name of Jesus.

9/20/06 *(Withdrawing From My Heavenly Account)*
I was listening to a CD of a pastor who spoke about how to reap the seeds we have sown over the years. During one of his teachings, he mentioned that we had a heavenly account with things laid up for us in this lifetime. The Holy Spirit let me know that I needed to make a full review of my account; which included everything I have sown and given up for the kingdom's sake. So, I put together an account ledger and listed everything the Lord told me to do and what He said I could expect because of my obedience. Then I found a scripture to support every item on my ledger. When I finished, I had seven (7) typed pages of things I was expecting from heaven; not when I get there, but things I can expect in this lifetime on earth.

The Lord also brought to memory things that the enemy took from me by force. Back in the day, the Lord had me sow these things. At first, I thought it was so I would hold no offense for them being stolen from me. The Lord made it clear back then that what He would give me in the future would be so much more than what was taken, and what He would give me, no man could take from me. Even my job was a seed. God let me know that I was sowing my time as a faithful employee in another man's business, performing my duties as unto God, doing the will of God from the heart. As a result, I would reap a harvest of faithful employees for my companies, who will also perform their duties as unto God. My eyes were opened!

285

9/06 *(Heavenly Account, Continued)*
Even my marriage that ended in divorce was a seed. It was the Lord that told me to leave because my life was in danger. Now I am entitled to reap a new marriage to a godly man and God promised the return of my son, and even more sons. Now, I realize, when I gave up my life to follow God, He invested it in the kingdom for me. And now it's time to make a withdrawal from my account. I meditated on my heavenly account and lifted it to God in prayer, fully expecting to get all I asked and more.

9/21-30/06 *(Confirmation on Withdrawal)*
The Lord repeatedly confirmed by His Spirit that I could expect my withdrawal to come forth. Every time He brought it up, I thanked God for bringing forth a full withdrawal from my heavenly account.

9/25/06 *(Preparing to Receive My Withdrawal)*
There was a sense of urgency to receive from my heavenly account. The Lord had me finish the addresses of the recipients for the foundation. I was eager to distribute the remaining $500,000. The Lord also let me know that it was time to finish the nonprofit business plans. I also wanted the money before Christmas. It would be the perfect gift for so many who are in need.

9/28/06 *(Prayer for Heavenly Account)*
I woke with a concern in my spirit that the devil would try to interfere with my account withdrawal. I asked the Lord to reveal if anyone or anything was in the way of my withdrawal coming forth. He responded by saying that His Word was sent out like a *'**Mine sweeper to destroy the hidden/deep traps of the enemy.**'* I thanked the Lord for watching over my account request and knew that money was on the way.

10/1-15/06 *(Much Work on Business Plan)*

Putting together the business plan for the relief organization consumed most of my time during these days. The more I wrote the more questions I encountered. These questions were submitted to God in prayer. He gave me ideas and plans I had not considered. It has been an enjoyable project to plan for this trust and other businesses that God has developed.

10/1-2/06 *(Prayer for Bin Laden)*

For two days straight, the Lord had me praying intensely for Osama Bin Laden. During that time of prayer the Lord warned, *'**War is Here!**'* No further utterances were forth coming. No instructions were given.

10/04/06 *(Heavenly Account Manifestation)*

The Lord responded to my claim from my heavenly account. He said, *'**It's here. I will restore all things to you and recompense you for pain and suffering for my name's sake.**'* He also let me know that I pleased Him. The Lord told me that I was in *'**full obedience**'* to His Word.

I began to praise God. My spirit replied, "Thine Hand stretched forth to judge my enemies and send me a blessing." Praises filled my heart to overflow.

10/5-7/06 *(The Lord Called Forth the Vision)*

My spirit has been flooded day and night with the word that the Lord spoke to me about the creation of outreach centers. I called the center and all its needed resources into being according to the word and will of God. I thanked God for showing forth His glory in that which He planned for the center.

10/7-8/06 *(The Lord Called Forth another Vision)*
Again, my spirit was flooded day and night with God's word concerning the creation of the companies. I call the corporation, its subsidiaries and auxiliary companies, all projects, needed staff, volunteers, resources, buildings, transportation, all stock inventories. I called forth all the financial resources necessary to start, sustain and perpetuate strong economy with all budgets sufficiently filled. I called it all forth in the Name of Jesus, to glorify God the Father, who destined its existence before the foundation of the world.

10/8/06 *(Curse on Amalek)*
In wake of the calling forth of what the Lord has given me, and His order to take the land, He reminded me that Amalek was lurking in the distance and would try to ambush those going in to possess the land. Amalek was cursed by God (Numbers 24:20) because they ambushed the Children of Israel as they headed to the Promised Land. Amalek had claimed the land illegally. The Lord vowed to war with Amalek from generation to generation. He said He would blot Amalek out of remembrance from under heaven (Exodus 17:14-16). I spoke those words of God in prayer concerning Amalek and vowed to blot this imposter out from under heaven. He will not prevent any of God's people from possessing the land that was promised to them.

10/12-14/06 *(Command to Write the Book)*
The Lord gave me instructions for my time off from work. I had planned on finishing the business plans, but He told me to write this book instead.

10/17-18/06 *(Command Concerning War)*
My spirit heard repeatedly, ***'War is here!'*** This time I got instructions to, ***'Prepare yourselves for disaster.'***

10/21/06 *(Victory over the Bear)*
While praying in the spirit, the Lord brought up my heavenly account on more than one occasion. Then I saw this big mean bear taking swipes at me. I took what looked like a cave man's club and beat that bear senseless. He fell to the ground dead. The angels came with a sword for me to take his heads and I said, "No!" I took out a long knife and jumped on the bear's back. I split his scull opened and ripped him all the way down the back and started to gut him. The angels were perplexed. I replied, "I want a bear skin rug for my floor. So every time I walk in my house, I can step on his head and remind myself of today's victory."

10/21/06 *(Heaven's Pouring Out Blessings)*
After the bear vision, I saw numerous shafts opening from heaven pouring out what looked like solid gold coins wrapped in gift packaging. Gold was pouring out so fast that I had several lines of people carrying huge wheel barrels. When one wheel barrel was full, the next person would come. I was somewhat frustrated because the people were hesitant about taking the gold that I gave them. Some were in disbelief of what was happening to them. Others could not figure out what to do with the gold. While these concerns were apparent, I did not stop bringing more people and barrels, because I knew that if heaven is pouring out blessings, I needed vessels to capture all of it. I did not want the blessing to stop like the widow who ran out of vessels and the oil stopped running (II Kings 4:1-7). There was no way I was going to let this blessing stop on account of a few ignorant people who could not figure out what to do with God's blessings.

10/21/06 *(Beauty from Ashes)*

Today, I went to the Natural History Museum in Los Angeles. There was a display entitled, "Chaparral". It talked about the unusual plant life in Southern California that relies on forest fires to germinate. The Lord told me to sit and listen to the videotaped story about these plants. Most plants can germinate and bring forth buds under normal seasonal changes, but in Los Angeles and other areas in the state of California, there are plants whose seedlings cannot break forth from their kernels without intense heat generated from a forest fire. They actually need the rain washed ash in order to grow. Within a few short weeks after a major fire has left a terrain charred and barren, beautiful seedlings appear.

Then the Lord explained that He uses fire to purify in order to bring forth new life. In Isaiah 4:3-4, the Lord wanted to bring Jerusalem back to holiness, but He needed to get rid of the filth and purge the blood from the midst of the city. So God sent the spirit of judgment and the spirit of burning (fire). Likewise, the Lord will bring judgment and fire upon the United States to purify our filth and purge the innocent blood that was shed in our midst. And from the devastation and barrenness, God will give to those who mourn, beauty for ashes, the oil of joy for mourning, the garment of praise for the spirit of heaviness; that they might be called the trees of righteousness, the planting of the Lord, that he might be glorified (Isaiah 61:3).

10/22/06 *(Another Word on Heavenly Account)*

The Lord said that the money and other things were coming, *'early this season.'* I got confirmation on how to distribute gifts to those on my list, Willy Wonka[19] style. It would be a golden ticket with the inscription: *Thanks for Everything from Paula!!*

10/23/06 *(Prayer for the Nation)*
Out of my spirit came these words, 'We take the City of Los Angeles for the Kingdom. We utterly destroy the enemies of God. We tear down their altars and their groves and burn their idols. We don't marry them. We don't covenant with them. We destroy them so that we can live peaceably in the Land you promised to give us Lord. Amen.'

10/23/06 *(Vision about California Politicians)*
Governor Schwarzenegger was heavy on God's heart. The Lord is maneuvering him to do great things. I saw the Lord turning him in ways the governor never thought he'd go. God has exalted him as a man of power, distinction and honor in the eyes of the state and the nation. He is a mighty man of valor. The Terminator[20] series was only a warm up for what God would call the governor to do. I also saw Villaraigosa fail miserably. He is in politics to exalt himself. The Lord is blessing the governor and his wife because they have a heart for the people.

10/24/06 *(Word about Nonprofits)*
The Lord told me to talk to staff at the California Apartment Association about gathering housing data in Los Angeles. He also told me to make an appointment to see specific individuals at the Los Angeles Homeless Services Authority. He told me to go during the day next week. I forgot that I had asked for November 2-3 for vacation. The Lord reminded me that there was more research to do in working on the housing proposal for the area.

10/24/06 *(Prayer for Co-Workers)*
The Lord gave me numerous visions during prayer. Several of my co-workers were in need of prayer. The Lord also told me that they were all part of the kingdom. He even let me know that one of the men at the office was praying for my protection. The Lord called him my armor bearer.

10/27/06 *(Intense Prayer at Work)*
The Spirit of the Lord fell heavy upon my heart around noon. Rather than going to the bank and running errands, I shut myself in an office and prayed. It was not only prayer, but also heavy travail came forth for the company and for one co-worker. Something broke in the spirit after about forty minutes. My co-worker was very sad and I picked it up in the spirit and God intervened.

10/28-29/06 *(Intense Prayer for Nation)*
I cast my absentee ballot this weekend and went into prayer for elections around the nation. My ballot was my seed for a righteous victory. God's hand is upon our city, state and nation. I declared His Kingdom operation in our city, state and nation.

10/30/06 *(Vision of Housing Program)*
The Lord clarified more on the housing program. He let me know that this project must be presented to both ministries and corporations. He showed a willingness on both sides to solve a problem that the city and state are not equipped to do. Ministers appreciated working with corporations, especially housing experts. Corporations enjoyed giving to a nonprofit that was solving a public problem. Many corporations gave tithes to this project and were blessed abundantly as a result.

10/31/06 (*Corporate Assistance with Research*)
I spoke with my General Manager about the housing research project. He was very supportive and said there were some sources of information he could give me. The key in our conversation was his question about whether poor people were willing to leave their lifestyles to take on a job and move into a decent home. As he spoke, the Lord reminded me about the dream of the wheel barrels of gold. I shared the dream with him, but knew I had even more work to do in this area. My desire is to reach those who want to change. But I remember that those with the gold wanted to change and were overwhelmed and shocked that someone responded.

10/31/06 (*Prayer for Gold Vision*)
The vision of the wheel barrels of gold was heavy on my heart. I asked the Lord to reveal to me how to handle those who needed wealth, but were unable to accept it. These people could easily go from sleeping on the streets one day to sleeping in a beautiful apartment the next day. How could people be prepared for the change? Then the Lord reminded about the outreach centers.

They are designed to be rehabilitation centers. The Lord had given me a series of programs to help the transformation from a downtrodden mentality, to that of a prosperous new life in Jesus. In addition to these programs, He said there will be training and personal counselors to help people set up bank accounts, do household budgeting and other normal functions that will be expected of them in their new life.

11/2-5/06 (*Time with the Lord Called*)

The Lord called me off work for a few days to write books, do research and pray. He placed me on a modified fast while I was on vacation. He did the same this time as well. Time was spent praying for elections, my projects, the war, and my first installment from my heavenly account.

11/2/06 (*Daytime Prayer Session*)

The Lord burdened me to pray from 8am until about noon. I prayed heavily for my co-workers. The Spirit of the Lord took me throughout the office mentioning specific people and His plans for their lives. One of my former co-workers also came up in prayer. The Lord told me to call her, and reminded me that I had her cell phone number.

Also during this prayer time I saw visions of people bringing money to me to do the work God is calling me to do. It's not what I fully expected, but the Lord called it an, *'__Early Withdrawal__'* from my heavenly account. The Lord said it was my reward for being faithful to the work He gave me to do. I gladly received whatever the Lord desired to send.

11/03/06 (*Prayer for National Elections*)

The Lord had me dedicate several hours to pray for the elections occurring next week. He showed me President Bush, Governor Schwarzenegger, and various others. The Lord was speaking, but nothing was given in my understanding. He also spoke about the upcoming war and terrorism. God was setting the stage for what it to come.

11/03/06 *(A Reason to Praise)*

I was writing this book and the Lord had me write about King Jehoshaphat and the victory in the Valley of Blessing (II Chronicles 20:26-27). The Lord filled me with joy by declaring victory over the enemies that have plotted to take away the possessions that He gave me. Not only did He destroy them, but also I got the spoils of the battle. Praise the Lord; for His mercy endures forever!

11/04/06 *(Multiple Dreams about Babies)*

Last night I had a series of dreams about babies. The first was a dream about a baby of about two or three months old. I was bathing it and talking about its purpose in God. The dream was so vivid, that I remember the feel of the little fingers and toes in my hands. This was the second time I have had this dream.

Then another dream came where I was holding many babies of different nationalities. They all had different looks and sizes, and all very happy to receive my attention. After the dream immediately came another. I still saw different babies, this time I prayed over them and lifted them in my hands to dedicate them to God. This dream repeated itself, but rather than dedicating them to God with words, I placed each baby in Jesus' hand. And, yet another dream came where I saw myself picking up babies and giving them directly to the Lord. I was picking them up carefully and quickly because there were so many. I sensed in my spirit that these were abandoned babies. Then I saw, as if a camera were pulling out and widening the view, babies that were on a conveyer belt ready to be disposed. My heart ached as I watched myself scooping up the babies in my arms at a rapid pace and making sure none went past my grasp on the conveyer belt.

11/04/06 *(Babies, Continued)*

These series of dreams ended with my holding the same baby and finishing the bath. I did not ask the Lord to interpret the dream, but I committed it to prayer. I saw the arms of Jesus filled with these babies and a smile was on His face. In past dreams, babies represented ministries that were not fully developed. Then I remembered that some of the babies that I took off the conveyer belt were walking and talking, some were newborn, and none were over the age of five years old. Whether these were ministries, or real babies not does matter. What does matter is that they were rescued and placed in the arms of Jesus where they would live forever.

11/04/06 *(Vision of the Crucifixion)*

I was praying in the spirit and was pressing against demonic forces that were trying to defeat me. I never felt close to defeat, but in my spirit, I wondered how long before God destroys those who intentionally harass me. Then I saw Jesus carrying the cross. I barely recognized a human form. He was so covered with ripped and deformed flesh. I looked into His swollen eyes and wept. All I could do was thank Him for taking on so much for me. The least I could do is endure so that His death and resurrection would not be in vain. After the vision, I heard the words in my spirit telling me to look to Jesus, who endured the cross and despised the shame, lest I become weary and faint in my mind (Hebrews 12:2-3).

11/04/06 (*Word about Disaster to Come*)
The Lord had me study how Joseph was led of God to deal with the famine on the earth. While reading I realized that when the famine was at its worse, the money failed in Egypt. There was little food to buy, and no money to buy what was available. The people gave their cattle, then their lands, and finally, their lives as slave labor just to be able to eat and live. When the money failed, they exchanged what they had left (Genesis 47:13-20). It hit my spirit like a bolt of lightning; this is why the Lord had me create the relief organizations. Then the Lord spoke, *'**Money will fail in the United States.**'* I had a greater understanding of how severe conditions would become.

11/05/06 (*Message about Change*)
Twice today the Lord said to me, *'**Prepare to Leave.**'* I don't envision leaving LA, but I knew He was telling me to prepare to leave my job. There was much preparation needed before disaster comes.

11/05/06 (*Intense Prayer for the Nation*)
I was led into hours of prayer for the nation. The Lord took me by the spirit to speak with President Bush about what was to come. He also showed me several actors that will be key players in the emergency work. There was one in particular that comes up every time I pray. I asked the Lord what the purpose was for him being so close to what I was doing. The Lord said that he was a business and a ministry partner called alongside me to work.

11/06/06 (*Prayer for the Office*)

I was in travail over my co-workers. The Lord is moving mightily upon their lives. God identified one of them as being my armor bearer; one who will pray and cover my back. While praying, the Lord showed that trouble would break out on the grounds during war. The staff must be fortified now, in order to withstand what is coming. I saw a gunman (probably not a terrorist), staging an act against the office. There was much fear, but the Vice President stepped up to the plate. The outcome was not revealed, but I kept them in prayer until the Holy Spirit released me. I will not be there when trouble hits, but the presence of God will abide there.

11/06/06 (*Reflections on the War to Come*)

A heavy spirit consumed my heart while at work. I remembered the vision about what was to happen at the office. I thought how blessed these people are to have me working for them. God sent me ahead to protect them from trouble to come, and now they go about their lives totally oblivious to the war that is upon their heels.

I see so much and understanding the things that God says so clearly now. People around me are totally ignorant and unconcerned that they are not right with God. My thoughts and feelings, on the other hand, are centered on God and His will for my life. It is my life, my passion to live for God. I want nothing more in life! He is my all. I don't belong with these people on earth. They are so feeble and mentally unstable, and so ungrateful to God. Yet, He loves and protects them because of my obedience. This is why I love God. He is good and His mercy endures forever even upon those who do not know Him.

11/09/06 *(War, Continued)*

I am a reflection of God's love. The fact that I am alive is enough to be grateful for, but also I have a reason to live now. I know my exact purpose for being alive. My life has been totally transformed. I had many days where there was nothing but darkness. Now I see the light and it is wonderful!! Yes, darkness is covering the earth, and more darkness is coming. The light within me is greater than any darkness that comes upon me. Greater is He that is in me, than he that is in the world; therefore I am more than a conqueror in whatever situation besets me.

11/06/06 *(Heavy Burden for Prayer for Nation)*

At about 4:30 pm, I knew that I should be praying. I heard the words, *'perfect peace'* in my spirit. I opened my Bible at my desk and read Isaiah 26:1-4, which reads, "We have a strong city; salvation will God appoint for walls and bulwarks. Open ye the gates, that the righteous nation which keepeth the truth may enter in. Thou wilt keep him in perfect peace, whose mind is stayed on thee: because he trusteth in thee. Trust ye in the Lord forever: for in the Lord Jehovah is everlasting strength." I continued to read through chapter 30 about God's vengeance and salvation.

11/06/06 *(Word about the Elections)*

While riding the bus home, I began to quietly travail in the spirit. I kept hearing, *'justice will be done at the polls.'* The Holy Spirit brought to my memory that the Lord said that justice meant fire in the sky and on the earth. I had a knowing that God would execute justice. Glory Hallelujah! In my spirit I heard *'Justice'* echoing over and over again. My spirit began rejoicing on the bus. I again heard, *'victory at the polls.'*

11/07/06 *(Election Day Thoughts)*

There was no significant prayer in my spirit for this day. I did have frustration that the Democrats have taken the position as the antichrist party. The Republicans have long stood for godly values and have come short of performing those values themselves. Why can't we stand for godly values in both parties? I was concerned that the Democrats have two black preachers in their leadership, and not once has either of them stood publicly for God. If they had, how different things would be at this time of election. As it stands now, if Democrats win nationally, they will vote against what God loves. God is bipartisan; yet Americans have made Him a Republican. How sad.

11/08/06 *(God's Team Still United in Spirit)*

Election victory for Governor Schwarzenegger was eminent. The Lord reminded me that he and President Bush were in key positions for the coming war. God will use them mightily. Nancy Pelosi on the other hand opposes God. The Lord had me praying for her. He says that she is *'**misdirected in her thoughts and actions.**'*

11/08/06 *(Vision about President Bush and Waterloo)*

I had a vision twice about President Bush. There was no detail except for the military outfit he wore. He had a red military jacket and grayish pants. There was a white powdered wig on his head, and he was holding up a powerful sword. My first thought was that this was the image of George Washington, when the Holy Spirit said, *'**Waterloo.**'*

11/08/06 *(Waterloo, Continued)*
The Holy Spirit told me that the president had a mighty sword in his hand. Then I heard the words, *'War of 1812.'* Vaguely I recalled the 1812 overture by Tchaichovsky.[21] I had no earthly clue what the Lord was telling me. I got up and researched Waterloo and the war of 1812 on the Internet. I thought that America fought Britain in 1812, but then I found out that Napoleon invaded Russia in 1812 and was defeated at Waterloo in 1815. I also realized that Tchaikovsky's 1812 Overture depicted the defeat of Napoleon in Russia. So, the common denominator in what the Lord showed me was Napoleon. Now, I had to know if God was comparing the defeat of Napoleon to what was to happen to our president.

When I went back into prayer, the Holy Spirit told me plainly that this was George Bush's Waterloo. Then He said the most unexpected thing, *'This is my plan.'* He said that God was victorious with Bush. The sword that Bush upheld was the Word of God. The nations will encompass around Bush and revolt against God. The Lord repeated, *'This is my plan.'* He revealed that President Bush was armed with the Word and the nations would turn against him for the Glory of God. The Lord will strike Americans, and every nation that comes against Bush!! His Hand is on the president for our nation's good. The ways of the Lord are certainly not our ways. We cannot conceive of what God is doing through the lives of those who will obey the word. It was necessary for the Lord to have George Bush as president during this season. Throughout the Bible, as long as the king of God's people yielded to God, the people were victorious. The leaders did not have to be perfect, they just had to know how to turn to God in prayer and ask for His help.

11/08/06 *(Waterloo, Continued)*

George Bush has indeed done so and had publicly said that he talks to God about the state of our nation. Because He honored God before men, God will honor President Bush when the enemies flood our soil to overtake our nation.

I now declare that in righteousness American shall be established. We shall be far from oppression, because we will not fear; and far from terror for it shall not come near us. Surely our enemies will gather together against us, but not by God. Whoever gathers together against America shall fall for our sakes. No weapon formed against us shall prosper, and every tongue that rises against us in judgment, we shall condemn. This is the heritage of the servants of the Lord, and their righteousness is of me, says God (Isaiah 54:14-17). America will be saved from the plots of the enemy and we will live to glorify God!

11/09/06 *(Vision of Knocking Through a Door)*

I was praying about money coming when the Lord showed me knocking at a door. I was knocking with a large log that had demons tied to it. Every time I hit the door, it caused a gaping hole, and the demons heads were used as a battering ram. I kept hitting the door and making more and more holes until I could walk completely through the opening. On the other side of the door was a gold refinery coming out of heaven. Gold was just beginning to trickle through the shafts coming from heaven.

11/09/06 *(Door, Continued)*

I began speaking to everything that was holding up production in the refinery. I even asked the Lord to search my heart to see if there was anything I was doing to hinder the production. Nothing was revealed, but the gold started to flow a bit faster, but I told the Lord that I needed trucks full just to sow into the lives of others in the kingdom. I came out of prayer knowing that God would honor my request; it was just a matter of His timing. The truckloads of gold were on the way.

11/10/06 *(Confirmation of Money Coming)*

While in prayer, I had flashes of images in the spirit of money being in my possession right now. The images flashed so quickly that if I had not been paying attention, I would have missed them. Then I was reminded of the Lord telling me to prepare to leave my job. Three and one half years ago, He told me that I would leave my job when my settlement check cleared the bank. So, this means that my check must be on the way very soon. Thank you God!!

11/10/06 *(Enemy Distractions Set Against Me)*

The enemy sent hoards against me to distract me from what is to come. I prayed in the spirit until the darkness broke. I recalled these words; he that regards the clouds shall not reap (Ecclesiastes 11:4). The Lord let me know that the enemy wanted me to be distracted and not focused on pulling in my financial harvest. I rebuked every hindrance and distraction that was sent to me. I have sown faithfully, and the Lord said I have won many battles, therefore the spoils and the harvest are my and I receive them now, in the Name of Jesus!

11/11/06 (*Focus on the Harvest*)
I thanked God much this day for the financial harvest that is coming my way. The hindrances were gone for sure.

11/11/06 (*Warning about Coming Disaster*)
The Lord told me to prepare for disaster and stock up on water and a few can food items. I immediately obeyed.

11/12/06 (*Another Confirmation of Money Coming*)
I was speaking to my father about money coming soon. When I hung up the phone, the glory of the Lord filled my spirit and I saw the check in my hand, and my spirit soared with praise. It was as though I was releasing the money from my spirit. I cried and screamed and saw myself holding the check at my office. A co-worker asked what was wrong and I showed him the check and declared that my divorce settlement check finally came. I saw myself going immediately to the bank next door and asking them to open an account. It is just a matter of moments before that vision would be a reality. God is good and His word is true. I receive my financial harvest and glorify God with all that is within me!

11/13/06 (*Instructions for Money Coming*)
The Spirit of the Lord reminded of what I was supposed to do when my money comes. I saw it all as if it were already happening. My first business account to open was for the publishing company. The Lord also reminded me of the distribution list for my book. He told me to rework the publishing budget to increase the staff to three people: a web designer, a publisher and editor. Also I was to include budget for a graphics designer.

11/15/06 (*Directions Given for Publishing Website*)
The Lord had me to prepare details for website. He also told me to create all the storyboards that would be needed for the flash media presentations.

11/16/06 (*God's Team Coming Together*)
My prayers for workers were starting to be answered. The Lord gave me names for His team of players. I have no idea what most of them would do in my company.

11/18-30/06 (*Book Research Completed*)
The Spirit of the Lord urged me to complete the appendices for The War Journal. There was much time spent in the library rechecking sources, which also lead to more research about our nation's Christian roots; and the religious persecution in England.

12/05/06 (*Money Confirmed Again*)
Early morning prayer was made for deliverance for my brothers in ministry. They are eager for God's will to be manifested in their lives. I know in my spirit that He will set them free from all bondage because their hearts are turned to heaven for help. During evening prayer, the Lord proclaimed, *'It's here!'* He said that my money was here.

12/7/06 (*God's Judgment on Our Enemies*)
The Lord woke me from a deep sleep with these words, *'**Judgment, it is here! It is done!**'* Then the Lord showed that everyone who stands in our way of completing His will would either be moved or destroyed in His judgment.

12/8/06 (*Word about Truth Seekers*)

While at work, I was in the midst of explaining that God was doing something special through the company. Many of us were being drawn together for prayer and talk about spiritual things. Some were Muslim, Jew, Christians, yet at this point in time; we are all hearing God speak the same thing. We don't agree on religious doctrine, but we are in agreement about God's having a purpose for us to fulfill. As I was speaking, I was also questioning in my heart how this was possible. The Lord spoke the words, '***Truth Seekers.***' Later that evening, the Lord woke me from sleep and spoke about truth seekers. He said that no matter where one begins, if he or she diligently seeks after the truth, they would always find Him. The Lord gathered together those of us who seek to do God's truth. He is revealing truth by His Spirit, apart from religious doctrine.

12/9-10/06 (*Taking Up My Cross*)

The Lord pulled me aside and talked to me about being a '***human shield***' against the enemies of God. He spoke about martyrdom and separating from this world and aligning myself with the one to come. Spiritually, it was if He was cutting all ties of this world off my life. The Lord spoke to me about an evil power in which one is willing to give all to die for Allah. Christians are called to be a living sacrifice, holy and acceptable to God (Romans 12:1). We are called to give up all for God. This is true martyrdom. We live to save other's lives from eternal death. The Lord is preparing me to deflect the evils of the jihad by standing in the full power of the Holy Spirit. He wants me and all believers to be a shield against the works of darkness that will be directed toward our nation.

12/9-10/06 *(Cross, Continued)*
While writing, I was reminded of Hebrew 12:22-25, which speaks, about salvation bringing us to Mount Zion, to the city of the living God, to the heavenly Jerusalem, and innumerable company of angels, to the church of the firstborn, and to the spirits of just men made perfect, and to Jesus the mediator of a new covenant. I am seated together with Jesus in the heavenly places (Ephesians 2:4-10).

I have come into a new position that is greater than any force that rules this present world. It is in this new place in God that I live, and move, and have my being (Acts 17:28). My spirit constantly bears witness that I am the child of God and therefore an heir of God and joint heir with Christ (Romans 8:14-18). Therefore I am to suffer like Jesus suffered in order to be glorified with Him.

The same spirit that raised Jesus from the dead will quicken my mortal body to complete the will of God even through suffering. I am being moved to become dead to self and alive only to Christ: utterly and completely sold out for the kingdom; no turning back; an obedient soldier for Christ.

12/11-24/06 *(Special Ministry Projects)*
The Lord directed me to perform special individual ministry for several people. It was an intense time of intercession, Bible lessons and personal times of sharing. The Lord is positioning people for what is quickly to come upon the earth.

12/24/06 (*A Calm Quiet Christmas Eve*)
I was scheduled to work the holiday rush for a friend of mine, but there were few customers. She let me go shopping and asked that I return or call to see if her situation had changed. While at the Beverly Center, I also noticed there were few customers and very little traffic. It was about 11am. By 1pm, I stopped by her store one last time and decided to go home. On the way home, I noticed that not only were the streets quiet, but the spirit realm was also quiet. There was none of the typical Los Angeles demonic activity. I questioned in my spirit what was going on and the Holy Spirit spoke, **'*It is the quiet before the storm.*'** After arriving home, my heart was heavy for prayer, and for a few hours I prayed about the approaching storm.

12/25/06 (*Another Day of Work*)
The entire day was spent in intercession for various ministries. The remainder of the day was spent writing notes for a new book. The Lord spoke much about how He communicates with men on earth.

12/29/06 (*Word for the New Year*)
While quietly praying in my spirit at work, the Lord gave me a personal word for 2007. He told me to stand on Isaiah 49 for the New Year. These passages confirm God's call on my life. It also confirms the restoration of all things to me, and the satisfactory completion of my call on earth. He reassures me in this word that no one who waits on Him will be ashamed.

12/31/06 (*Exhortation to Victory*)
My spirit was heavy with prayer for hours. I saw my ministry brothers also praying. Two were involved in intense intercession; another was about to open a door that the Lord had placed before him. The Lord was moving upon all of us. Then I heard in my spirit, *'**full throttle lift off into orbit.**'*

I saw tremendous spiritual activity that caused us all to move miraculously in the things of God. He told me not to worry about detractors or hindrances because at the speed we are traveling, it will burn off all the evil in the ascent. As we moved upward with supernatural speed, everything else fell with an equally powerful plunge downward. Then He told me to, *'**celebrate the victory!**'* I saw my ministry and brothers all in the flow of God's will. God's Kingdom was rising to power, as all others were coming down and being destroyed. It was fantastic!!

THE WAR JOURNAL
YEAR 2007: *A Day Of Rest*
For The People Of God

THE WAR JOURNAL
YEAR 2007: *A Day Of Rest For The People Of God*

1/1/07 (*Word about A Day of Rest*)
The Lord spoke to my heart about calling the 2007 Journal Chapter, **'*A Day Of Rest For The People Of God.*'** When I first heard this, I was perplexed. My body and spirit seemed overworked and God was talking about a day of rest; which is what I thought I needed more than anything. Then I remembered that Hebrews 4:10 says that one who entered into God's rest has also ceased from doing his own works just like God did from His. God did not rest because He was tired; He rested because all of His works in the earth were completed.

Then it dawned on me that if God called me from my mother's womb as Isaiah 49:1 says, then everything in my life and call was completed in God, when He completed all His works at creation. Ephesians 1:1-12 basically says the same thing. It says that God chose us and predestined us to be His children. It continues to say that He had kept us hidden in Him (Isaiah 49:2) and equipped us with wisdom and grace to be the praise of His glory. All of this was hidden in a mystery before the foundation of the world, for each of us who are called of God.

This all has new meaning for me if God's will for my life was completed and is being revealed by His wisdom via His Spirit, then why do I need to continue in my own works? If I know His will, then resting in that will is all I need to do. My only labor should be to let God have complete control of my life by obedience to His word, knowing that there is nothing that I am going through that He does not know about and He has not perfected. Everything in my life is naked and open before His eyes. So I can boldly go to the throne of grace and obtain mercy and grace in my time of need (Hebrews 4:10-16).

1/7-17/07 *(More Extra Ministry Work)*

This New Year started not with fasting and prayer, but with numerous assignments that the Lord said had to be completed immediately. Prophecies came forth out of my spirit at rapid-fire speed for several people. There was a sense of urgency to get the messages to them.

1/5-14/07 *(Word about Publishing)*

The Spirit of the Lord told me in November to get my storyboards ready for production. He told me that I needed to interview a specific artist no later than January 15th. The storyboards were done in fast sketching and must be put in presentation form for the artist. We scheduled to meet on Sunday January 14th which gives me about one week to prepare.

1/12/07 **(*Word about the Artist)*

I had just two days to finish the sketches, scripts etc for Sunday's presentation and the pressure is on. The minute that I stepped off the property at work, the Spirit of the Lord fell on me and began speaking about the artist. He said, *'it's all about Yvon.'* I knew at that moment that the Lord was moving upon the heart of the artist.

1/14/07 *(Meeting with Artist a Success)*

Meeting day arrived and God took control. The artist saw what I had prepared and said they could do it. They just wanted me to give them a budget to work with. Yvon and I were on the same frequency at all times. The meeting lasted one half hour. At around three o'clock that afternoon, the Holy Spirit said, *'they're in.'* I knew that they were ready to work on the project. My heart soared with rejoicing.

1/15/07 (*Artist Confirmed*)
I called the Yvon's wife to thank her for setting up the meeting. She confirmed what the Lord had told me the day before. They are ready to work with me; I just need to bring the budget to get started. My heart rejoiced even more when I got this confirmation.

1/18-19/07 (*Solemn Intercession*)
After such elation with getting the artist on board, the Lord took me to a strange low place in intercession. For the next few days, He spoke to me about the faith of Isaac, but He would not explain why. God asked if I could let Him bind me with cords and place me on a burning altar with a knife to my neck. He asked if I had the faith that Isaac had in his father Abraham. Again, the Lord would not explain why. I don't ever recall responding with a yes or no; I just kept wondering why He was asking me this question. In my heart I knew that He is preparing me for something ugly.

1/20/07 (*Rebuke from the Elders*)
I was awaken from sleep with several renowned ministers rebuking me. These were people I knew, but their attacks took me by surprise. The word of God says not to rebuke an elder, but I knew that if they continued to attack, something had to be done. I turned my head from their faces and asked the Lord to talk to these men of God. Their words and actions were shameful and uncalled for. They accused me of hideous sins and asked the Lord to send wrath against me. I don't know what they were talking about, but I knew that I had successfully blocked their attacks, but I was still furious.

1/21/07   *(Attack Ensued)*

The attacks continued and this time I struck back in anger. I was appalled that they would ignorantly strike me and not inquire of the Lord first, but they persisted and so did I. I distinctly remember a vision the Lord showed me twice and I was not paying attention. The Lord showed me and a few faithful soldiers isolated in the midst of enemy territory. The Holy Spirit reminded me that these ministers were supposed to rescue us, but instead, left us, *'**to die on the battlefield.**'*

1/21/07 *(Final Death Blow)*

The fighting continued and their ugly accusations were hurled in the spirit. My spirit blew some deadly blows in defense. The men who were called to protect me were now trying to destroy me. This is crazy. I don't understand what is going on. My spirit hurled out power and I asked the Lord to state my case and remove them from my path. We have work to do and their hindrance has to be removed.

1/21/07 *(Prayer of Peace to God)*

I spent time before the Lord recalling the tumultuous events over the past day. I asked the Lord to check my heart and make sure that I was not out of line in defending myself.   Whatever God's judgment warranted, I would accept. I knew that my actions could have caused me to abort my entire assignment, if I had made a mistake in fighting back. But, at no time did the Spirit of the Lord try to stop me from fighting back. Then the Holy Spirit said to my spirit, *'**this is about the book.**'* He then revealed that these men attacked me because they felt I was unqualified to write this book. They were commanding me to abort my assignment and give up the book.

1/22/07 *(Funeral Procession)*
In a vision, I was at a military funeral. There were military soldiers everywhere I looked. I did not know who they were; there were so many of them. Then I saw myself wearing a white shroud over what looked like a white-laced aviator cap. Then one soldier appeared wearing his soldier's uniform. He took me by the arm and marched me slowly to the edge of a gravesite. I looked down and saw a coffin draped in the American flag. I tossed a red rose on the coffin, turned and walked away from the gravesite. The soldier escorted me back to the place where I had been standing. I paused in tears for a brief moment and then turned to walk away. As I walked away, my shroud disappears and I am now dressed in complete military attire. I walked into a room with several top brass military leaders. I addressed the one by saying, 'reporting for duty, sir!' The vision ends with me asking the Lord who or what was in the coffin. The Lord responded by asking, **'*Why do you need to know?*'**

1/22/07 *(Back on Track)*
The remainder of Sunday evening was spent getting back on track with my regular projects. The ledger was completed and status reports for the book and the company were also updated. The Lord also told me to write, work on my network flow charts and put together a housing study.

1/23-26/07 *(Recollection of Past Visions)*
The Holy Spirit clarified everything I just went through with the men of God. He showed the coffin draped in the U.S. flag, this time I knew who it was in that coffin. I heard Him say the name of the man to whom I was supposed to marry. To my horror, the Lord explained that this man led the attack on me out of jealousy.

1/23-26/07*(Past, Continued)*

The Lord revealed that the minister was so jealous of men who came to help, that he commanded that I get rid of them. This was an insane request given the fact that the devil was trying to kill me; and the man of God was not doing anything to help. So why would I get rid of the one person who obeyed when God called him to pray? The Lord said that the minister conspired with other men of God to tarnish my reputation and accuse me of having an affair with my armor bearer.

Before I could finish comprehending what the Lord was saying, in a vision He flashed before me the face of a redhead that I knew. She has worked for the minister for many years. Then I understood that this man was accusing me because of what he was doing with this other woman. Out of my spirit I reminded the Lord of what He told me about this assignment. He said that if I decided not to obey, He would find someone else more faithful to complete the assignment. I told the Lord that my heart's desire is to complete the assignment regardless of who is going with me. I asked him to honor my request and give me a new line up of faithful men who will honor Him. As I spoke, I knew in my spirit that my request was granted. I proceeded to finish writing.

1/26/07 *(Word about Jihad)*

The Lord spoke boldly to my spirit about jihad, and began separating me from people and things of this world. He said that I had that jihad-type determination inside my spirit. The Lord said that they are committed to killing for Allah. He asked me if I was prepared to be a **_'human shield'_** against their weapons and their attacks. The Lord reminded me that my mission was to give my life so that others could also live.

1/27-30/07 (*Spiritual Retreat*)
I spent much time in prayer, in the word and listening to faith tapes. Much prayer went forth for co-workers. The Lord said that my money was here. All seemed to be on track. The remaining time was spent journaling and writing the book.

1/29/07 (*Scriptures Revisited*)
My heart was yearning for more of the word of God. I spent time reading the Psalms, then the entire gospel of Luke. And still, I wanted more. I ran across Isaiah 49 again. This time when I read it, it spoke directly to my heart. After everything that happened last week, I needed some reassurance that I was still on target with the Lord. He reassured me that I was still in His perfect will.

The Lord let me know that unusual warfare came because of what I am writing. This also explained why it all happened immediately after I met with the artist and set publishing in motion. I prayed that no one be allowed to interfere with the publishing of my book; that all those destined to work with me are also unhindered. I covered everyone and everything with the Blood of Jesus.

1/30/07 (*Word about Jihad*)
The Lord spoke to my spirit, *'**Jihad is here!**'* He gave me no further instructions. I received the word and kept it near my heart awaiting more details.

1/30/07 (*Spiritual Release from Marriage*)
The Lord told me by the spirit that the man of God is officially released from my assignment.

2/1/07 (Another Word about Jihad)
I was walking home from the train station when I heard the Lord say again, *'**Jihad is here.**'* This time my spirit responded, 'if it's jihad they want, jihad they will get. But in the end, they will bow their knee to the God of Abraham, Isaac and Jacob.' When I finished speaking, the Lord revealed that many Muslims would be converted during the war in America. They will see the power of our God and recognize that He is the True and Living God.

2/9/07 *(Command to Edit Journal Entries)*
The Lord told me to take out of the journal all entries that refer to the man of God, our ministry and life together. As I began to edit, it was like uprooting the depths of my soul. In all it was about twenty pages of text, and hours of painful tears, not so much for him, as it was for what could have been if he had obeyed. The Lord had given me many details about our two children and us. I had been told to keep those visions close to my heart and speak to the children about their call in this earth. I saw their faces in a dream more than twenty years ago, long before I knew who their father was. Now the Lord is telling me to uproot years of prayer and meditation for what was promised. My pain was great yet, I could not imagine how many similar dreams were aborted because people would not obey. Then I recalled the vision the Lord gave me about babies and thought, 'how many children could not come to earth to fulfill their purposes because their parents married someone other than the one appointed?' I thought about the pain God must feel every day. How difficult it must be to design wonderful plans for your children and never see them come to pass. I prayed that for every seed of mine that was aborted, that the Lord would let me keep what I could and resurrect the dream inside someone truly faithful.

2/10/07 (*Command to Finish Writing*)

Warfare has greatly intensified, yet the Lord told me to finish writing the book and put together a draft of the manuscript for friends to read. I could tell by the nature of the demonic activity that the end is near. Right before God makes His final play, Satan and his demons start to kick up dust and harass the people of God with more intensity. It's okay, because I know how it will end with them. The plans of God will go ahead unhindered. Those who get in the way will be destroyed. The writing continued and a final manuscript prepared.

2/12/07 (*Purging the Pain Once and For All*)

This day found me with despair in my heart. My head was confused as well. The spiritual climate was changing and it was like everything was being severely uprooted. I no longer felt secure about my assignment or my life. It was though I was scrambling to gain some sense of composure. When I began praying in the spirit, the Lord showed me that there was much deliverance going forth. I had much pain concerning the loss of children promised to me. I had just uprooted the visions and prayers for the one that was to come, when it connected in my spirit to the one I lost years ago. I had a stillborn child that happened to be a girl. It was such a trying time that all I remember was staring at her peaceful face and wonderful what she could have been. She was so beautiful. It was as though she was sleeping and did not have a care in the world. That day I gave her back to God, but that is all I remember. There was suppose to be a gravesite service, but nothing was done. All I remember was seeing her and signing the death certificate. It was time to let go of the past and move into my future. The Lord told me that in the future I would have sons. I thanked Him for those words of comfort concerning having children, but my mind and heart could handle no more.

2/12/07 (*Effectual Door with Adversaries*)
The Lord showed many people of God waiting on answers to prayer. They were waiting on promises from God. Doors were opening everywhere, but the warfare at the entries of these doors was fierce. There were evil giants in the land that had to be slain in order for the promise to be obtained. The Amalekites wanted the things of God for themselves and refused to leave without a fight. The only ones able to walk through the doors were those willing to take on the enemy. They did not necessarily have to fight, they just had to show up armed with the promise of God and stand on that word with all boldness.

2/14/07 (*Times of Visitation Missed*)
During prayer, the Lord showed me that the church is in total ignorance of who He is. They have read about and sang about the Lord, but will not recognize Him when He shows up in the coming season. Many in the church miss God because of their religion and arrogance. Some have been in the church so long that they think they know all there is to know about God, and yet they know nothing.

It was if the Lord will use their blind spots to hide the open doors before them. I saw that many hearts were hardened against God and they were destroyed utterly and completely. How sad to be confessing a promise of God and then miss it because you were too stubborn to obey God. So many will believe the lie of Satan over the truth of God and this deception will cause them to forfeit the promise.

2/14/07 *(Word about a New Team)*
Panic hit my spirit as I realized that the man of God originally assigned to help me with this book, was suppose to use his company, lawyers and staff to help me. In fact, the publishing company name the Lord gave me, was the same name of a publishing company the man had lost years ago. God had planned to give the company back to him through marriage. I asked the Lord to send forth those appointed to help me with this project. In one act of disobedience, many decisions and people are affected. I needed to write and not worry about how to put together the business end of things. There was no choice but to give this one to God and let it alone.

2/14/07 *(A New Momentum)*
Finally, the Lord gave me hope about picking up and continuing with the project! He told me '***do what's in your heart to do concerning. You won't go wrong in whatever you do.***' This was just the boost I needed to keep going. The Lord also told me that I did not need the man of God's resource to get this book published. He said that I was given a '***true word of prophecy***' that would come to pass just as He spoke. God said <u>that</u> was the only thing I needed.

2/15/07 *(Word about Two Sons)*
I asked the Lord how it was that the man of God failed to fulfill his call. The Holy Spirit spoke to me about the parable of the two sons (Matthew 21:28-31). A man had two sons and asked that they go to work in the vineyard. The first son who said he would not go, but later changed his mind and went. The man of God was the second son said he'd go, but did not. The one that actually went to do the work did the will of his father. The man of God said he would do the work, but then refused to go.

2/15/07 *(Two Sons, Continued)*

The Lord also reminded me of the words I prayed sometime back. Out of my frustration for getting no assistance while on my assignment, I told the Lord that if the man of God did not want to go with us to do the work, then raise up sons from the stones who would be faithful. The Lord told me that my prayer request had been granted. He put together a lineup of faithful team members who will do the work.

2/20/07 *(Perilous Day Are Ahead)*

Fear took hold of my heart as I saw what was coming to the enemies of God. Pain and suffering beyond human imagination was about to be unleashed in their midst. All this is coming because people think they have outsmarted God. They are reveling in their sins to no avail. Sinful men are bolder and more sinful; thinking that God cannot see. In short order, there will be a rude awakening in America: so much bloodshed, so much loss and devastation. Every foundation will be shaken. Every household divided by fear of what will come upon the nation; grief too much to bear. Only those anchored in God will survive.

2/22/07 *(Vision of the Open Door)*

The Lord showed me an open door. He reminded me that I had seen the door before, but for some reason I did not record the vision in my journal. Then it came back to me in detail. I was in a basement room surrounded by demons. There was an open door that had a bright light shining through. As I started walking, I noticed that there were two steps leading to the door. When I stepped on the first step, a host of demons began grabbing at my legs and pulling me down on the ground. The more I struggled to get up; the more they began attacking the bottom half of my body by inflicting pain and perversion.

2/22/07 *(Open Door, Continued)*
The Lord reminded me that the man of God saw me head for the door. He also saw the demons attacking my body with perversion, and he did nothing. The man of God did not pray nor did he ask anyone to pray for me. He stood around to watch me die. That was his plan. I clearly see why he attacked when the Lord gave me an armor bearer. If I had died, as Satan had planned, then he would have been free to legally marry someone else and carrying out this assignment without me. I realized that the Lord gave this man a chance and he blew it.

2/25/07 (*The Open Door Revisited*)
I was listening to the song "I believe I can Fly."[22] I have listened to that song numerous times, but this time when I heard the words, 'I see me running through that open door', my spirit spoke the same words with a passion. Yes, I literally saw myself running through that open door.

3/1-5/07 (*Ready for Take Off)*
The Lord reminded me of the vision of the space rocket. He said, *'it's time.'* Every day that He repeats these words, my spirit sings a song. It's the same song. I sing it at work. I sing it in my sleep. It's a happy song. It's a song of freedom. The Lord had me write my letter of resignation from my job. I am just waiting for the go ahead. I know it's any day! Then I can do what the Lord is calling me to do full-time. Oh, yeah, I also asked for a much-needed vacation on a sunny island in the South Pacific. It's time!!

3/07-6/07 The journal was to be published and distributed during this time frame, so the writing was complete, or so I thought.

6/07 *(Dream Delayed One More Time)*
As I finished the book for production, jealousy arose on our day job. We never told anyone what was going on either between us or about the project. But rumors began to circulate that my book would make me famous, and then all hell broke loose. This chapter was supposed to be a day of rest, yet, the enemy was more ferocious than ever.

There was a man on my job who from the moment he was hired began harassing me in the most vulgar way. Someone stepped in a couple of times to help me. Since God had my back, I did nothing more until the Lord commanded me to tell the company management. Things ceased for a few weeks, then erupted even more dangerous. The Lord told me to report him again, but this time He said, *"**Don't be fooled, this man will kill you.**"* The company did not respond and the Lord told me to report it to EEOC; two days later, the company fired me. The attorney spoke on behalf of the company management (three of whom were present) when I was told that I was being fired because they believed there was never any harassment, but only a religious difference between me and the alleged perpetrator. I was being escorted off the premises like a common criminal.

6/07-8/07 *(Dream Delayed, Continued)*

These months were difficult because no one would hire me because of the EEOC investigation. Also, the harassment did not stop and the Lord told me to file for restraining order. On the day of the hearing, none of my witnessed appeared. The Lord told me that one of the witnesses had found naked pictures of me in this man's possess, yet they were afraid to come forth because they knew what happened to me when I told the true.

8/07 *(The Enemy Going For the Kill)*

It was about 7pm one evening when the Holy Spirit commanded me to sit down and open my mouth. I fell into a chair, as if pushed down by a supernatural force, and I began praying feverishly in tongues. This went on about forty-five minutes. When it was over, the Lord showed that the man from my job, was in the hotel where I was staying. He had an oversized briefcase from which he pulled out a huge gun and was preparing to use it. The Lord showed that when I began praying, confusion hit the man and he dropped the gun and began holding his head as if he were under attack. The Lord showed how the man had planned to come to my door and shoot thru the room with a big gun. He wanted to make sure the job was done thoroughly. But God intervened when I prayed and he left the hotel. The next morning, someone reported seeing a man that fit his description in the hotel at the time the Lord showed me. The manager said the face may have been the same, but the name I knew was not on the register.

9/07 *(Our Assignment to Europe Revealed)*
In early July, the Lord put Europe on my heart. In particular, He talked to me about a family inheritance in the Riviera. God told me to call a friend and talk to her about going. She was willing to go. When the Lord explained what he had for us in Europe, I was eager to go. The Lord's assignment became **our** project. The Lord gave approval for us to go with Marilyn Hickey. He spoke by saying,
"I have work for You and Your Family in Europe."

10/07 *(Heading to Europe)*
Before heading out of town, we agreed to meet to pray. The Lord brought up family and marriage again. He said, The Lord responded by saying, *". . . I won't leave you alone, I have someone waiting for you in Europe. You have permission to marry him, and he will do the work. There is so much work in Europe, you don't ever have to come back to America."* I hang on to every word. This project was bigger than any two people. We need a full time team. God was giving us hope that help was available in that place.

10/31/07

At 3:30am, the Lord said, *"__Head to the Airport, now!__"* I called my friend and she was already to go. We headed to the airport as commanded. We had no tickets, but we had a deadline to arrive in Spain by the following Saturday. Twelve hours later, we were able to get a last minute flight to New York that we could afford.

11/01/07*(Supernatural Move Overseas)*

At JKF, we prayed in the spirit until the Lord gave us an opening and the resources to make it to Barcelona. While praying, I could feel God's spirit covering us strongly. It was like he was actually on the plane heading to Paris. I knew he really wanted to come with us, but for some reason, he could not. Although, I remember what God said about having someone waiting for me in Europe, my heart was for only one the work. What God has is supernatural love. It makes you stick things out no matter how you feel. This will be a new and exciting challenge in Europe.

11/03/07

It took another 12 hours, but we made it to Paris, and missed our flight that would have arrived in Barcelona by noon, instead we waited for hours and finally arrived in Spain late afternoon. We met our ministry team in Spain and went to the crusade that evening. It was glorious. I fell in love with the Spaniards! You could feel their love and see it on the children's faces. There was a pastor from the US that prophesied about God's work for us in Europe. As the pastor spoke, the Lord said, *"__Make a home base in Nice.__"* So, the next day, we got tickets on the train and headed for Nice, France.

11/05/07 *(At Home in France)*

The heavens confirmed our residency in France. In my many travels in Europe, I never had a desire to see the Riviera and now God is telling me this is where He wants me to be. The people were welcoming and the Mediterranean Sea was majestic! I could hear God's voice so clear at the Sea. It became my place of meditation and prayer.

11/07 *(Amazing First Revelation in Prayer)*

My first night in prayer was crazy in France. Anytime the Lord sends me to a new region, I encounter the principalities and demon rulers usually within the first 24 hours. I encountered the demons of Spain before I left the US, because it was El Dia de Los Muertes (Day of the Dead) and they were conjuring up every demon to walk the streets of Spain. But, what I saw in France beats all.

This gigantic creature appears in the spirit and tries to bully me with his size and ugly appearance. I was not moved and told him to go. He was shocked that he could not scare me. I repeated myself and told him to go. The demon's head spun all the way around. He then turned his head back to me and lowered it in shame. The demon was in tears and said, ***"We heard you were coming and we know we have to go. It's not fair!"*** The demon turned to walk away and behind him stood four other spirits and they all left together. This was a major confirmation that God had given us authority over this region for His Good.

11/07 *(Much Prayer for President Sarkozy)*
My main purpose in France was to pray for the work God has for us there, and the first order of business was the president, Nicholas Sarkozy. I saw God's Hand mightily on that man. God has such promise for France, Europe and the Economic Union through this man. I saw a strong reunion with the US, one that had not been seen ever in our history. God let me know that the relationship with France would be crucial in the hard years to come.

11-12/07 *(Company's World-wide Purpose Revealed)*
While in France, the Lord revealed that America was going to have a severe financial fall and the company would have to be in place to help get things on a firm footing. God said I had to connect with people and projects in Europe in order to help America during this time of trouble. He had me work on the organizational structure and told me to set up a home office both in the US and in Europe. God also reminded me of a prophecy. It was about my family having great wealth around the world and that we needed to find vessels to finance in order for the overflow to keep flowing out of our house.

12/07 *(Federal Investigation Goes Forward)*
The investigation into my former employer was expedited and I was able to make statements from Europe to help the investigators. But, then the Lord let me know that the attorney got rid of the witnesses and they remodeled the office before the investigators got there. And the response from the reports confirmed that evil was on the move in LA.

12/17-12/31 *(Legal Victory in Sites)*

After sending a legal response to the investigators, the Lord gave me three visions and two scripture passages to stand on. In the first vision, I saw the owner of the company in a meeting with about ten people and he asked them to find out who I was. He suspected that I had secret government ties because no one could have exposed what they were doing unless they were undercover. In the second vision, I saw the attorney getting rid of the security guard witnesses and employees. The security men were still on payroll, just hidden. In the final vision, I heard one of my co-workers shouting for joy saying, ***"Paula won, y'all. She did it. I knew God was going to have her do it!"*** The Lord then gave me Psalm 58 and 35 to stand on. This was prophesying God's vengeance upon the company for lying and devising evil against me and others like me.

12/31 *(Confirmation of God's Promises)*

The Lord revealed to me that all he had promised for me, it would come to pass just like He said. It took coming to Europe for me to see and start to understand that no matter what I encountered, I was in agreement to complete what God started. Things were coming together just like God promised.

I also saw the promise coming to pass for my family. It was amazing how the Spirit of the Lord rallied around my family and they all pitched in to help with our expenses for this trip. And the biggest blessing is that my mother finally understood what God was doing, and she called the family to get them involved. I saw answers to my prayers unfolding before my very eyes. God said that if we went to the Riviera He would remove family bondages and release the fullness of His blessings upon us, and so He did just that!

THE WAR JOURNAL

YEAR 2008: *The European Connection Defined*

THE WAR JOURNAL
YEAR 2008: *The European Connection Defined*

1/1/08 (*New Year in France)*
This was the month that the Lord gave me much detail about setting up for business in France. He opened doors and sent people to confirm His word. I saw God's Hand move upon the people of France and they received Him greatly. They don't reject God like Americans do; the French just have never heard the truth about Him or His importance to their lives. That is a message they are ready to hear.

1/08 (*Call to Return to LA*)
The Lord dropped in my spirit that I had to return to LA for a brief period to wrap a few things up. As soon as I saw it, I felt sad. I love France and Europe because I feel more accepted there than in America. Europeans welcome other cultures and delight in meeting people who are different. I appreciate a place, where you are treated as a person and not as a member of a race. The South of France is filled with interracial couples and beautiful mixed cultured babies. It was wonderful to see.

1/08 (*Final Welcome to Our New Project in Europe*)
While praying on the last day in France, the Lord showed that I was returning. I didn't understand what that meant, but I heard God say to the continent, ***"Prepare for her arrival!"*** Then I saw prayer warriors arising from across the continent as far away as Russia. They all stood up as to receive a dignitary. There were no more than seventy-five people, but the Lord said this was His army that was ready to battle for the kingdom. We praised God for what He was beginning in France and in the world!!

1/16/08 *(Return to LA)*

We arrived LAX and it was like being in a foreign land. The people were ugly and the demons were everywhere. It was my plan to stay only thirty days and return to France in time for a conference in Paris.

2/08-6/08 *(Headed for Federal Court)*

The Lord told me to file charges in federal court against the company. After filing, the Lord told me that I gave the government what they needed to go after them on other charges as well. I was unable to get an attorney, so I had to represent myself. On first meeting with their attorney, I got there early and so did the client. They tipped their hand, by inquiring how special my relationship was with co-workers. I let them talk and they bragged about getting rid of the witnesses and evidence and told me I didn't have a leg to stand on. They began to make threats and it didn't work.

As their attorney came in, the Lord asked me, ***"what is their motivation?"*** Then their attorney echoed that I had no case and they had a solid witness who will swear before a judge that I lied. I immediately told them it was impossible. Then it hit my spirit. Now, I understand why I had to go to Europe. Someone had threatened me and my co-workers. Their attorney was shocked to find out that there was a relationship in the middle of the conflict. And, she asked who would have done this, and out of my spirit came the name of the boss. I told them that he did this because he wanted to date me and I turned him down knowing that he could have fired me. As I spoke, the client jumped up and began screaming for me to shut up. Their attorney was rattled to know she had been deceived into taking the case.

9/08 (*Preparing to Return to France*)
I spent most of my time working on the plan for Europe. We knew all about what we were supposed to do in Europe. God told us what to do, but we originally didn't want to leave LA, but now we were changing our minds. In any case, I was moving ahead. The Lord gave me a team of people and gave us an itinerary for Europe. I spent much time making job assignments, budgets and job descriptions.

10/08 (*Vision about Gross Darkness*)
The Lord showed me and others together and it looked like we were lying on our backs on the ground outside somewhere, possibly in LA. There was a thick black cloud that permeated the air. I felt horror as this black cloud came upon us; it didn't over take us, but it was hovering an inch or so above our bodies as we lay on the ground. I could tell that God wanted to give us instructions.

After this vision, I wondered why I was so horrified. God had shown me these things before. Then it dawned on me. I was horrified because my preparations for shielding victims from the darkness were incomplete. Between the court case and other retaliation, evil people had interfered with what God told me to do, and now many will die needlessly and without hope. This was more horrifying to me than the darkness itself.

11/05/08 *(Obama's Win A Sign From God)*

Election results came in announcing Barack Obama as the 44[Th] President of the United States. Television sound bites from across the world displayed tears of joy and embraces among the races. God began flashing before my eyes, His Dream for America and the world. It was confirmation of all the company was ordained to do: the nations coming together to help one another.

As President Obama gave his acceptance speech,[6] I heard God speaking to my heart. The first thing out of Obama's mouth was a declaration that ALL THINGS ARE POSSIBLE in America. This is what God had me stand in faith for America in the tough days and years to come. This the entire premise of this book.

The President talked about healing, restoring, and reclaiming the American Dream: about all of us working together to achieve this goal. It echoed God's Kingdom message coming out of mouth of a prophet. Then Obama declared that CHANGE HAD COME TO AMERICA, and I saw in the spirit, the Hand of God realign the leadership for the country and for the church. I saw a path in the spirit, opening up what looked like a transition from Moses to Joshua; a change from people waiting for God to drop food from heaven, even murmuring and complaining about their leaders; to a mighty army eager to unite the people, equip them to slay the giants and possess what God promised.

I also knew that just like in Joshua's day, the judgment of God would swiftly fall on all that oppose God's ordained leaders; and the battle in America was about to begin.

11/08 *(God's Purpose for George Bush)*
God has placed a special burden on my heart to pray for President Bush. Although no longer in the White House, God still has a great purpose for this man. His leadership was a transitional one; a bridge from the old guard to the new leadership of President Obama, but there is so much more that God has for Bush. I will keep praying that God reveal to him what else he is to do, and pray he has the courage to obey.

11/08-12/08 *(Still Making European Plans)*
I made new contacts in France, also waited to get a specific return date. It is difficult being in LA. It does not feel like home any more.

12/08 *(Pains of My Heart)*
The holidays can be very difficult for me because I am alone. God won't let me go see my family and my mom wanted me to come home after I left Europe earlier this year. I thought I would have a break, but this court case has taken up my time. Between missing my family, not knowing the whereabouts of my son, my heart is a bit overwhelmed, but God declared a year ago that He would restore my family and marriage. He declared that nothing was lost, so I have to believe God, protect my heart and keep moving forward with the work God gave me to do.

THE WAR JOURNAL
YEAR 2009: *A Better Understanding*
Of Things To Come

THE WAR JOURNAL
YEAR 2009: *A Better Understanding Of Things To Come*

1/1/09 (*Return Date April or May*)
All of my team members received my offer letters and were excited about leaving for Europe for an introductory visit. I gave them all detailed production schedules for their specific assignments. Then the Lord said, *"**Morocco. Take the team to Marrakech Morocco. Get six tickets.**"*

Spring 09 (*Perpetrator Admits Guilt*)
The Lord showed me a vision in which the perpetrator in my case admitted guilt and asked for forgiveness.

After showing me this vision, God told me to re-file and charge the company with criminal neglect. It just so happened that we had a hearing and the company had filed a motion to dismiss, but I was never notified about their action until I showed up for court. The judge sensed something was wrong and rescheduled. Out of my spirit I asked the judge if I could re-file my claim as well. There was silence in the court room as the judge paused, thought for a moment, and then said yes.

Spring 09 *(Date of Hearing)*

There was a court date set for a hearing and that night before the Lord showed the boss paying cash to some man. When I woke the next morning, the Lord told me not to go to court; an assassin's bullet would be waiting for me. I obeyed God. Then the Lord said I needed to move because they were going to kill me to make sure we don't bring the evidence to court. My landlord moved me to a safer apartment for short-term. They were also alerted to look out for suspicious characters looking for me.

3/09 (Destruction at the Hand of God)

I saw destruction in LA that left huge craters in the ground where buildings once stood. I did not see the enemy only explosions and the aftermath of something that hit us. When the dust totally cleared, I saw what appeared to be the back portion of a huge foot standing in the midst of the destruction. I also saw our team and many saints of God being shielded from the destruction by thousands of huge powerful angels with swords drawn to protect us. Everything outside the angel's protection was destroyed. And then I saw more.

The angels appeared to be about 10 feet tall, but the foot was so much larger. I realized that this was no angel, but the foot of God standing in the earth. I could not tell you where the other foot landed, but I knew that if one foot caused so much damage, the other one would have too. I never saw His entire body, just a portion of back of the foot and ankle. And then, I saw God's hand pulling things out of the clouds of heaven. He was pulling things out of the clouds both good and bad.

3/09 *(Destruction, Continued)*

Then I saw someone watching me and the team praying and this person began to pray against us because they thought we were causing the destruction. Before they could strike against us, the Hand of God crushed them to the ground and the Spirit of the Lord said, ***"You are on the wrong side and will be replaced."*** I knew that God was dead serious about protecting us against those who hate us.

4/09 *(God Opens All the Doors)*

Within a two day period, everything the Lord told me to do was made available. This was a sign it was time to move forward. The temporary office space became available immediately and at a discounted rate. The language learning system I was told to get was also offered to me by a complete stranger. Then I was at a fast food restaurant in Hollywood and a woman came to me and offered her services to help me buy commercial property. Before I could say anything, she told me her area of expertise was in Carson. I knew that God was talking because that is exactly where He told me to find a warehouse. The flights to Europe were ridiculously cheap and there were also decent rates to Morocco. All I needed was the money that God promised would be here. But nothing appeared in my mailbox yet. So, I kept pressing in the spirit, but still nothing came forth.

Something was very wrong. This is not how things go with God. He gives us a plan and when we see the promise coming to us, God provides all that we need to obtain the promise. But now, the money was not coming forth. I enquired of the Lord. I asked Him what it was I was missing. God responded that team mates were missing.

(4/09) *(All Doors, Continued)*
This was not the answer I wanted to hear. I cannot make people obey God and neither should anyone be allowed to prevent me from being obedient in what I have to do. This was the craziest thing I ever heard. The Hand of God was giving me provision that God said would come, but I can't partake of these provisions because the man was out of position.

Now, I see the pattern of attack from the enemy. I keep getting saddled with men who hear God tell them what to do, but then they don't obey which sabotages this project and endangers everyone on my team. I begged God to give me a solution because I have all these people depending on me, and a plan without money to execute it is not acceptable. I am loyal to God and have always been obedient and followed through with perfection the will of God when I was single. Being linked up to men has only caused me frustration and grief. I don't get it. I understand God's military rank and subordination. I understand that lives depend upon me to be obedient. If I get it, what is wrong with these men that they don't?

I began to wonder if it is because I am an attractive woman and they are distracted by what they see and revert to treating me like every other woman out there. But, I am no ordinary woman. I have been called to lead and train up generals around the world for God's Kingdom Army. They are waiting for me because the season is evil and the troops need reinforcements. God gave me the most precious thing He has on earth; His people and His plan for their lives. We can afford no further delays. I asked God to do whatever is necessary to get me through this open door. I don't care how it's done, but we **are** going in!!

4/09 *(Word to Go Back to France)*

The Lord told me to meet with my team and reassure them that the project will go forth no matter what happens. Then He commanded me to go to Europe and buy property so, we will have a place to stay on future trips to France. I made plans to leave.

5/09 *(Hired Killer on the Move)*

The Lord showed in a vision that a witness in my case was under attack by two hired killers. They were beating him in an alley somewhere in LA. Then the Lord said to me, ***"Speak to their guns!"*** As I commanded the guns to cease their action, I saw flashes of light, but knew that he was going to survive. If God wanted him killed why would he have told me to stop the guns?

5/09 *(Vision of Murder Plot Against Me)*

I was awaken at 2 am with face of the company's attorney smiling at me in a vision. He pretended to want to talk but there was gun concealed behind him. He pointed the gun at my head and my reaction in the vision was of fear and helplessness. This was my first clue that this vision was not from God. I have never been fearful of someone killing me, nor am I ever helpless. I belong to God. He is my protection! This was witchcraft, an evil attempt to send messages of fear and death against me. God let me see the entire plot. My spirit rose up in me and I declared that the devil is a liar. The Lord warned me that this man would try to find me and pretend to want to talk, but murder is his mission. He got away with murder before and he plans to do it again, but I'm not the one; not now, not ever! In Jesus' Name.

5/09 *(Murder Plot, Continued)*
For the first time, something made sense. My first day on the job, the attorney followed me around. He acted very suspicious and I knew he was a criminal; it was all over his spirit. Then, I recalled people dying on our property and no one seemed to care. Many supposedly jumped from the towers. But I recall an ex-wife of one of the victims calling the office and asking me how we did it. Something had her convinced that our company had killed the man.

And then there was one persistent reporter who kept coming around asking about the tragic events that happened on a regular basis. He wanted me to tell him why there were no police or news reports, yet our residents were calling his office to complain. The management never responded.

I also remember before I was hired, how eerie it was just to drive thru that property to go across town. The place had an evil feel about it. The employees said the residents were evil, but I soon learned that the residents were only responding to the perceived evil from the company. It became such a battle field, that our boss developed a hit list of all the people he wanted gone.

Most times all you had to do to get on his list was be a long-term resident and aging. And now, I was number one on his list and on the receiving end of his evil schemes. God told me to take the job there, but now He is telling me to leave LA and return to Europe. I obeyed God.

5/09 (*Enemy Plans Made Clear*)
While at LAX, I began praying in the spirit about whether or not to wait for more money to come. In the spirit, I heard the company boss yelling at witness (co-worker) saying, 'I OWN YOU. YOU AREN'T GOING ANYWHERE. It was approaching mother's day and my cousin offered to fly me to Phoenix for the weekend. I agreed to meet her, hoping that would buy some time before heading for Europe.

5/09 (*Final Exit from LA*)
It was a great reunion with my cousin and sister in Arizona. They wanted me to wait there before going to Europe, but God had other plans. As soon as my plane landed LAX, I went directly to the prayer room at Crenshaw. I needed to know which way to head next. I also called one of my team mates to have her meet me in the prayer room.

As soon as I passed the guard and headed to the prayer room, the Lord told me that the guard alerted someone on staff that I was on the grounds. Within five minutes, I was joined by a somewhat hostile woman who approached me while I was praying. But, it did not stop me from crying out to God for answers. Then the Spirit of God began to move upon me and He spoke, ***"Go to New York and wait there."*** Then I heard the woman pray for God's safe passage for me to complete His will for my life and I knew that God was confirming my trip to NY to stay with family.

5/09 *(Final Exit, Continued)*

After I finished, I noticed my team mate also sitting in the prayer room. The three of us left together. I thanked the woman for joining us in prayer. She asked where I was headed and I explained that I just flew in from Phoenix and needed to hear from God about where to go next, and He confirmed that I am to head to NY today. The woman looked at me amazed. She had entered the prayer room with one purpose and left with another. God is indeed in control!!

5/09 *(Still Harassed By the Enemy)*

After arrival in NY, the alleged perpetrator started sending me witchcraft messages stating that the witness had been killed and now I belonged to him. The devil had no idea that God had protected the witness. God gave me the music and arrangements for our wedding, and the Lord told me where we were to be married. All this occurred just a day before the witchcraft began. I am so glad that I know God and can hear him. I am nobody's fool. God is watching our backs!

6/09 *(Bad Witches from Home)*

The Lord woke me up and showed that the evil prayer warriors from my church in LA were back on the war path. They were trying to stop me in whatever they thought I was doing in New York. This craziness has to end. Too many people are dying and going to Hell and these leaders are trying to kill me over a position. The Lord woke my brother and had him praying to protect his family from the 30 or so witches who were in LA wanting to kill me. But, the Lord sent me to pray at Crenshaw before I left, so He had to know that rumors were going to start and the devil was going to send them after me.

6/09 *(The Open Door Revisited)*
Then the Lord showed me the open door again, this time He zoomed in to the bottom of the door way. Right along the threshold were armies of small demons ready to trip me as soon as I stepped through the open door to Europe and the plans for the company. So, I just prayed in the spirit and asked God to destroy the evil ones intent on hurting those desiring to do His will in this earth. The Lord responded with Matthew 18:6, saying that it would better for these evil ones to have a millstone hung on their necks and they be drowned in the sea.

7/09-9/09 *(Racist Church Leaders Attack Obama)*
I have to stop listening to Christian television because the white preachers have been really speaking evil about President Obama. This grieves the Spirit of God because these men are leaders who are supposed to teach the people by example. You can hear the racial undertones in their words. The Lord said that He was going to deal head on with the devil of racism in the church. Dr. Price started preaching against racism back in the early 2000's.

Racism will be cast out of God's church once and for all. God had me pray for the leaders who are espousing racism in their congregations. God calls them murderers who will have no place in His Kingdom. If they don't get delivered, they will die in their sin and spend all eternity in Hell.

7/09 *(Prayer for Men Pleasers)*

I got a call from one of my team members saying she wanted me to pray for her, but needed to call me back with more details. As soon as she hung up, the Lord started talking about her problem. He took me to I Kings 13. This is one of those Bible stories that I never liked nor understood, until today.

It's the story about a young prophet who had a specific word to deliver to a King. This was the last chance for this king to repent for the sake of God's people. God gave this young prophet specific instructions saying, don't go home with anyone, nor eat or drink with them, and don't go back home the same way you came. So, the king was happy he was being restored to God, and offered to thank the prophet with food and drink, but the prophet said that God would not let him.

Then, there was an old prophet who heard about what the young prophet had done, and he sent men to invite the young prophet to stay and eat with them. The young prophet said that God forbid him to do such, but the old prophet said that he also heard from God, and God said it was okay for them to spend time together.

So, the young prophet visited with the old prophet and while they were eating, a curse fell upon the young prophet. God used the mouth of the lying old prophet to curse the young prophet. God said that the young prophet would die that day and on the way home, and indeed, the young prophet was killed by a lion and never made it home.

7/09 *(Man Pleasers, Continued)*
In the past I always felt it was unfair that the young prophet died and the older one lived. This day God corrected me. The younger yielded to the authority of the elder prophet, rather than obeying God. He honored the old prophet and dishonored God. The fact that the old prophet lied did not matter. As the story ends, the King heard about the young prophet's death, and no longer desired to repent. He turned from God and was cut off and destroyed from the face of the earth. So, the young prophet's behavior caused the king to sin further against God.

The Lord explained that His purposes are more complex than ours. We cannot comprehend the reasons why He gives us strict instructions, but we can be assured that someone's salvation and eternal destination is attached to our obedience.

The message to my friend was to obey what God had told her and separate herself from those who would cause her to stray. Just because someone has a title in God's house, does not mean they are hearing or even know God. God then had me pray for others who esteem the opinions of men above God's word. I left a message for my friend. She called me back amazed that God told me the problem before she could tell me what to pray for.

8/09 *(Mighty Women of Valor)*
God showed me the most amazing thing after prayer today. I saw women taking leadership and upholding the men in battle. It was like when Debra undergirded Barak, the leader of God's army (Judges 4-5). Debra was a judge and the prophetic voice of God guiding the people. Barak had the military strength. Together, they led the People of God to victory over their enemies. In particular, the Lord showed Black women leading alongside their husband's and doing mighty works for the kingdom. Even as I am writing the Lord is revealing more. God is saying that the first family is a prophetic sign of what He is doing in the spirit. God put a powerful Black woman in the White House next to her husband, the Commander and Chief of the United States Armed Forces. Her husband's name is also, Barack. In the Hebrew language, the name Barak[7] *(Baraq)* means *lightning flash*; as in the lightning flash of a powerful sword.

10/09 *(Command for the Team)*
The Lord spoke a word of readiness for my team, saying, ***"The Team is here! They are here and ready to go!"*** This was a confirmation that we are about to go forward. I'm ready!!

10/12/09 *(Warning of Things to Come)*
The Spirit of the Lord sounded an alarm at 8am. He warned, ***"Get Ready! Brace Yourselves! Embrace My Glory! It is Here!"***

10/21/09 *(Purpose of the Gospel is Change)*
The Lord had me praying for the transformation of the church into His image. He says His people are resistant to change and that is the very essence of the gospel. It's a message of transformation: transforming the sinner into a believer; transforming the believer from faith to faith and glory to glory, until he or she is conformed into the image of God's son. Without a change of heart one cannot be saved. But this is just the beginning of our change. In Christ, we are a new creation; a species certified capable of doing God's will in the earth.

When we change our plans and follow Heaven's plan for our lives this glorifies God. Our transformation shows the world that not only is there hope for their situation, but it is evidence that the gospel message is true. What a bolster to one's faith, to see someone completely transformed by the power of God!

Jesus Christ gave up the riches of heaven and exchanged His heavenly form to live as a man on earth. Then He changed again when He died on the cross and then resurrected with a glorified body. As Jesus is, so are we in this world. God is calling the church to submit their bodies for His service and be transformed by renewing their minds with His Words and His Thoughts. According to the Lord, this is the duty of all God's Kingdom citizens.

10/25/09 (*Intense Prayer against Sexual Perversion*)
The Lord had me praying to break the spirit of sexual perversion off the church leaders. They appear religiously pompous and strict on the surface, but in their private lives they are plagued with homosexuality, pedophilia, adultery, and pornography. These same men have no guilt for their sin, or fear of retaliation from God. These are wolves dressed in sheep's clothing. They look like servants of God, but secretly prey upon the innocent; using shame and fear to abuse others in the name of God. It's a conspiracy of sin that has to be broken.

God blames the church for the sexual perversion of our society. He made His people the keepers of the world, just like He made Adam and Eve keepers of the Garden of Eden at creation. God gave them authority to bless or curse. How they obeyed God determined if the earth was blessed or cursed. Adam and Eve sinned against God causing the entire earth to be cursed. Likewise, the American church is promoting and condoning sin in the house of God and the curse can be seen on the people around our nation. God said, *"**This Sexual Perversion Must Go Now!**"*

Leaders are placing rules on people to control them, but they are not eradicating the evil in their hearts. Men are being defiled because they meditate on evil in their hearts. The heart needs to be cleaned by meditating on and obeying the Word of God. Whatever a man spends time meditating on, will come to pass in their lives, bringing along with it either a blessing or a curse.

10/09 *(Conspiracy Confirmed)*

During prayer about my court case, the Lord said that the company boss paid the killer. Then I saw the attorney with the gun. But how did the perpetrator know about the hit? Then the Lord showed that they were all in on the plot against me from the beginning. Money exchanged hands among them. This was a plot more wicked than first believed.

Week of 11/07/09 *(Warning of Nuclear Attack)*

I was awaken by a vision of at least one nuclear bomb headed straight at us here on the East Coast. There was an earlier prophecy about two nuclear bombs that God had me cancel, but this felt different. This attack felt like an inside job. I asked the Lord who was responsible for this attack. The Lord mentioned the name of Dick Cheney. I began to pray in the spirit while the Lord spoke about war crimes against America. I prayed half the morning for Dick Cheney and whatever he had done. The Lord would not command me to stop the bomb; it was coming straight at us. The Lord instead commanded me to spend all my time finishing up the book, the business plan and figures. He indicated that things were moving very fast and any day we could be under attack. I obeyed God.

11/16/09 *(Prayer for the Hurting Masses)*
I was preparing for bed when travail came into my spirit. At the moment I could feel the pain and suffering of millions of people. It over whelmed my spirit. All I could do was ask God to comfort all that mourned. It was a cry to end injustice and suffering at the hands of evil people who want to hurt others for profit. The travail was for the young children and elderly and all who were being abused and enslaved by brutality. It was for all who cried out for justice in the most remote and desolate places. And God heard them all. The spirit of God responded, ***"I will comfort all that mourn for this is the day of My Vengeance!"*** My heart could only praise a God who hears even the faintest cry in the midst of darkness. He will give them beauty for ashes, the oil of joy for their mourning, and the garment of praise for the spirit of heaviness (Isaiah 61:2-3)

11/21/09 *(Prayer for Marriages)*
God had me praying for marriages. And then He began to speak about gay marriage in a way that touched my heart. He did not blame gays for wanting to marry. God put the desire for marriage inside of human beings. What grieved Him was that they were looking for love; and they have no idea that God is Love. God, who is Love, created human beings to experience the heights and depths of His love in marriage. That is why God created marriage. But, until people honor God in their unions, marriage won't work. It doesn't matter if the two people are heterosexual or homosexual; without God (Love), it won't work.

God blames the church for the confusion about gay marriage in America. He says that these people are looking for love anyway they can, but the church is responding to gays with hatred. In our zealousness, we have blocked the path of God from those who are desperately seeking love. Jesus commanded us to act in love towards one another because this is how the world will identify us as His followers. It's is our love that draws people to Jesus, and those who follow Jesus **will** find God (Love).

11/24/09 *(The Secret Things Belong To God)*
The Lord woke me early this morning and kept showing me evil plots and schemes against his people; things being done secretly, keeping them from doing His will. I began to pray for God to reveal these things and do justice for His people. The Lord responded immediately, ***"The Secrets Things Belong To Me. I will expose that which is hidden in the earth; every unknown resource and bounty AND every lying scheme and plot against man in the earth: lies and plots against My People."***

11/24/09 *(The Secret Things, Continued)*
"__What was done in the dark will be brought into the Light.__ __That__ __which was spoken in secret closets will be shouted on rooftops.__ __Likewise every secret plan, I will reveal to My People to make clear__ __their inheritance. I will manifest my secret wish to bless and prosper__ __you this day! Yes, The Secret Things Belong to Me, says God and I__ __will reveal them all: both bad and good.__"

I was overjoyed by this response from God. But I remember that there was a specific scripture that described the secret things. It was Deuteronomy 29:29 that echoed what God was saying. Then another scripture came into my spirit: Ecclesiastes 12:13-14, it summarizes clearly what God was saying about the fear and judgment of God.

12/21/09 *(Final Command about the Book)*
At 4am this morning the Spirit of God shook me awake and told me to go downstairs and pray. I was so startled that I tripped and fell down the stairs. When I sat to listen to His command, He told me to, *"__Finish the Book.__"* From the moment God spoke until 1pm later that day, Satan and his demons fought to keep me from obeying God. But, I subdued the enemy by continuing to move forward to finish as God commanded. Something terrible is about to happen, yet for the people of God; it will be a relief from the demonic oppression that has kept us from obeying God to the fullest. It is Time!!

THE CONCLUSION OF THE WHOLE MATTER

'Fear God, And keep His Commandments:

For This Is The Whole Duty Of Man.

For God, Will Bring Every Work Into Judgment,

With Every Secret Thing,

Whether It Be Good Or Whether It Be Evil.'

Ecclesiastes 12:13-14 (KJV)

Final Exhortation

You have heard the prophecies; you have heard the teachings. If you were not stirred in your heart to get right with God and seek His plan for your life, then the message of this book was not for you. But, if you have found any convicting truth in this book, then I exhort you to study what the Word of God says about what you have read. Then, commit what you have read and studied to God in prayer. Ask Him to reveal to you, further truths about the events to come. Remember that discernment is essential for end-time survival. There are many deceivers and false teachers in the world, and many more will come before Jesus returns.*

The most disturbing prophesy in this book stated that the violence that is occurring in heaven would be played out on the earth before Jesus comes.$^{\alpha}$ God said that His people would be deceived into thinking that the violence was from the devil when in actuality, the violence would be God's Hand shaking the heavens and the earth.$^{\beta}$ Rather than repenting and getting right with God, His people would continue in their deception, fight against God and be destroyed. They would be sincere in their hearts, but they would be greatly deceived by their own ambitions and false prophets. Many of God's people will be destroyed because of lack of knowledge,$^{\chi}$ not because the truth was not available to them, but because they rejected the truth, believed the lie, and refused to repent. In this chapter, we will show how to overcome deception and stand boldly in the evil day.

The Apostle Paul said that there are many voices in the world, each having their own meaning.[*] This passage was about understanding the spiritual gift of tongues, but it could also be applied to any spoken word as well. We are bombarded by many voices including that of our upbringing, our present lifestyle, our religious beliefs or lack thereof, advertising, political rhetoric, news and media propaganda. Each has a specific meaning and purpose to persuade, or move us to carry out some predetermined action. Not all voices edify our spirits nor do they glorify God and His Kingdom. Jesus warned us to be careful how we hear.[α] Again, these verses were about the way we receive the Gospel of the Kingdom, yet they can be applied to how we receive any message that we hear. The heart of a man is like a fertile ground: it has the ability to hear and receive a message like a seed that will take root and grow in our minds and spirits.

How we hear a message determines the manner in which the message is received. For example, if a child hears that he is no good and that he will grow up to be like his no good father, and the child honestly believes what he has heard, he will indeed grow up to be just like his father. Now, imagine the same words spoken to a child who heard that if he made Jesus his Lord, he could have a new life in God's family. If this child believes God's word instead of his family's word, he could indeed grow up to be like his father God, and transform his earthly heritage.

366

Jesus told his disciples that unless a man receives the kingdom like a child, he could not enter in.[β] It is commonplace for children to believe without question the things parents say. This is the kind of heart God desires from his children. He seeks to do wondrous things for those whose heart is committed to Him.[*] Such a heart is good ground to produce heavenly results in any situation. Although Jesus wants us to come into the Kingdom with faith like a little child, He does not want us to be ignorant. He repeatedly warned about deceivers in the world. The Bible has plenty of warnings about deceivers, those who are deceived and those who deceive themselves. Jesus told us to heed warnings about false prophets and evil leaders who would bring death and persecution to a troubled and chaotic church. Because of this hatred and chaos, many people will leave the faith.[α]

To arm yourselves against deception, you must know the truth. God's word is truth.[β] Jesus told his disciples that if they continued in His word they would know the truth.[χ] When the Pharisees rejected Jesus, He said that they rejected God's word because they were children of the devil. They wanted to believe a lie and not the truth.[δ] So, if we use this same method for detecting deception we would do well. If a teacher or prophet habitually speaks or acts against the word of God and defends his right to do so, beware. They are making the choice to reject God's word. But, if you read, study and obey the word, you will be able to discern truth from err and avoid being led astray.

Dear Christians who think you know the word; Beware! The deceiver knows the word too. Remember that Satan's job is to steal the word of truth before it takes root and grows within you.[*] He battled Jesus over God's word in the wilderness,[α] and anyone who names the name of Jesus must be prepared for a similar battle. The Lord gave me the following steps that would help us win the battle of truth versus deception:

1. Inquire of the Lord Before Going to Battle
2. Hear and Obey the Word From God
3. Stand Boldly in the Face Persecution
4. Be Still, The Battle Belongs to the Lord

We look at each of these steps using examples from biblical characters such as David, Saul, Moses, Joshua, Jehoshaphat and Ahab. These stories will teach us, warn us, and inspire us to fight the good fight of faith, and win.

1. Inquire of The Lord Before Going to The Battle

It was common during Old Testament Bible times for the people of God to seek the Lord before a battle. Many times the king would inquire whether the Lord would deliver the enemy into their hands. When young David went up against Goliath he did so by faith.[β] The Philistines were terrorizing King Saul and his armies and all the people of Israel. No one was brave enough to go up against Goliath, the champion of the Philistines. David boldly stepped forward by declaring to King Saul that he slew a lion and a bear and that the Lord would deliver Goliath over to him as well.

David also spoke bold words of faith to Goliath by saying *'Thou comest to me with a sword and a spear, but I come to thee in the name of the Lord of hosts, the God of the armies of Israel, whom thou hast defied. This day the Lord will deliver thee into my hands, and I will smote thee and take thine head.'*[*] David did exactly what he declared by faith, and the Philistine armies fled after witnessing Goliath's death. David displayed great faith in the face of great danger. He stepped out in faith knowing that His God was with him.

Years later, when the Philistines heard that David was anointed King over Israel they begin searching for him.[α] They encamped against David at the valley of Rephaim. This time David did not step into battle based on his previous faith, but enquired of the Lord whether he should go up against the Philistines. The Lord told David to go up against them and He would deliver them into his hand. King David and his armies defeated the Philistines. Then the Philistines boldly came up yet another time against the armies of God.

Again, David enquired of the Lord. This time the Lord told him not to go directly up against them but to encircle the enemy from behind and come upon them in front of the mulberry trees. They were instructed to advance quickly once they heard the sound of marching in the tops of the mulberry trees. That would be their signal that the Lord had gone out before the armies to strike the camp of the Philistines. King David led the armies just as the Lord instructed, and they defeated the enemy.

369

In these examples we see how David went to battle armed with the wisdom of God. He did not to rely on his own ability to go up against his enemies. He fought Goliath by faith in the first battle, but David was not so arrogant to go up against the enemy again in the same manner of faith. He was no longer the brash young man armed with a slingshot. Now David was king of Israel and his powerful armies slew many. His enemies were even more determined to stop David's reputation of having slain tens of thousands.* When the Lord told him that He would deliver the Philistines in the valley of Rephaim, David did not expect the enemies to come back at them, so the Lord had to instruct him how to fight with a different strategy.

How easy it could have been for David not to enquire of the Lord a second time. After all, God said he would deliver the enemies over to him. But, David had the wisdom to see that another battle had ensued and therefore further instruction was needed.

A word from God is vital when going into battle, but if things are seemingly going opposite to the word, it is best to inquire a second time. It is always good to know if God has further instructions, or if a change in circumstances requires a different course of action. Inquiring a second time is not an act of unbelief, but a way of getting clarification.

2. Hear and Obey the Word From God
(Lean Not to Your Own Understanding)

Hearing from God is a great blessing, but not obeying what you hear is just plain dumb. The Lord said that His people are in the habit of selectively obeying what they hear. In the coming season of glory, selective obedience will kill you. We will see death, destruction and famine all around us, but know that a thousand may fall at your side and ten thousand at your right hand; it will not come near you, if you abide in God's word. When you habitually hear and obey the Lord, you abide in the will of the Father, and are hidden under the shadow of the Almighty. Only when you abide in the word can you claim these and other protections from Psalm 91.[*] Your ability to hear and your willingness to obey will save your life and the lives of those around you.

In the Bible, we find that when the men of God inquired of the Lord about the battle, the instructions they received were at times unconventional. The Children of Israel were waiting to escape from Egypt, and the Lord gave His people specific instructions.[α] Their safety and escape from the enemy's bondage depended upon their obedience to those instructions. They were told to stay in their homes until morning, dressed and ready to leave. They put blood on their doorposts and lintels so that when God in His wrath came thru the city, none of their first born would be killed. Because of their obedience, the death angel passed over them and they were freed from the hands of Pharaoh. When war comes to our nation, we will see the Lord make a distinction between His people and all others.

God wants to bless those who obey His instruction. Our collective obedience will cause millions to see our good works and glorify our Father in Heaven. God is allowing war to come to our shores not to destroy us, but to show His power over all other gods of this universe. And, those who will fall down and worship God and God alone will be protected and blessed. Before Joshua took Jericho, the Bible said that the entire city was shut up in fear of the Children of Israel. The harlot Rahab helped Joshua's men survey the city before they took it. She said that the people of Jericho's hearts melted because of the Children of Israel's God. Rahab's faith caused her family to be spared when all of Jericho and its inhabitants were killed.[*]

When Joshua led God's people into Jericho, the Lord gave him specific instructions on how to destroy the enemy. He told them to encircle the city walls once a day for six days. Seven priests carrying trumpets of ram's horns were told to go before the Ark of the Covenant. On the seventh day, the people were told to encircle the city seven times with the priests blowing the trumpets. When the people heard the trumpets, they were told to shout, and when they did, the walls of Jericho fell down, and they seized and burned the city.[α] Another great example of following God's word before the battle was the story of Jehoshaphat, King of Judah. The enemies of Judah gathered against them for war. The king led the people into fasting and prayer before God. The Lord told them to go up against the enemy, but they would not have to fight because the battle belonged to Him.[β]

The people of Judah were instructed to send praisers before the army. As they began to sing, the Lord sent ambushments that caused the enemy to turn on each other. By the time Judah made it to the battlefield, all the enemies were dead. So the people spent the next three days stripping the enemy of all its spoils.[α]

Just like Judah, America will be attacked by severl enemy nations who want to take over the land that God gave us. This will be the time for us to go before the Lord with fasting and prayer and ask Him what we must do. If the Lord prepared His people for war in Bible times, why wouldn't He do the same for us who are under a better covenant? Like Judah, America needs to recognize the sovereign rulership of God over our nation. Then we will know that the battle belongs to the Lord. We will not fear the enemy, but we will praise the Lord for His mercy endures forever.

Finally we will show an example of what happens when the instruction (word) of God is not obeyed. Now, after Jericho was taken, Joshua went up against AI, but did not inquire of God.[*] Instead, he listened to the advice of the men who went to spy out the land, and sent only three thousand men to battle against AI. The results were disastrous. The men of AI slew thirty-six men of Israel and others fled for their lives. They went to battle and lost because they did enquire of God. If they had prayed, they would have known that the camp was cursed because of one man's sin. God's people were warned not to take property as booty, because it would cause the camp of Israel to be cursed.

Now, the camp was cursed because someone indeed took what God commanded them not to touch. They were instructed to find the guilty party and stone him and his family to death, and burn them and all of their possessions in order to appease the anger of the Lord. After they released the camp from the curse, the Lord told Joshua to go up against AI again, and this time they took the city.[*] Ai and Jericho were cities in the Promised Land, but no one was allowed to possess what God had promised until sin was dealt with. It is important to God that we receive the promise with honor and not reproach. In our day we will go up and take the promise as a unified body, holy and acceptable to God.

If Christians do not see God's promises manifested in their lives, it is often because they choose not to obey God. Instead, many are under the control and manipulation of the enemy and have become weary and discouraged about the promises of God. Some are unequally yoked with unbelievers who have spoken evil over their promise. Others have willingly submitted to sin without repentance. Whatever the reason, these people have chosen not to obey God, and all disobedience is sin. They may say they love God, but their disobedient heart says they don't.

War is coming and the Lord is expecting His people to be spiritually fit like Olympic athletes are physically fit. We are expected to be at the top of our game for the kingdom's sake. God is calling us to a zero tolerance for sin and disobedience. So, lay aside every weight and all sin and run with patience the race that is set before you.[α] Run to win!

3. Stand Bold in the Face of Persecution

I exhort all of you whom God has given a strong prophetic word, to stand boldly on that word regardless of what people say or do to you. Not many have been chosen to hear what God is saying. Those who are listening are being given detailed instructions on how to survive what is coming upon the earth. God always gives a warning about trouble, and gives instructions of what to do before trouble comes. Hold fast to what God gave you because it will save the lives of many! Remember how Noah built an ark, years before God's wrath brought rain and floods upon the earth?[*] Joseph [α] prepared an emergency food program for the world years before famine hit the earth. Why think it strange that God would tell His people how to prepare for war in their own nation?

Let's take it one step further, John the Baptist warned men about the wrath of God to come, urging them to repent for the kingdom of heaven was at hand.[β] John told the people how to prepare for Jesus, Who would bring unquenchable fire upon the earth. Then, Jesus came preaching the kingdom and telling men to repent before the wrath of God comes upon the earth.[γ] Before His crucifixion, Jesus warned that not only was God's wrath coming, but He (Jesus) was coming back in the glory of God, to reward all men for their works on the earth. He told them to deny themselves, take up their cross and follow Him, if they wanted to survive the wrath to come.[δ]

Now, when you decide to stand on the word from God, please know that Satan will stir the hearts of your family and friends to rise up against you. But, understand this; it is because of the word that tribulation and persecution come.[*] It's not about you; it's about the word of God you received! Therefore, have no offense in your heart toward those that hate you. If they persecuted Jesus, they will persecute you.[α] If they plotted to kill Jesus, they will plot to kill you too. Jesus told the disciples that whoever killed them would think they were doing God a service.[β] They do these things because they don't know God. But, you who know God stand boldly and speak the word!! Fear not those that can kill the body, <u>but fear Him</u> who is able to destroy your soul and body in Hell.[γ] Stand on the word in the face of persecution, and in doing so you will be blessed. The Lord declares that you are blessed when men persecute you and speak evil of you for His name's sake.

So, REJOICE AND BE EXCEEDINGLY GLAD. LEAP FOR JOY, for great is your reward in heaven.[δ]

4. <u>The Battle Belongs to the Lord</u>

If you are a Christian, you know that the Bible says that our battles are spiritual. Therefore, our weapons of warfare are not of human strength, but mighty through God to destroy every evil thing that exalts itself against the knowledge of God.[ε] It takes more than an army of physical force to tear down an evil empire that threatens your existence. You better know spiritual weapons in God's arsenal and how to use them.

Because the battle is spiritual, it belongs to the Lord and must be fought His way. Obey the word; hold your peace and the Lord will fight for you.* God's word is a called a sword of the spirit that is sharper than any two edged sword.ᵅ If you use the word, you better be compliant with what it says, or the same weapon you use against another will swing around and cut you. The season we are embarking upon requires strict obedience to the word. You may recall the vision from the Journal Entries in which Jesus was destroying every demonic force within His path.[8] There was tremendous destruction, but Jesus was not angry, or sorrowful, and He was no respecter of persons. It was all about the word. If you obeyed, He rewarded you. If you disobeyed, He destroyed you. It was cold and ferocious, but it was the word.

There was another vision in which the Hand of the Lord shook the entire earth with such power, that the demons cried for mercy.[9] Inhabitants of the earth beware! None of us will be able to escape when the Lord shakes the earth. Get in the kingdom, obey and stay there!!ᵝ Therefore, if someone does you wrong, do not avenge yourself, but let God's wrath have its place. Vengeance is the Lord's and He will repay.ᵞ So, get out of God's way and let Him fight for you. Disobedient Christians are out of order, and therefore become a powerful demonic influence in the earth. If they do not repent, the wrath of God will be their reward. Remember how God took His people out of Egyptian slavery and then destroyed those who disobeyed in the wilderness. Please understand that if God didn't spare them, neither will He spare us who disobey.

Earlier in this chapter we mentioned the battle between Saul and David. That battle was the result of God choosing David to be the new leader of His people. During our upcoming shaking, God will raise up His chosen leaders. And a similar battle will erupt in the Body of Christ. The Lord has to shake off the evil operations of the church and raise His obedient church in the midst of turmoil. The Lord has declared that a battle like the one between Saul and David would come to pass, so it is necessary that we take a look at how the original battle was won.

Saul was jealous because the Spirit of God departed from him and rested upon David. He also hated that David was loved by the people and always behaved himself wisely.[*] Saul was jealous and an evil spirit took over him. In spite of Saul's attempts to kill him, David's works and thoughts toward Saul were always good.[α] This caused the people, and especially Saul's son Jonathan, to love and admire David even more. Because there was no evil in David, the Lord protected him from the plots and schemes of Saul. The rivalry between the two began after the fall of Goliath. Young David arose to become a brave warrior with great faith when the King Saul and his armies were too afraid to fight.

There is also a Goliath coming to wage war in America. He is coming to defy the armies of the Living God in this nation. The present day leaders will be too afraid to fight, but the Lord has reserved for Himself, many valiant warriors who will use unconventional methods to take this Goliath down. These will be covenanted people of God, who know Him and will do great exploits in His Name! When God is with you, and you hold your peace, He will fight the battle and win.

David never had to fight in his battle with Saul, yet the king persistently pursued him to kill him. Saul had persistently sinned against God. The Prophet Samuel told Saul that because he had rejected God's word, God had rejected him as king.[*] God told Samuel to anoint David king, yet Saul chose to fight God's judgment. Saul did not confront God; instead, he chose murder as his course of action against what God was doing. He relentlessly pursued David from city to city to destroy Him.

The Bible makes it clear that Saul was under demonic control and could not see God, nor did he desire to obey God's word. David, on the other hand refused to kill Saul even when he had the opportunity to kill him. David loved God and followed God's order of leadership. He vowed not to touch Saul because he was still on the throne. David knew that the judgment of God would cause Saul to fall in death. He was determined that Saul's blood not be on his hands, but that God would be the judge between them.[α]

Because David did not avenge himself, the Lord's wrath fell upon Saul and he along with his sons were killed. When David heard about the deaths of Saul and Jonathan he did not rejoice, he wept and mourned.[β] David did not render evil for good, if he had, he would have been condemned right along with Saul, and his prayers for deliverance would not have been heard by God.[γ] David followed the commands of the Lord and God honored him and gave him the throne.

Now, knowing that God's wrath will fall on all unrighteousness, how should one behave? We should all be imitators of God like dear children, and walk in love one to another.[*] So, how does love behave? Love suffers long and is kind. Love does not envy. Love does not parade itself nor is puffed up. Love does not behave rudely, nor does it seek its own. Love is not provoked. Love thinks no evil. Love does not rejoice in iniquity, but rejoices in truth. Love bears all things, believes all things, hopes all things, and endures all things. Love never fails.^α

The righteous person walks in love. This is also the person who dwells in the secret place of the Most High and abides under the protection and provision of the Almighty.^β And like David in his battle with Saul, whatever the righteous person desires will be done of God for him.

Will you be one who loves and obeys God? Will you walk honorably before God and His people? The Bible says that the eyes of the Lord run throughout the earth desiring to show Himself strong on the behalf of the man or woman whose heart is loyal to God.^γ Are you that person?

God is looking for people who will dare to hear His voice and obey His commands. God is looking for those who will leave their country and familiar mindset to go to an unknown land. He is looking for those who will enter onto the holy ground to seek His face on the behalf of others, and then command them to obey.

God is looking for people who, when commanded to take the city, won't automatically use man's war tactics. They would rather seek and obey the wisdom of God no matter how unconventional. These are those who understand that God's ways are not our ways, neither are His thoughts are thoughts.

God has always looked for sons who will imitate Him: men and women, boys and girls who will speak like God speaks to create what He desires in the earth for all mankind. What could make a father more proud than to have his sons and daughters walk in honor as he walks?

Before Jesus returns, God's sons will be manifested in the earth. They have no choice. All of creation is yearning for them to come forth. Won't you be that person God is seeking? Trust Him, and watch God move miraculously through you to win mighty battles before your very eyes.

It will be such a glorious feat that His praise will continually be in your mouth. You will join in the chorus of mighty men and women of valor, singing; *Praise the Lord, for His mercy endures forever! Hallelujah!*[10]

Conclusion

Although Jesus declared that there would be many wars until He returns to earth, this war in America is of particular interest to God. The Lord wants us to understand that He never ordained war with either Iraq or Afghanistan. It was pride and arrogance that brought the United States to war. But when our prayers bombarded heaven and President Bush finally turned to God in prayer and then publicly stood firm on godly values for our nation, we as a nation captured the heart of God. Now the heart of our nation's new leader, President Trump is also securely in God's hand. The Lord will therefore end this war for His Name's Sake and for those of us who believe in His Name.

This war will not be won by US Military strength, but by the supernatural power of Almighty God. Before this can happen, the Lord will bring America to her knees once again. God must execute judgment against the United States because of our nation's historical acts of terror against the nations of the world. Much blood will be shed in America. The Lord says we must pay for the innocent blood that has been shed under the guise of freedom, free enterprise and fair trade.

In the eyes of God, America is a bloodthirsty and adulterous nation. America wants God to bless her but she continues to rebel against Him. In fact, as a nation we have all but erased God from our daily lives. We find it politically incorrect to serve one God; therefore America has not one, but many gods. We have played the Harlot with many gods: money, power, and the pride of American life, just to name a few. America only turns to Almighty God when she is in trouble and feels she has no other choice.

Conclusion

The American political system is corrupt and full of adulterous men and women. These elected officials have only one true loyalty, and that is to doing whatever it takes to get elected. There is an absence of bold leadership and integrity in American politics and industry. We have groomed many 'yes men' and 'that a boys' who do what they are told. We are experiencing the fallout of this conspiracy of corruption that has resulted in the current financial downfall of our major corporations nation-wide. The average American has had to forfeit their dreams because our political and business leaders have devised wicked plans that promote their own political and financial profit at the expense of all others.

Worse yet are America's religious leaders who are also adulterous and lacking integrity, but they do so in the name of the God of Abraham, Isaac and Jacob. They praise God with their mouths, but their hearts are far from Him. When we esteem people and things more than we value God, we are considered idolatrous. These people and things become gods in place of the true and living God. When we are not loyal to God but share our loyalties with other things, then we are considered adulterous. We promise ourselves to God verbally, but in our actions, we give ourselves to other people and other things. No one tolerates that kind of behavior in a marriage, yet in a relationship with God we consider it acceptable. America let me remind you that the Living God said that He is a jealous God. We are not to serve anyone but Him, lest He allow our children and us to be cursed for generations. [*]

The United States and its leaders (political, business <u>and</u> religious) as a manner of doing business have mastered the things that God hates and finds disgusting.[*]

1. A proud look
2. A lying tongue
3. Hands that shed innocent blood
4. A heart that devises wicked plans
5. Feet swift in running to do evil
6. False witnesses who speak lies
7. One who sows discord among brothers

In this journal we have seen that if someone feels that his or her position is threatened, hatred erupts and they plot to discredit or kill you in the name of God. This is true with the Christians that came after me and the terrorist who have targeted America. And, if someone becomes jealous because of a project you have or the husband or wife you have. In their pride, they may lie and devise evil plans against you; turn your friends against you, and look for others who will join in their plots to harm you. This was my personal war story, but the same thing happens in families and social groups around the world, but God's concern right now is America. We are the ones standing in the crosshairs of the enemy.

Should we be surprised that our government threatens other nations who have resources we need, and we devise a reason to go to war with them? Our public face is innocent, yet we are always devising war to sustain our position of world domination. How many plots and assassin's mission have we financed? And, the guilty have no remorse. That was the old leadership that God is casting out of America! No More says God!

You know, the Golden Rule which says, do to other what you would like them to do to you? It's not just a nice saying, it's a warning; you will reap what you sow; both the good and bad. It's God's law that exists in all He created.[11] And now, God says that it is harvest time!

So, as a nation and as individuals, we are guilty of transgressing God's Laws. What can we do? Repent. We must turn from our evil ways and ask God to forgive us, and forgive our nation for the crimes we have committed against Him, against each other, and against the nations of the world.

I am reminded of King Solomon when he prayed on the behalf of the people of the nation of Israel for God's intervention in event of tragedy.* Solomon was very specific in his request of the Lord. In each case he asked that God would look from heaven, forgive their sins and bring the people back into the blessings of God. Several of these specific requests are appropriate for the United States in this time of war:

1. When famine, or pestilence or plague come upon the people because an enemy has besieged the cities,
2. When the people go into battle against an enemy, and,
3. When the people would be captured by the enemy because of their sin against God

Solomon asked that God hear the prayers of His people and save them from destruction. America needs to bow before the Holy God and pray that if famine, nuclear or biochemical weapons or other plagues are unleashed upon us because our enemies coming to our cities, that God would hear from heaven and forgive our sins and bless us once again.

America also needs to pray that while we go to battle against our enemies abroad and at home, that we be protected from harm. We need to pray that if the enemy captures us because we have sinned against God, that he would hear our prayers, forgive our sins and bless us once again as we humble ourselves before Him in repentance.

If we do these things, then God will indeed hear the cry of America and save our country. God's response to America will be the same response He gave King Solomon. God spoke from heaven in response to Solomon's prayer. He told them,

'If my people which are called by my name, shall humble themselves, and pray, and seek my face, and turn from their wicked ways. Then will I hear from heaven, and will forgive their sin and will heal their land.'*

So, who are those that are called by His name? Those who are called Christians: those who obey the Word of the Living God. If that is you, then humble yourself, seek Him and pray for forgiveness for yourself and the nation, and watch God heal America.

Now if you are not a Christian, with a simple confession you can receive the salvation that Jesus offers. Your confession should not be in words only. It should come from a heart that is deeply remorseful about sin and has an honest desire to change. This is what it means to repent. It should come from a heart that truly believes that his or her only hope at a better life is through Christ Jesus.

A new life in Christ means that you no longer want to do things your way, but desire to be led by the Spirit of God to fulfill His purpose in the earth. If this is what you are feeling right now, then read this prayer out loud and tell God your decision to return to Him:

Dear God,
I am sorry for sinning against you. Please forgive me. I need you to guide my life. It is impossible for me to live pleasing to you, without your help. Please help me. I am tired of messing up my life and I want to live a whole new life in Jesus. I renounce Satan and his hold on my life. I want Jesus to be my Lord and Savior from this day forward. I want to follow Him and let Him guide my path to fulfill your purpose for my life. Please fill me with Your Holy Spirit so that I can successfully perform all that you have for me in this earth. Thank You for giving me another chance at pleasing you. I look forward to loving you, serving you, and spending an eternity with you in heaven.

I ask this all in the Name of Jesus, who is now my Lord and Savior. Amen.

If you prayed this prayer, you are now in God's family. You are now called by His name. God is your Father, and He sees you as a son, just like Jesus is His son. Now go out and make your papa proud, by loving Him and loving others. Obey the Bible and everything God speaks to your spirit. Spend time with God everyday by reading the Bible and talking to Him in prayer. He wants to be involved in every aspect of your life. Talk to God often, and expect Him to respond. He will teach you things no man could ever begin to imagine. A family relationship with God is the best decision you could ever make. Enjoy it!

PRAYER TO HEAL OUR NATION

Almighty God in Heaven,

We come to you as a nation bowed in the clutches of death and despair because we have forgotten the God of our fathers. Instead we have chosen gods of our own making; the gods of money, power and pride of our American life. We have faithfully served these gods with our whole hearts believing that they would fulfill the needs of our longing souls. In doing so we chose not to remember that it was <u>You</u>, the True and Living God that gave us power to get wealth, not to lavish upon ourselves, but to fulfill the covenant in the earth that you established with our forefathers.

Our forefathers vowed before heaven to establish a nation committed to serving God[12], and we, their children have broken covenant with you. By your law, the penalty for breaking covenant is death, but You God, in your infinite wisdom and mercy, vowed that if we would humble ourselves and turn from our wicked ways, <u>You</u> would forgive our sin. Now God, we who are called by Your Name, humble ourselves before <u>Your throne</u> in prayer.

We also confess that we have sinned against our neighbors and shed innocent blood to build this great nation. Your law requires that our blood be shed to satisfy the innocent bloodshed, but Jesus Christ shed His blood for all our sins and we ask that His blood cover the sin of murder our nation has committed. We also repent for trespassing against ours neighbors and nations and ask that You would hear from heaven and forgive us and bless us once again.

We pray that if You shut up the heavens with drought, or open the heavens with floodwaters, open the earth with volcanoes, tsunamis, earthquakes, and other disasters because we have sinned against you, and we turn our hearts in forgiveness, please hear our prayers from heaven and forgive our sin.

We pray that if famine, nuclear or biochemical weapons or other plagues and destruction are unleashed upon us, and our enemies besiege our cities because we have sinned against you, and we cry out in repentance to You, hear from heaven and forgive our sins and bless us once again. We pray that our troops battling our enemies abroad and at home, are protected from harm, and every heart that turns to you is heard. We pray that if the enemy, or the stranger who does not know You, yet turns their hearts to You in prayer, that You hear from heaven, forgive their sins and give them the petitions of their hearts, so that all nations of the world will see the Hand of the Lord and give You praise.

We, who are called by your name, have humbled ourselves in prayer and have sought your face and have turned from our wicked ways. We believe that You, Oh merciful God have forgiven us, and will heal our hearts and heal our great land America! May Your eyes and Your heart be upon our nation perpetually, for You have chosen us and set us apart to be an example of Your liberty and grace,

For Yours is the Kingdom, and the Power and the Glory forever Amen.

APPENDIX

BIBLIOGRAPHY

Howe Hall, Florence. *Story of the Battle Hymn of the Republic*. New York: Harper & Brothers, 1916.

Webster, Christine. *Pledge of Allegiance*. Cornerstones of Freedom™, Second Series. New York: Children's Press, 2003.

Berlin, Irving. *"Irving Berlin's God Bless America and Other Songs for A Better Nation"*. Milwaukee: Leonard Press, 2008.

The Holy Bible Authorized King James Version. Nashville: Thomas Nelson ,2003.

RECOMMENDED BOOKS

American Ideology

Faith and the Presidency; Smith, Gary Scott; Oxford: Oxford University Press; 2006.

One Nation Under God, The History of Prayer in America; Moore, Jr., James P.; New York: Doubleday, 2005.

One Word From God Can Change Your Nation; Copeland, Kenneth & Gloria; Tulsa: Harrison House, 2000.

The Audacity of Hope, Thoughts on Reclaiming the American Dream; Obama, Barack; New York: Crown/Three Rivers Press, 2006.

Christianity

Christ is All; Murray Andrew; London: Marshall Pickering Publishing, 1990.

Foxes Book of Martyrs; Foxe, John; Nashville: Thomas Nelson Publishers, 2000.

Hard to Believe; MacArthur, John; Nashville, TN: Thomas Nelson, 2003.

Christianity (Continued)
The Elijah Task; Sanford, John A. and Paula; Strang Communication Company, 2007.

Tortured for Christ; Wurmbrand, Richard; Westchester, IL: Crossway Books, 1987.

Islam, Terrorism and Western Thought
Islam and the West; Lewis, Bernard; New York: Oxford University Press, 1993.

Prisoners of Hope; *The Story of Our Captivity and Freedom in Afghanistan;* Curry, Dayna; Mercer, Heather; with Mattingly, Stacy; New York: Doubleday; Colorado Springs: Waterbrook Press, 2002.

Terrorism, Jihad, and the Bible; *A Response to the Terrorist Attacks;* MacArthur, John; Nashville: W. Publishing Group, 2001.

Racism in Christianity
Race, Religion & Racism, Volume 1; A Bold Encounter With Division in the Church; Price D.D., Frederick K.C.; Los Angeles: Faith One Publishing, 2002.

OTHER RESOURCES

<u>Websites for Free Online Bibles:</u>
Ethnic Harvest
www.ethnicharvest.org/bibles/
(Parallel language bibles in over 250 languages)

The Blue Letter Bible   www.blueletterbible.org
(Reading, study tools and commentaries)

The Bible Gateway   www.biblegateway.com
(International versions w/commentaries)

Audio Version of Bible   www.audio-bible.com
(Read and listen to King James Version with special tools for the
visually impaired)

<u>To Order a Personal Copy of the Bible:</u>
Faith Comes By Hearing   www.faithcomesbyhearing.com
(Free mp3 downloads in over 400 languages, or Purchase digital
audio players loaded with the Bible)

Free Bible   www.freebibles.net
(For sick, poor or imprisoned individuals in the US—allow 4-6
weeks)

<u>To Order Large Quantities of Bibles for Personal or Ministry:</u>
The American Bible Society   www.americanbible.org

Biblica Direct   www.ibsdirect.com

HOW TO FIND A BIBLE TEACHING CHURCH
IN YOUR AREA

The best source of information about churches in your area is the people you know. If you don't know anyone that goes to church, then feel free to use the following resources.

The Believer's Voice Of Victory Network (BVOVN)
Kenneth Copeland Ministries
Fort Worth, Texas 76192
Prayer Line (877) 281-6297
http://www.kcm.org/church-listing

Christian Broadcasting Network (CBN)
977 Centerville Road, Virginia Beach, VA 23463
24hr Prayer Line (800)759-0700
www.cbn.com (Search Church Finder)

Trinity Broadcasting (TBN)
PO Box A, Santa Ana, CA   92711
24hr Prayer and Request Line (714)731-1000, (888)731-1000
www.tbn.org/contact/

Or better yet, pray about it and let the Spirit of God lead you to a church. It may indeed be a denominational church and the only church in your area.

Just remember, no matter where you choose to go, it's not about the church or the people, it's about your relationship with God, the Father. So, go to church to fellowship with like minded believers, but spend the rest of the week communing with God and reading His word.

TOPICAL INDEX

Causes of War in America:

America's Rejection of God	iii,17,116,205,206,226
Capitol Hill Corruption	165,234,385,386
Corruption in the Church	xvi,167,213,220,226,238-239,322,351
Hatred	xv,7,32,75,76,115,118,123,136,146,159,212
	228,229,235,359,369,389
Judgment of God	vii,27,71,73,74,76,79,85,131,136,151, 167
	168,169,197,205,206,213,225,238,251,264
	290,302,338,359-60,385
Muslim Jihad Declaration	v, xii,306,318,319,320

Enemy Tactics:

Artillery Fire	10,58,174,181,183,186,187
Biochemical Weapons	187,188,196,197
Bombs	9,10,32,154,160,173,176,180,182
Cities Occupied	9,157
Ground Troops	157,174,185,187
Hostage Situations	165
Military Planes	10,28,157,158,160,162,173-4,177,188
Missiles	9,178
Nuclear Bombs	9,161,174,175,178,243,357,386,390
Plane Crashes	165,187
Poisoned Water and Crops	158,178,198
Tanks	9,185

God's Views On:

Abortion	237,296,320
Homosexuality	118,145,169,170,224,356

God's War Strategy:

Enemy Thwarted	10,123-24,147,159-60,165,173
	175-7,179-80,184-5,277
New Leadership	v,xiii-xvi,1,5,196,338,339,354,387
Provision for His People	28,45,61,84,85,91,108,124,152,347,382

Nations at War:

Afghanistan	v,383
America	v,vii,viii,ix,2,6,7,9,10,16,18,27,28,73,165,383,384-5
China	10,57,173-4
France	179,331
Germany	179,259
Iraq	v,xii,202,203,234,383
North Korea	10,173
Russia	10,173,174,301,335

Political Influences:

Arab Leaders	9,256
Bin Laden	v,9,287
Bush	16,166,182,188,198,208,209,210,229,230,232,234,236,239 241,242,243,257,294,297,300,301,302,339, 383
Cheney	182,357
Gephardt	182
Hussein	v,9,175,178,202,215
Kerry	226, 232,235,236,241,242
Obama	338,339,351,354
Partisan Politics	300
Pelosi	300
Powell	182
Rice	208
Sarkozy	331
Schwarzenegger	209,210,212,236,241,257,291,294,300
White Supremacy	163
Trump	x, 383

ENDNOTES
Listed By Chapter

Chapter: Dedication

[1] Matthew 24:6-8
[2] Isaiah 60:2
[3] *"50th Anniversary of Our National Motto, 'In God We Trust', 2006"*, proclamation, by the President of the United States of America, www.whitehouse.gov.
[4] *"The Declaration of Independence: A Transcription,"* The U.S. National Archives & Records Administration, www.archives.gov.

[*] John 14:6
[α] I Peter 2:8

[β] Matthew 10:34
[χ] p. 25, Webster, Christine, *Pledge of Allegiance*, Cornerstones of Freedom, Second Series, NY: Children's Press, 2003.
[δ] p. 41, Hall, Florence Howe, *The Story of the Battle Hymn of the Republic,* New York: Harper, 1916.
[*] p. 25, Webster, Christine, *Pledge of Allegiance,* Cornerstones of Freedom, Second Series, NY: Children's Press, 2003.

[α] p. 17, Webster, Christine, *Pledge of Allegiance,* Cornerstones of Freedom, Second Series, NY: Children's Press, 2003.

[β] p. 26, Webster, Christine, *Pledge of Allegiance,* Cornerstones of Freedom, Second Series, NY: Children's Press, 2003.

[*] p. 50, Hall, Florence Howe, *The Story of the Battle Hymn of the Republic,* New York: Harper, 1916.

[α] p. 49, Hall, Florence Howe, *The Story of the Battle Hymn of the Republic,* New York: Harper, 1916.
[*] p. 49, Hall, Florence Howe, *The Story of the Battle Hymn of the Republic,* New York: Harper, 1916.
[*] John 14:6
[α] II Corinthians 3:17
[β] Deuteronomy 8:11-20; Isaiah 61:2
[*] I Chronicles 28:9
[*] Isaiah 9:6
[α] p. 86, *Irving Berlin's God Bless America and Other Songs for A Better Nation,* Milwaukee: Leonard Corporation, 2001.

Chapter: Dedication p.22
* Revelation 21:24; 22:2

Chapter: Special Acknowledgments
* Genesis 37:3-4, 8
α Ecclesiastes 5:6-7

Chapter: Labor of Love
* Matthew 12:35
α Luke 17:21

Chapter: Counting the Cost
* *See Year 2001, Preparation For War, 7/01; p. 180*
α *See Year 2001, Preparation For War, 6/01; p. 178*
β *See Year 2002, The Enemy Exposed, And God's Plan Revealed, 3/02; p. 199*
χ *See Year 2001, Preparation For War, 9/14/01; p. 181*
* *See Year 2001, Preparation For War, September-October 2001; p. 184*
α *See Year 2002, The Enemy Exposed, And God's Plan Revealed, 1/09/02; p. 197*
* Matthew 4:1-11

α Blue Letter Bible. "Dictionary and Word Search for *rhēma (Strong's 4487)*". Blue Letter Bible. 1996-2009. 24 Nov 2009. < http:// www.blueletterbible.org/lang/lexicon/lexicon.cfm? strongs=G4487 >

* *Luke 21:14-15*
α *Matthew 10:17-20*
β *John 14:16-18*
χ *John 16:12-14*
* *See Year 2002,The Enemy Exposed, And God's Plan Revealed, 12/02; p. 222*
* Luke 14:33
α Luke 17:33

Chapter: Notes About the Journal
* See *Year 2002, The Enemy Exposed, And God's Plan Revealed, 5/02*; p. 203
α See *Year 2001, Preparation For War, 3/01*; p. 173
β See *Year 2001, Preparation For War, 7/01*; p. 180
χ See *Year 2001, Preparation For War, 9/07/01*; p. 180

Chapter: Warning to the Skeptic
* Genesis 3:8
α Hebrews 10:16-23
β I John 1:1-7

Chapter: Warning to the Skeptic (Cont.)

* Blue Letter Bible. "Dictionary and Word Search for *koinōnia (Strong's 2842)*". Blue Letter Bible. 1996-2010. 24 Feb 2010. < http:// www.blueletterbible.org/lang/lexicon/lexicon.cfm? Strongs=G2842&t=KJV

α John 14:21-23
β Hebrews 3:12
χ I Corinthians Chapter 12

* John 20:30-31	α John 21:25
β Isaiah 55:8-13	χ Psalm 147:5
δ Romans 10:17	ε Luke 8:8

* Luke 2:41-50; 4:16-17
α Matthew 4:1-11
β John 10:4-5
χ John 17:3
δ John 5:17-18, 37-40
* John 3:32
α Matthew 4:1-11
β John 4:4
χ John 11:4
δ Romans 8:29
* John 14:17
* Ephesians 1:14
α I John 3:2
β I Corinthians 13:12
* Revelation 21:22-25
α II Timothy 3:5-7
β John 1:12
* Hebrews 11:6
α Daniel 2:18-22
β Matthew 5:8

Chapter: Warning to Those Eager

* I Corinthians 2:6-13
α John 14:15-16
* John 14:21
α John 10:9-10; 14:6
β John 10:7-14
α Psalm 23:1

Chapter: Warning to Those Eager (Cont.)

β Psalm 25:12-14

α Romans 6:16

* Blue Letter Bible. "Dictionary and Word Search for *pythōn (Strong's 4436)*". Blue Letter Bible. 1996-2010. 24 Feb 2010. < http:// www.blueletterbible.org/lang/lexicon/lexicon.cfm?Strongs=G4436&t=KJV >, The New Testament reference scripture is Acts 16:16.

α Deuteronomy 18:10-19; Acts 3:22; Hebrews 12:23-25

ε John 6:33, 63

* Ephesians 2:18

α James 1:5-6

β Colossians 1:11-17

* Daniel 1:4,17-20; 2:19-23

α I Corinthians 1:19-20, 24; 3:19

β Colossians 1:16; Psalm 147:5; Isaiah 55:8-9

Chapter: The Real Matrix

* Acts 8:39-40

* Matthew 9:11-13

α Matthew 15:6

β Mark 4:2

* Blue Letter Bible. "Dictionary and Word Search for *'matrix* H7358'* in the KJV". Blue Letter Bible. 1996-2010. 24 Feb 2010. < http:// www.blueletterbible.org/search/translationResults.cfm?Strongs=H7358&Criteria=matrix%2A&t=KJV >. Old Testament Scripture Reference is Exodus 13:12.

α I John 4:16

β Revelation 4:11

* Genesis 1:26-28

α John 4:24

β Genesis 2:7-8, 15-17

χ Genesis 5:2

δ Genesis 3:17

* I John 3:8   α Luke 19:10

β John 18:37; 14:6   χ Matthew 28:18

δ Matthew 16:27

ε Romans 8:29, Colossians 1:18

Chapter: The Real Matrix (Cont.)

* John 3:3-5, 16   α John 10:9; 14:6
β II Corinthians 4:6-7   χ II Corinthians 5:17
δ Romans 12:1-2

* Colossians 1:13
α Romans 8:2, 29-30
β John 1:12
χ John 8:44; Ephesians 5:1
δ Romans 8:14; Genesis 12:1-4; Hebrews 11:24-29; Philippians 2:5-8
ε Luke 14:27
φ John 15:12; 14:21,23

[1] *The Matrix.* Dir(s) Andy Wachowski, Larry Wachowski. Warner Home Video, 1999. DVD

[2] Film Ratings."What Each Rating Means". Motion Picture Association of America. Web.10March2007. <http://www.mpaa.org/ratings/what-each-rating-means>

[3] *The Matrix: Reloaded.* Dir(s) Andy & Larry Wachowski. Warner Brothers Entertainment, 2003. DVD

[4] *The Matrix: Revolutions.* Dir(s) Andy & Larry Wachowski. Warner Brothers Entertainment, 2003. DVD

[5] *The Matrix.* Dir(s) Andy & Larry Wachowski. Warner Home Video, 1999. DVD. Scene 8, "Morpheus' Proposal"; Scene 11, "Nebuchadnezzar's Crew"; Scene 14, "Training Begins."

[6] *The Matrix.* Dir(s) Andy & Larry Wachowski. Warner Home Video, 1999. DVD. Scene 13, "The Search is Over."

[7] *The Matrix.* Dir(s) Andy & Larry Wachowski. Warner Home Video, 1999. DVD. Scene 12, "The Real World."

[8] *The Matrix.* Dir(s) Andy& Larry Wachowski. Warner Home Video, 1999. DVD. Scene 17, "The Gatekeepers."

Chapter: The Real Matrix (Continued)

[9] *The Matrix.* Dir Andy & Larry Wachowski. Warner Home Video,1999.DVD.Scene 4, "The Question."

[10] *The Matrix* Dir Andy & Larry Wachowski. Warner Home Video, 1999.DVD.Scene 22, "Choices…and a Cookie."

[11] *The Matrix.* Dir Andy & Larry Wachowski. Warner Home Video,1999.DVD.Scene 8, "Morpheus' Proposal."

[12] *The Matrix.*Dir Andy & Larry Wachowski. Warner Home Video, 1999.DVD.Scene 12, "The Real World."

[13] *The Matrix.*Dir Andy & Larry Wachowski. Warner Home Video, 1999.DVD.Scene 9, "Down the Rabbit Hole"; Scene 10, "Slimy Rebirth."

[14]*The Matrix.*Dir Andy & Larry Wachowski. Warner Home Video, 1999.DVD.Scene 14, "Training Begins"; Scene 15, "Morpheus/Neo Match up"; Scene 16, "First Jump."

Chapter: The Darkness and The Glory Part I
[*] See *Year 2002, The Enemy Exposed, And God's Plan Revealed, 6/02; p.* 205
[α] Revelation 20:11-15
[β] Isaiah 9:7
[χ] Daniel 2:44
[δ] II Timothy 3:13
[*] Malachi 4:5-6
[α] Zechariah 5:3-4
[β] Revelation 19:11-21
[*] Habakkuk 2:8
[*] Matthew 24:6-14
[α] Genesis 4:8
[*] Psalm 18:30
[α] Genesis 4:7-16
[β] Romans 12:17-19
[χ] Genesis 4:3-4
[*] Genesis 2:17
[α] Exodus 20:3-5
[β] Matthew 5:21-22
[χ] Romans 13:1-3
[δ] I Timothy 2:1-2

Chapter: The Darkness and the Glory Part I (Continued)
* Luke 13:1-5

α Luke 17:26-28
* Genesis 6:13-14
α Exodus 8:23
β Daniel 3:16-30; 6:18-28
∂ Matthew 3:2
χ Matthew 3:7, 11-13
* I Peter 4:17-18
α Hebrews 12:25-29

* Luke 23:3
β John 4:24
χ Genesis 1:1-3
δ Luke 1:35; John 1:14

Chapter: The Darkness and the Glory Part II
* John 14:20-23
α Luke 4:1; Romans 8:14
β John 8:29
χ John 14:10
δ Mark 16:15-20
* John 13:13-15; 15:10
α John 14:12
* John 14:15
α Hebrews 10:26-29
β I John 1:9
χ I Corinthians 9:24-27; 10:11
* John 12:23-28
* John 17:15-22
* Genesis 6:3
* Matthew 21:1-3
α John 11:4,11
β II Corinthians 5:8
χ John 16:33
* II Timothy 3:11-12
α Matthew 5:10-12; Luke 6:23
β John 11:40, 43-44
* Romans 12:2
α Romans 10:17
* I John 5:3-4

Chapter: The Darkness and the Glory Part II (Cont.)

α Luke 1:37
β I Timothy 2:4
χ John 8:31-32; 17:17
δ Ephesians 5:26
ε Ephesians 4:24
5 Luke 24:36-43; John 20:19; Luke 24:31; Acts 1:9
* Matthew 13:45
μ Luke 9:23

CHAPTER: Year 2000: *Move To Ohio*

1 Roberts, Oral. *My Story*. Tulsa: Summit Book Company, 1961.
2 *Faith*. Kenneth Copeland Ministries. 1980.audiotapes. (Tape 6)
3 Giordano, Geraldine. *Everything You Need to Know About Wicca*. New York: Rosen, 2001.

CHAPTER: Year 2001: *Preparation For War*

4 King James Version, Luke 8:26-39.
5 Acts 2:46.
6 Voice of the Martyrs, is a not for profit organization that exposes worldwide persecution of Christians <http://www.persecution.com>
7 Trinity Broadcasting Network (TBN), is a California based Christian Television Network. TBN has a 24hr prayer line.
<http://www.tbn.org>
8 *Rambo: First Blood*. Dir Ted Kotcheff. Per. Sylvester Stallone and Richard Crenna. Warner Brothers,1982. DVD.

CHAPTER: Year 2002: *The Enemy Exposed*

9 Revelation 6:12-17.
10 ISBN, International Standard Book Number, is a book identification number assigned by publishers and administered through the International Standard Numbering System for the Information Industry.
<http//en.wikipedia.org/ISBN>

CHAPTER: Year 2003: *The Storm Is Coming*

11 *"President Says Saddam Hussein Must Leave Iraq Within 48 Hours,"* March 17, 2003 White House press release,
<http:/www.whitehouse.gov/news/releases/2003/03>
12 *"The Recall Election. Governor Davis is Recalled Schwarzenegger Wins"*, Los Angeles Times; Michael Finnegan; Main News Part A; Metro desk; newspaper; Oct 8, 2003 <http//articles.latimes.com/2003/oct/08/local/me-recall8>
13 *"War Enduring Freedom from Tikrit Iraq Saddam's Farm"*, CNN Breaking News 12/15/03, 12:36 p.m. EST.<http//archives.cnn.com/TRANSCRIPTS/0312/14/bn.06.html>

CHAPTER: Year 2004: *The Year of Completion*
[14] *The Ten Commandments*. Dir Cecil B DeMille. Paramount Home Entertainment, 1956. DVD

CHAPTER: Year 2004: *The Year of Completion (Continued)*
[15] "The Wake Up Call". The Believer's Voice of Victory Broadcast. Kenneth Copeland Ministries. KCAL TV. Los Angeles. 27Mon2004.
<http//www.kcm.org/media/webcast/kenneth-copeland-oral-roberts-and-richard-roberts/040927-the-wakeup-call>

[16] "Candidates Tighten Focus on Battleground States". American Morning. Anchors Bill Hemmer & Soledad O'Brien. CNN. New York. 25Oct2004.
<http//archives.cnn.com/TRANSCRIPTS/0410/25/itm.06.html>
[17] "Kerry Concedes; Analysis of Election". American Morning. Anchors Bill Hemmer & Soledad O'Brien. CNN. New York. 03Nov2004.
<http//archives.cnn.com/TRANSCRIPTS/0411/03/itm.07.html>

Chapter: Year 2005: The Glory is Here!
α John 3:3,5; Matthew 18:3
β Mark 10:24; I Corinthians 6:9; Galatians 5:21
∞ Matthew 7:22-23; 8:10-12
[18] Blue Letter Bible. "Dictionary and Word Search for Shalowm (Strong's 7965)". Blue Letter Bible.1996-2007. 10March2007.
<http//www.blueletterbible.org/lang/lexicon/lexicon.cfm?strongs=H7965&t=kjv7>

CHAPTER: Year 2006: *Possessing the Land*
[19] *Charlie and the Chocolate Factory. Dir Tim Burton. Warner Home Video,*2005. DVD
[20] *The Terminator*. Dir James Cameron. Orion Pictures,1984. DVD
[21] Ilyich Tchaikovsky, Pyotr. *"Festival Overture 'The Year 1812'" in E flat major, Opus 49; French Ouverture solennelle 1812),* an orchestral overture.

CHAPTER: Year 2007: *A Day of Rest*
[22] *"I Believe I can Fly"*. Performed by R. Kelly. Space Jam: Music from and Inspired by the Motion Picture. Atlantic Records, 1996.

Chapter: Year 2008: The European Connection Defined
[6] http://edition.cnn.com/2008/POLITICS/11/04/obama.transcript/

Chapter: Year 2009: A Better Understanding

[7] Blue Letter Bible. "Dictionary and Word Search for *'barak'* in the KJV". Blue Letter Bible. 1996-2009. 24 Nov 2009. < http:// www.blueletterbible.org/search/translationResults.cfm? Criteria=barak&t=KJV >

Chapter: Final Exhortation

* Matthew 24:11

α See *Year 2000, Move to Ohio,* **1/00**; p. 137

β Hebrews 12:25-29

χ Hosea 4:5-7

* I Corinthians 14:7-11

α Luke 8:11-15, 18

β Mark 10:15

* II Chronicles 16:9

α Matthew 24:9-12

β John 17:17

χ John 8:31-32

δ John 8:39-44

* Matthew 13:19

α Matthew 4:1-11

β I Samuel 17:32-37

* I Samuel 17:45-46

α II Samuel 5:17-25

* I Samuel 18:7

* Psalm 91:7, 1

α Exodus 12:21-30

* Joshua 6:1; 2:1-21

α Joshua 6:1-27

β II Chronicles 20:1- 19

αII Chronicles 20:20-25

* Joshua 7:1-13

* Joshua 7:14-26; 8:1-29

α Hebrews 12:1

* Genesis 6:14-22

α Genesis 41:32-40

β Matthew 3:1-12

γ Matthew 1:15

δ Matthew 16:24-27

* Matthew 13:21

α John 15:20

Chapter: Final Exhortation (Cont.)

John 16:2
Matthew 10:28
Matthew 5:11-12; Luke 6:22-23
II Corinthians 10:3-5
Exodus 14:14
Ephesians 6:18; Hebrews 4:12
See *Year 2006, Posses the Land,* 1/02//06; p. 293
See *Year 2001, Preparation for War,* 12/12/01; p. 190
Hebrews 12:25-29
Romans 12:19
I Samuel 18:10-16
I Samuel 19:4
I Samuel 13:13-14; 15:18-26; 16:1-13
I Samuel 24:9-13
I Samuel 31:1-6; II Samuel 1:11-12
I Peter 3:10-12
Ephesians 5:1-7
I Corinthians 13:4-8
Psalm 91:1
II Chronicles 16:9
II Chronicles 20:21

Chapter: Conclusion
Exodus 20:1-6
Proverbs 6:16-19
Genesis 1:11; 8:22; 9:6
II Chronicles 6:19-42
II Chronicles 7:14

Prayer to Heal Our Nation
See Excerpts from the Mayflower Compact, page 7